Quality and Education

Quality and Education

By
Christopher Winch

Blackwell Publishers/The Journal of the Philosophy of Education
Society of Great Britain

Copyright © The Journal of the Philosophy of Education Society of Great Britain 1996

ISBN 0-631-20085-1

First published in 1996

Blackwell Publishers
108 Cowley Road, Oxford OX4 1JF, UK
and
238 Main Street, Cambridge, MA 02142, USA.

British Library Cataloguing in Publication Data
A CIP catalogue record for this book is available from the British Library

Library of Congress Cataloguing-in-Publication Data
Quality and Education/by Christopher Winch
p. cm. — (Journal of Philosophy of Education Monograph series: 2)
Includes Index. ISBN 0-631-20085-1 (alk. paper)

Printed in Great Britain by Redwood Books, Trowbridge.
This book is printed on acid-free paper

Contents

Editorial

This book, which is also the second Special Issue of the *Journal of Philosophy of Education*, could hardly, in the UK at least, be more timely. As it goes to press issues of quality, of standards in education and how they are inspected and evaluated, are again in the news. Schools are said to be setting insufficiently high standards; universities and colleges are complaining that standards cannot be maintained with current levels of resourcing. In a culture where accountability has become a watchword (and where accountants of various sorts are increasingly powerful) it is obviously of the first importance to clarify what these 'standards' are and to examine critically the way in which education is measured against them.

Among the many questions which analysis of quality in education must deal with is what might be called the *qualis* question: what sort of thing is education? It makes all the difference, for example, whether education is a commodity to be traded in the market, or something else altogether. Some would claim that while other services must respond to consumer preferences education is distinctive, and perhaps unique, in that its role is to shape those preferences.

Here the long-standing preoccupation of philosophy of education with the concept of education itself shows its continuing, and even growing, relevance to contemporary political and philosophical debate. Christopher Winch's discussion of Quality takes account of earlier work in philosophy of education while moving on to deal with more recent developments in political and economic thinking and game theory. He analyses crucial features of the accountability to which contemporary schools and other educational institutions are subject. Further philosophical debate on quality in education seems bound to be stimulated by his work, for which this Journal would like to record its gratitude.

Richard Smith
Journal of Philosophy of Education

Chapter 1
Introduction

I WHY QUALITY IS A MATTER OF CURRENT CONCERN

The issue of quality dominates much current educational debate in the western world. Yet it is not clear what quality in education is. This book aims to show why quality issues are currently such a matter of concern in public and political debate, and how the concept of quality shapes discussions of educational worthwhileness. In doing so, an account of education will be offered that marks something of a break from quite a long liberal philosophical tradition of theorising about education.[1] I make no apology for doing this, as I think that it is a move which is both desirable and long overdue. But the main reason for doing so in the context of this book is that without a reconsideration of what education is, educational thinkers will be so out of touch with current public and political thinking about education that they will become irrelevant and so any philosophical or conceptual writing about quality and education will be largely a waste of time. This perhaps would not matter so much if the liberal tradition was the source of all wisdom, although it would still be a matter of serious concern to all who cared about education. But, as I hope to show in Chapter 3, that liberal tradition needs re-evaluation, and since that is necessary in itself and also necessary to understand the quality debate, it is a pressing task that can be ignored no longer.

II ACCOUNTABILITY MATTERS

The main issue driving current concerns about quality is that of *accountability*. This is a particular issue for publicly funded education and the main, although not the exclusive, concern of this book will be with publicly funded educational services. The time has long passed, if it ever existed, when governments concerned themselves solely with defending the populace against internal and external enemies. They are expected in addition to promote economic growth, preserve the cultural heritage of the country that they govern, and provide protection and help against sickness, poverty and unemployment.[2] It is plausible to suggest that education has a part to play in all these functions, including the first. Furthermore, the education of a country's population has been seen as an essential means of promoting personal growth and self-fulfilment.

Most modern societies devote a considerable proportion of their expenditure to the provision of educational services of one sort or another.[3] The revenue raised to provide these services comes from taxes, either direct or indirect, raised from individuals and corporate bodies. The services provided are held to benefit individuals, families, enterprises and the wider community. There are a number of different social groups which have a stake or interest in education. Few would argue that taxation in modern democracies is either a gift, or the payment of a tribute, to government. Popular thinking and most political theory concur in believing that the raising of taxes by government confers reciprocal obligations on a government to provide the services for which the taxation was raised and to provide good services with a wise and careful deployment of the revenue raised to do so.

One does not have to believe in a social contract version of the political obligations of citizens and of governments to see that the accountability of governments is a major condition of the long-term allegiance of their citizenry, certainly of their willing and enthusiastic allegiance.[4] It follows that modern governments must, in some way, account for their provision of expensive services to those who pay for them and to those whom they are intended to benefit. The principle of accountability is a moral, as well as a political, issue; it is based on the idea of mutual obligation and the keeping of promises. If someone undertakes to carry out a service in return for payment, an obligation is placed on him to do so to the best of his ability.

Admittedly, this obligation has sometimes lain lightly on the shoulders of governments, but it is always there as a background concern. In recent times, however, it has become much more than a background concern: it has come to dominate political debate. This in turn has meant that attention has focused on education as one of the main recipients of tax revenue and as the partial provider of some of the most important functions with which governments are charged. Education is sometimes regarded with almost mystical importance by the public, the media and governments. Moral, religious, economic and even military decline are, on occasion, attributed to the supposed failure of educational systems; at the same time educators are often held in low esteem and enjoy low status, particularly in the English-speaking democracies, where the concern about educational quality is currently at its most vocal and fervent. However misconceived these concerns may sometimes appear to be, teachers cannot escape the expectations (often exaggerated and therefore disappointed) that are placed on them. One thing that they can no longer do is to pretend that accountability is something which they have always welcomed gladly and discharged adequately, because not only will they not be believed, but they will be brushed aside in the rush to implement new procedures for ensuring accountability. Better for them that they accept the way the world is turning, but take part in the debate and strive to ensure that the interests of the education system and its users are protected against ignorant and ill-conceived reforms.

Three historical pressures have made accountability in education a major issue. The first has already been mentioned, namely the hopes that are placed in education. Even if these hopes are sometimes exaggerated, it remains the case that public education systems are financed in order to promote cultural continuity, moral order and economic growth and there is an expectation that they at least contribute to the provision of these public goods. The second has been the rise of neo-liberalism as a major political and ideological force, particularly in the United Kingdom and the United States. Neo-liberals believe that the role of governments should be kept to a minimum and that, wherever possible, both public and private goods should be provided by the market. In this way, both freedom of choice and quality of service are best ensured, because the mechanism of accountability is immediate and transparent in its operation. Those who provide an expensive or poor quality service will go out of business. There is a direct and rapid correlation between price and quality on the one hand and popularity on the other. A third factor has been a decline in deference towards professional people on the part of the general public and less preparedness to assume that they always know best. Arguably this is part of the development of democratic ways of thinking.

Most neo-liberals accept that the state should provide the means for a people to defend itself from internal and external enemies, although there is some debate as to whether these services should be provided directly by the government or indirectly through contracting out. Education is usually accepted reluctantly as part of the remit of the state, but with the proviso that means of accountability should be made more vigorous and, wherever possible, pursued through some form of market mechanism.[5]

If Aristotle is right in thinking that man is a political animal, then it is part of his nature to be concerned about the kind of society he lives in and the values which that society stands for. Therefore, debate about political society and its values is an intrinsic part of political life, even when that life is conceived as the playing out of interests (see the next section). So it is not at all surprising that ideas and ideological movements such as neo-liberalism play a large part in educational debate. At the time of writing, neo-liberalism remains a dominant strand in contemporary politics and political thought, although there are signs that it is on the wane, even in conservative circles. This book will, therefore, be concerned with neo-liberal ideas about education, together with their critics and the successors of neo-liberalism. The current signs are that, although the successors of neo-liberalism have modified their views on social and environmental policy to some considerable degree, even new conservative thinking about education remains radically neo-liberal in character.[6]

III POLITICS AND INTEREST

The provision of education is, then, a political issue. But what does this mean? In this book a broadly Aristotelian view of politics is taken. Politics is seen as the conflict between and negotiation of different interests within a political society. However transient and shifting they may be, different interest groups are part of the furniture of any political society and the relationship between the satisfaction of interests of particular groups and the principal values of a society is the main business to which a politician must attend.[7]

It is helpful to consider interest groups as representing *different points of view* which are often, although not always, linked to material interests and which often, although not always, come into conflict with each other in a way that demands a resolution. This is not to claim that the acts of interest groups are always self-interested in the narrow sense that they seek to maximise the material gains of their members. More generally, they strive to put forward a point of view which may or may not encompass material interests. It may contain an ideology or political point of view to which its members subscribe just as easily; the teaching profession and educational professionals generally constitute, it can be argued, such a group.[8]

This book is concerned with the political philosophy of education. The major interest groups involved in the politics of education in a modern industrial or post-industrial society will be: those being educated (children, young people and adults); those responsible for those being educated (usually, but not always, parents); those concerned with providing education (teachers, teacher-trainers, civil servants, administrators, and inspectors); the state (which includes much of the immediately previous group together with specific departments such as the Treasury or finance ministry); taxpayers (both individual and corporate); and the government (which provides the legislative framework and sets budgets). One way of looking at the interests involved in education is to see them in terms of *consumers* on the one hand and *producers* on the other. This approach, not universally accepted, is largely the result of the influence of neo-liberalism.

The producers are not hard to identify: they are the teachers and other educational workers. But who are the consumers? One's first inclination might be to say that they are the children and students who are educated. This is a partial truth at best. Accountability means that education must justify its conduct to those who provide the resources for it. Children do not provide these resources: taxpayers do. Therefore it seems that education is acountable to taxpayers. There is then a sense in which taxpayers, too, are consumers of education. But the government cannot be responsible directly to such a diffuse body of people, so it must act as a representative of the taxpayers. Because taxpayers are such a diffuse body, they cannot be assumed to share common interests. Individual taxpayers belong to corporate bodies such as trade unions and churches, which have their own aims and interests, while different enterprises have their own interests and the interests of one enterprise may conflict with those of another. Governments have an agenda which, although dependent on accounting to voters and taxpayers, is to some extent independent of them, being concerned with such matters as party factions, electoral timetables, financial and economic constraints and political ideology.

Accountability is not just about the stewardship of money, however. Those who work in schools and colleges give two most precious assets, their time and their energy. Whoever takes these does not take them as a gift or a tribute but as something for which some benefit is to be returned. Thus teachers are under an obligation to students and children not to waste their time and effort. Children are under an obligation not to waste the time of their fellow pupils and their teachers. The government is under an obligation not to waste the time of teachers. All these obligations are moral ones that arise from the same requirement of reciprocal fairness and justice that animates the concern for financial accountability. The lines of accountability in education can become a little tangled, given the range and complexity of the interests involved, and the unravelling of them is often a matter of intense political debate. Simplistic talk of producers versus consumers will not be very enlightening.

IV   TOWARDS A BROAD VIEW OF EDUCATION

Much philosophical discussion of education has been conducted in the liberal tradition, which assumes that the main aim of education is some form of personal fulfilment and development, which in turn is achieved through following a liberal curriculum consisting primarily of traditional academic subjects such as literature, history, mathematics and pure science. On the other hand, liberal educators have tended to be sceptical about the role of education in promoting a universal or common good. While there are few people who would doubt the importance and value of personal fulfilment and development, it is not so obvious that these are the only aims of education or even that these aims are best achievable through the pursuit of a traditional liberal education. For reasons that will be articulated in Chapter 3, it is necessary to take a much broader view of education than has traditionally been done by most educational thinkers. This means that other aims of education will also be considered seriously, aims such as the promotion of economic growth or social cohesion.

It follows also that a broader view of the curriculum will need to be taken. The criteria for assessing the worthwhileness of education may well be seen in various ways by different groups with diverse outlooks and interests. If this makes a discussion of the issues more complex, it also has the virtue of making it more attuned to the concerns of the many people who do not work inside academia or schools. This may lead to accusations of philistinism from those wedded to the liberal ideal, but the accusation is worth bearing if the reward is an escape from the parochialism that affects much educational thinking.

V AGAINST EPISTEMIC PESSIMISM ABOUT EDUCATION

A complaint frequently made against philosophers (with some justification) is that they are better at destruction than they are at construction: that they are readier to show why someone is wrong than to show why he is right. Very often their fire has been directed against 'scientific' solutions to human problems. In an activity full of inexactitude such as education it is relatively easy to show how seemingly neat and quantifiable solutions do not measure up to the complexity of the problems they are designed to solve. This is particularly the case where educational achievement and educational practice are the questions at issue. It will be disputed, for example, whether judgements about achievement are objective and whether they can be reliable or valid.[9] Claims about the quality of teaching and learning will be just as vigorously contested on the grounds that they are the products of subjectivity and ideological prejudice. Since education is thought to be about the promotion of values in a world where people adhere to different and often incompatible values, the problem of subjectivity threatens to become insuperable.

One response would be to embrace a thoroughgoing naturalism and positivism that would seek to quantify achievement and performance and render judgement and comparison a matter of mathematical precision. But, quite rightly, such approaches have had their day in education. The dismal lessons of using psychometry and verbal deficit theory as instruments for the formulation of policy should have been learned by now.[10] But what is the alternative? One of the aims of this book is to show that it is very difficult to obtain 'quick fixes' for the measurement of educational quality. However, from the conclusion that an all-embracing optimism about the possibility of quantifying educational achievement and practice is misconceived, it does not follow that we should embrace pessimism about *ever* quantifying the success or otherwise of educational activities.

A complete failure of the possibility of measurement would throw into doubt whether the performance of teachers and students could ever be monitored in a satisfactory way. It is most important that such pessimism is, if possible, avoided. If accountability has the importance that I have already claimed for it, then the whole basis of trust on which a public system of education is based would be thrown into jeopardy. It is for this reason that the concept of educational standards and of performance against those standards is vital. If different performances can be compared against standards and if standards in different times and places can be compared with each other, then it is possible to create the framework for comparative judgements about such matters as pedagogy and added value. It goes without saying that not all aspects of education can be quantified easily: spiritual and moral development are just two examples of areas where judgements are likely to be more impressionistic. But academic achievement (one of the main desired outcomes of education, if not the only one), whether in the theoretical or the practical side of the curriculum, should be, and is, susceptible of quantification and comparison.

If educators are successful in denying this, then the whole enterprise of education, whether public or not, is likely to be brought into disrepute.

VI   OUTLINE OF THE ARGUMENT

The next chapter examines various ways in which quality control and quality assurance procedures from industry and commerce can be imported into education. It is argued that they do have some limited value. In Chapter 3 I explain and defend the contention that education should be conceived very broadly as a set of activities with diverse, although related, aims. The concern that philosophers have with language will be explained and the idea that a proper discussion of education, educational worthwhileness and accountability can take place in the context of a narrow prescriptive definition will be criticised. Instead the view will be expressed that education is a complex concept whose ramifications can only be understood in the context of the interest groups implicated in it and the ideological positions which they adhere to. The concept of *quality* as it applies to education shares these features and therefore any discussion of educational quality is bound to be problematic and complex.[11]

Chapter 4 is concerned with the aims of education. Given that education is an area that is linguistically, ideologically and politically contested, what sense is there in maintaining that education is a purposive activity with identifiable aims? I will maintain that education without aims is unlikely to be a coherent activity and that diversity of interests and values does not preclude the formulation of a set of aims that all can agree on. A distinction will be made here that is crucial to much of the argument of the book, namely that while it is not often, if ever, reasonable to expect people to negotiate away their values, it is reasonable and often necessary that they be prepared to compromise about the degree to which those values are implemented, particularly in the public sphere. This opens the way to a consideration of the desirability of diverse but clearly articulated aims for education, emerging from political debate. This is a point about any political society that manages different interests through negotiation and compromise rather than confrontation and open conflict, but I will assume that the context of the discussion is that of a liberal democratic society with a well-developed civil society and that the way in which negotiation about an implementation of values occurs is through a democratic debating and legislative process.

Chapter 5 builds on the conclusions of Chapter 4 and shows how a national curriculum can accommodate diverse aims through the construction of a common core with branches at the later stages. Chapter 6 introduces educational standards and performance against those standards. It is argued that the notion of standards is fundamental to any assessment of performance, which is itself fundamental to any notion of accountability. Standards can be compared, both historically and comparatively, and so can performance. The dangers of epistemic pessimism about standards are indicated and it is shown why such pessimism is not justifiable.

Chapter 7 takes seriously the view that raw performance scores in examinations and other tests are not a fair measure of how well a school or college is doing its job. Various ways of measuring added value, effectiveness and efficiency are discussed and it is argued that however well these are developed the notion of standards and performance against standards cannot be ignored. Chapter 8 is a critical examination of the idea of 'good practice' and takes the view that this is not just a technical matter. Teaching is about the implementation and expression of values in the classroom, but whose values and the extent to which they are implemented is a contentious matter. It is argued that ultimately it is a political matter and that views about the nature of good pedagogic practice need to rest upon a negotiation of the extent to which different parties are able to see their own values implemented in classroom practice.

Chapter 9 looks at the arguments of neo-liberals and conservatives for the view that the provision of education should be left to the market. Given the broad view of education adopted in Chapter 3, it is argued that the provision of public and positional goods through education cannot be left to market forces. Game theoretic models such as the Prisoner's Dilemma support, rather than undermine, this view. State involvement in the provision of education is unavoidable. In Chapter 10 arguments for and against the idea that education should be concerned with equality as a social goal are considered. The inegalitarian views receive cautious support, but are inadequate to prescribe arrangements for the diverse kind of education system that has been argued for earlier.

Chapter 11 returns to some of the more practical issues concerned with quality and accountability and looks at various ways in which education systems can make themselves accountable. The notion of inspection is given particular attention and the British OFSTED system of school inspection is analysed and discussed in a critical fashion. Chapter 12 concludes with a discussion of possible and desirable future developments in the field of educational quality.

NOTES

1. See R. S. Peters, *Ethics and Education*, 1966. For a more recent defence of a form of the liberal ideal see David Carr, *Educating the Virtues*, 1991.
2. For an early recognition of the role of the state in the promotion of economic growth, see Friedrich List, *The National System of Political Economy*, 1991.
3. For recent figures, see the *OECD Economic Survey UK 1995*, London, HMSO, 1995, which gives educational expenditure as a proportion of GDP for 1991. Figures for OECD countries range from Canada (6.7%) to Japan (3.7%); the figure for the UK is 5.3%, for the US 5.5% and for Australia 4.7%.
4. The classical statement of contract theory can be found in John Locke, *The Second Treatise of Government*. For modern statements see Robert Nozick, *Anarchy, State and Utopia*, 1974; John Rawls, *Political Liberalism*, 1993.
5. See John Gray, *Beyond the New Right: Markets, Government and the Common Environment*, 1993, for a discussion of this issue from a former neo-liberal thinker.
6. See for example John Gray *op. cit.*
7. Cf Aristotle, *The Politics*, especially Books III and IV.
8. In taking this line, I am in agreement with Hugh Stretton and Lionel Orchard in their *Public Goods, Public Enterprise and Public Choice*, 1994; they mount a sustained and detailed criticism of the utility maximising view of individual action, whether it be individual or within social institutions.
9. For a recent sample, see A. Davis, Criterion-referenced assessment and the development of knowledge and understanding, 1995.
10. See C. Winch, *Language, Ability and Eductional Achievement*, 1990.
11. For a recent discussion, see D. Aspin and J. D. Chapman, *Quality Schooling*, 1994, Chapter 1.

Chapter 2
Manufacturing Educational Quality

I INTRODUCTION

It was argued in Chapter 1 that concern with quality in education arose largely out of attempts to import concern about quality in the private sector of the economy into the public sector and, in particular, into the service section of the public sector. It is now time to examine the private sector and to see whether or not what has occurred there in the last fifty years or so has any relevance to education. The first sense of quality in products or services concerns the *species* of that product or service: is the product suitable for the purpose for which it was designed? We might, for example, ask whether or not a piece of earth-moving equipment was suitable in rough terrain. The second sense of quality concerns the *individual* product and whether or not it will work as it was intended to do without malfunctioning. In fact, both these senses of 'quality' are important and they will be considered together in the discussion of quality systems.

It is possible to identify four distinct approaches to quality.[1] First, there is a total approach, where 'quality' becomes synonymous with 'excellence'. This is the sense of 'quality' pioneered by Peters and Waterman, which has become very influential in the public sector.[2] Second, there is the approach that is product-based, where quality is precise, measurable and part of the characteristics of the product. This approach is perhaps most associated with Crosby.[3] The third approach is *user based*, where quality is judged according to whether it meets the needs and wants of the user.[4] Fourth, there is a *value based* approach, where quality is defined in terms of 'value for money'.[5] As we saw in Chapter 1, the protean and shifting definition of the term 'quality' as it is used about the education system is mirrored in its use in the commercial sector as preoccupations and fashions change. In education we have seen a shift to user-based approaches from the first two, with an increasing emphasis on reconciling the value-for-money approach with a user-based approach. As we shall see, one of the problems in applying this kind of approach to education is that of specifying *users*. This consideration is quite crucial because it obliges us to consider the overall political context in which considerations of the worthwhileness of education operate.

Nevertheless there are two broad approaches to quality in the commercial sector that have become very influential in state education and it is now time to look at these.

II QUALITY MANAGEMENT SYSTEMS

The division of labour in the production process, together with the disciplined operation of a production line, is known as *Taylorism* after the executive of that name who was one of the advocates of such a form of industrial production.[6]

Taylorist practices of work in manufacturing led to important gains in efficiency and productivity. The system has, however, been found to have certain drawbacks. It was predicated on a lack of trust for the working man and, following the prescription of Adam Smith, led to a requirement of minimum skill exercised in relentless and tiring conditions of pressure at work. In short, it led to an increasing alienation of labour along the lines predicted by Marx in the 1844 manuscripts. The result was a tendency for workers to develop a mental and moral disassociation from their jobs and a sense of antagonism towards management and owners of the enterprises in which they worked. This antagonism was sharpened by the division of labour between management and supervisory funtions on the one hand and the specialised production functions of the line workers on the other. The result of this was that the quality of the individual product manufactured tended to suffer. If workers did not care about or even deliberately tried to sabotage the products on the production line, then it was inevitable that the quality of the products would suffer. The problem could be rectified by tough systems of inspection and quality control but ensuring quality by this means adds to the cost of products and hence to a lack of competitiveness in the market place. It is estimated that the cost of rectification can in some cases be equivalent to 30 per cent of turnover, incurred through scrapping, rework of defective items, repeated quality inspections, warranty payments and discounts to aggrieved customers. In addition, there are less tangible costs such as cluttered factories, delay, strained relations with customers and suppliers and a heavy load of paperwork.[7]

Despite its association with the commercial world, the concern with quality of manufacture appears to have originated with the state and in particular with defence manufacture. This is, perhaps, not as surprising as it might first appear. The prime function of the state has always been seen to be defence and the very survival of a polity depends on the effectiveness of its ability to defend itself. The survival of individual soldiers depends to a large extent on the effectiveness and reliability of the equipment that they use. The modern concern for quality in manufacturing seems to have originated with the concern of governments to ensure that the right kind of equipment, properly manufactured, was given to soldiers.

It is by now well known that Japanese manufacturers first took up the importance of quality in the sense of product reliability and built a concern for it into their mass production techniques. They were influenced in this by the American thinker W. E. Deming (the Deming prize for quality has been awarded in Japan since 1951). The idea is to get the product 'right first time' and thus to eliminate the costs (mentioned above) incurred in maintaining quality. An important distinction here is between *quality control* and *quality assurance*. Quality control is concerned with the testing of products to see whether or not they meet specification. Thus batches of widgets may be tested and sent for scrapping or reworking if they are found to be defective. Quality control mechanisms may prevent defective products from leaving a factory, but they cannot of themselves prevent waste and loss of time and all the other frictions that may arise from defects in production. Quality assurance (QA) is concerned with ensuring that the production processes are such that defective products are not made in the first place, so that the need for extensive quality control mechanisms at the end point of production is not as pressing. QA relies on a variety of techniques, both statistical and human-based, to ensure that the quality of the product is guaranteed by the time it leaves the production line. The more fashionable 'total quality' approach adopts 'fitness for purpose' rather than 'conformance to specification' as the quality criterion, as this incorporates both design and customer satisfaction considerations into the overall assessment of quality.[8]

Although the maintenance of individual product quality 'right first time' does reduce manufacturing costs, it does not follow that the search for quality should be driven solely by cost. It could arise from *esprit de corps* or an ethical concern with getting it right, living up to ideals or serving the customer. Arguably quality in this sense is a by-product of concern with ideals at work. Many of Deming's recommendations for enhancing and maintaining quality involved getting the systems right, so that a concern for quality was reflected in management structures and in the use of statistical techniques for monitoring deviations from the norm in product manufacture. It would be a mistake, though, to see Deming's concerns as solely system-based. He emphasised that quality had to be a concern for the workforce as a whole and that workers worked best when they were not driven by fear but by a pride in their workmanship. Employee involvement was an important aspect of Deming's system and lives on today in Japanese-owned manufacturing. Several points follow from Deming's thinking, most of which are taken up in the approach known as 'Total Quality Management' which we will look at below.

First, it is difficult to *impose* a concern for quality: if achieving quality is an ideal for a firm, then it must also be held by the workforce; otherwise the problem of alienation alluded to earlier will not be eliminated. At the very least, therefore, a concern with quality will require a complication to Taylorist work practices, making individual workers less like automata and more like autonomous beings with their own powers of judgement.

Second, a concern for quality implies the availability of programmes of training and education, so that workers can have a chance to identify with the aims of quality improvement and learn how to improve quality and share experiences of improving it.

Third, it follows from the points made above that quality improvement is a long-term process: the willing and knowledgeable involvement of individual human beings has to be worked for over comparatively extensive periods of time. Half-hearted or 'bolt-on' programmes of quality improvement are not going to work. This point is related to one made by List (above, p. 8), that the human capital element of productive power takes time and effort to build up, sometimes over generations.

Fourth and finally, there is a difference between the service and manufacturing sectors of the economy in the maintenance of individual quality. Even if a manufactured artefact is not produced 'right first time', it can be improved within the factory, albeit at a cost. This is not the case with services: insofar as they exist only as a transaction with a customer or client, if they are not right first time they are not right at all. Once delivered they cannot be improved — only the next transaction can be improved. In this sense, education is more like a service than it is like a product.

There are two broadly distinct, although not necessarily incompatible, ways of looking at the management of quality within an enterprise. The first is that of establishing quality management *as a system*. This approach is associated with ways of documenting the process of quality assurance and arose from the way in which defence organisations specified both products and the processes that went into their manufacture. In Britain this approach is associated with British Standard 5750 and in the European Union with EN 2900. The idea is that documentation specifies and monitors each stage of a process and that the administration of the documentation is audited both internally and externally in order to guarantee that the processes run according to specification.

The second approach, known broadly as TQM (Total Quality Management), takes the requirements of purchasers (customers) as the starting point and says that the organisation, practices and attitudes (sometimes known as the 'culture' of the enterprise) should be tailored to those requirements. The notion of totality comes from the ramifications that follow from making the customer's priorities those of the firm. They extend through the organisation, from marketing to design for example, to ensure that the kinds of products that are designed are the kind that the customer is likely to want. They also extend from the manufacturer or provider of a service to his suppliers, since he is dependent on them for delivering well-designed and reliable products.

Total Quality Management is as much concerned with design as it is with production, and consideration of the culture of a firm shows how the success of the design function depends on the firm's culture. Here the question is whether or not the item fulfills a purpose well, how well it fulfils that purpose in relation to similar items on the market and the extent to which it is attractive to clients and customers. The issue is a much broader one than the question of whether or not a product comes up to specifications: it is also a question of what those specifications should be. A firm considering making a new product has first of all got to be persuaded that it is worth investing in the product before it commits significant resources to it. Design and testing have to take place and when major problems have been overcome the prospective product has to be tested by potential customers to see if it is attractive to them, to see if it works and to make improvements in line with their suggestions. There might also be a further stage of market research using a survey. Only then will be the product be considered ready for manufacture or operation.

It might be thought that large organisations with well-resourced research laboratories and marketing divisions will have the edge in product innovation, design and development. This is not always true: small firms are very often good at identifying a need and developing a product quickly in order to get it to the customer before the competition. Even large firms often adopt relatively decentralised structures in order to allow room for individual enthusiasts who are also in contact with customers to be given the opportunity to develop innovations without encumbrance from bureaucratic procedures.[9] Once again, a key feature of successful innovation in the commercial sector is often the enthusiasm of individuals and a concern on the part of companies to nurture such enthusiasm.

For both specific and individual quality there is some evidence that knowledge about and care for the type of product or service being sold is a highly significant factor in success.[10] It is enthusiasm about the product, knowledgeability about the competition and close relationships with the customer base that make for commercial success and quality, both in innovation and in manufacture. Remote management, a diverse range of activities that bear little or no relationship to each other and cumbersome and bureaucratic committees and paperwork are not associated with the kind of close and enthusiastic involvement that works, both in developing good, new products and ensuring quality of manufacture.

At least, this is the case made by some of the more influential management gurus such as those cited here. The Peters and Waterman study does seem to have a thin evidential base and a lot of its claims could be said to be little more than common sense. Nevertheless, if what they claim has some truth, then it is worth careful consideration in relation to the way in which concern with quality has had an impact on the world of education, because there is some evidence that the practices adopted to ensure quality in educational organisations are at odds with the way in which the movement for quality has developed among successful organisations in the private sector.

III   THE ANALOGY BETWEEN COMMERCE AND EDUCATION

We need to consider just how strong the analogy between education and the private sector actually is. Most educational activities, being largely sponsored through taxation, do not need to make a profit in order to survive in the way that commercial companies do. Neither do they have to survive in the same kind of competitive environment as commercial organisations. In this sense they are like other activities maintained by government: the administration of justice, health care, defence and social security. Neo-liberal thinking has moved in the direction of introducing the disciplines of the private sector into public sector activity by seeking to ensure that individual units are financially viable and subject to some kind of market for what they have to offer, so that the client group is able to choose among what is on offer. This view is taken by neo-liberals because they believe that human beings work at their best without interference from any discipline other than that of the market. It follows from this that the more like the commercial market sector one can make the operation of public services, the better they will become. Two questions now arise: how much like a commercial service is education, and will commercial disciplines improve it?

Since the term 'education' embraces such a wide range of activities, the answer to the first question is that in some cases the analogy is quite close. For example, training of short duration delivered to a company's employees in return for a fee is similar to other kinds of commercially delivered services. The effectiveness of such training can be judged comparatively easily in terms of performance indicators such as reduction in delays and in accidents at the place of work. But the further one moves from examples such as this, the less obvious it is that education is like a commercial service, still less like a manufactured product. This is evident even if we confine ourselves to the private sector of education. Even here, although schools are in competition with each other, they may well offer distinctive kinds of experience to prospective pupils. Their values and their ethos may be different, they may appeal to different abilities or different kinds of abilities, they may emphasise high academic standards, character formation, artistic pursuits and physical sports to different degrees. They may also be popular because of the social stratum that uses them; this is particularly the case with those schools that have traditionally prepared a future ruling élite for the business of running the country, but it may also be true of a much larger group of independent schools which are popular just because they *are* independent schools. Even if schools are compared directly for high achievement, judging whether schools are effective in helping pupils to achieve is not a straightforward matter, as we shall see in Chapter 5.

The purpose of introducing quality concerns into the private sector is not difficult to understand: it is to improve market share, profitability or both. The increasing sophistication of consumers has meant that they are unlikely to be satisfied with products that are unsuitable for their needs or which tend to break down. Since the Japanese made quality a major feature of their manufacturing effort, firms that are unable to compete on quality criteria are likely to go out of business. A concern with quality is not an option for many firms in the private sector: it is a precondition of survival and success.

The same concerns do not operate in publicly funded education or, if they do, they do so to a limited extent. There is certainly a sense in which schools, colleges and universities can increase their market share by attracting more pupils and students, and they can increase profitability by increasing the amount of income that comes to them from government funding and from fees. Many of the reforms instituted by the New Right have been oriented in this direction, so that income follows intake and, to some extent, is dependent on a quality criterion. There is also an important sense in which those who are educated (the 'consumers' of the service) have not had their views taken account of as much in the past as they now do. More generally there has been an increasing concern, on the part of government, with such matters as the appropriateness of the curriculum, progression and continuity, and the qualifications and ability of teaching staff. The reason for this is that it is thought that successful international competition may be compromised by a deficient system of education, leading to a badly trained, unadaptable and poorly motivated workforce. In one sense, therefore, governmental concern with international competitiveness has led to a concern with the quality of an aspect of the economic infrastructure.[11]

But this does not explain the importation of quality concerns into other areas of state-funded public service, such as the health service. Other factors that operate across the public sector are important here, notably the decline of deferential attitudes among the population and a general expectation that taxation should provide value for money. These attitudinal changes have affected education at all levels. So the concern with quality in state-funded education mirrors the concern in private manufacturing: it arises from international competition and an increasingly demanding public. But there is also the influence of public choice theory and the effect that this has had on imposing external forms of discipline on public sector activities. This will be discussed further later in this chapter.[12]

There are, however, important differences between the two sectors which should encourage caution about the possibility of a wholesale adoption of private manufacturing practice by public sector education. But first it is worth looking at some of the practices that have been taken over.

Formal mechanisms of quality assurance

Throughout the UK education system, the day-to-day operation of schools, colleges and universities has tended to take place on an informal, person-to-person basis. Whether in the hierarchical structures associated with schools and FE colleges or in the more collegial atmosphere of the old universities, trust and the customary recognition of authority in the person of the Headteacher or Principal were assumed to be sufficient to secure the smooth running of the institution. The most significant change in this system was the Council for National Academic Awards, set up in 1964, which instituted structured and well-documented procedures for the awarding of degrees, together with an auditing system to ensure that specifications were adhered to. In recent years, as the CNAA ceded powers to the institutions that it used to accredit, internal quality assurance procedures have taken over this role and the new funding body for higher education in England, the HEFCE, has assumed an inspectorial role. Elsewhere, in the school and further education college system, the tendency has been to extend inspectorial systems of quality assurance, in some cases (the UK) using a privatised system of inspection.

Customer response

There has been an increasing tendency to seek out the views of those perceived to be the users of education, students and parents in particular, and they have been asked to produce course evaluations and to sit on course committees and governing bodies in order to provide information on how they judge the quality of education on offer.

Increased market orientation

This has occurred at various levels of education systems, but particularly in the higher education sector. The income of universities is heavily dependent on recruitment, and in addition there is often intense competition between institutions for the best students and, sometimes, simply for students. This has led to a commercially oriented strategy of student recruitment and the role of the market has, to a considerable degree, been enhanced by governments. It is theoretically possible for universities and schools to 'go out of business' in the sense that they can fail to attract enough users to remain financially viable.

Increasing documentation

Not all quality assurance systems rely on extensive documentation, but formal systems have a tendency to generate paperwork. Since quality assurance requires access to appropriate information, this is not surprising. Techniques such as statistical process control and the involvement of suppliers in quality assurance procedures, together with the need for audit, make this inevitable. In addition, the use in the world of education of committees and documentary procedures along the lines of BS5750 makes the generation of documentation and reliance on its use very prevalent in education.

These four features of commercial quality assurance provide continuity between business and education. Perhaps the most important is the first. Traditionally, schools and universities have tended to take it for granted that procedures would work through custom, practice and the professionalism of those involved. But society has grown less deferential to professionals and has, to some extent, been encouraged to be less so. This means that error has been uncovered and people have become more aware of it. Maladministration can occur, for example, at any stage in the setting and marking of examinations, registration procedures can be sloppy or the qualifications of teachers can be neglected. There is room for correcting errors in educational institutions and quality systems may go some way towards doing this. The problem comes in deciding when the costs entailed by the operation of formal systems outweigh the benefits in error elimination that they produce. It is important that these costs are, as far as possible, the costs that accrue from the employment of properly trained personnel to service these functions, rather than the *opportunity* costs incurred by diverting teachers and lecturers from their primary duties. It is, perhaps, worth pointing out that although the production of error on the part of pupils and students is an essential part of learning and the possibility of it should not be compromised, administrative errors should be eliminated wherever it is possible to do so.[13] In this sense, education is on a par with industry.

IV   DIFFERENCES BETWEEN THE SECTORS

But there are also important differences between the commercial world and education (both private and publicly funded), which now need to be rehearsed.

First of all, government will still wish to control the activities it sponsors, even if it cedes some control to the operation of the market. Secondly, education is associated with values, both those by which individuals live and those espoused by the society, and cannot be considered as a purely commercial profit-driven operation. Thirdly, because of this different context, the introduction of commercially oriented quality systems is likely to have a different effect in non-commercial organisations from what it has in commercial ones. Fourthly, and finally, the concept of a 'customer' as it is used in the private sector can be misapplied when it is used for consumers of public services. Neither is it clear that there is just one consumer of these services who can be called the 'customer', to the exclusion of other interested parties.

Continuing state control

The continuing interest of the state in the maintenance of public services, even when they have been subjected to 'market disciplines', means that they will never operate in a completely independent way. They are simply too important to the maintenance of the basic functions of the state to be left on their own. In some ways, the need for the state to intervene and control actually *increases* with the introduction of market forces, since the market can be unpredictable in its effects, leading to consequences that are contrary to government intentions.

A good example of this is the way that the professions allied to medicine gained degree status for their professional training after the introduction of the 1988 Education Reform Act in the United Kingdom, which allowed individual institutions to offer whatever courses the market would bear, despite previous government resistance to these professions gaining degree status.[14] Another example is the conflict between Treasury pressure to reduce costs by rationalising school provision and a policy of open access to schools which may well lead to a proliferation of small schools each offering a 'niche' type of education. The most obvious way in which the state can exert overall control over a marketised system is by manipulating funding. Another is through the use of audit and inspection services, which may themselves be provided through the market but which may also be able to play a regulatory role.

Education and values

It will be argued in Chapter 4 that education services work according to aims which, even if they are not always stated explicitly, nevertheless profoundly influence the nature of the education provided. Commercial firms, too, have values that influence the way in which they behave and which often have a vital effect on their commercial success. But there is an important difference. The commercial firms have values that inform the ways in which they work, their relationships with employees and their relationships with customers. Educational institutions have values that they aim to inculcate within their students or pupils. These may very well have a strong religious or moral significance.

In a sense, then, educational institutions, expecially those that are concerned with longer-term phases of education, as opposed to short-term training packages, are seeking to *change* their pupils and students rather than just to influence them to come back and buy the product or service again. This means that what they do is very often contrary to the immediate wishes of the recipient of education. Yet it is also possible, and often likely, that the change is in the recipient's interest, whether he likes it or not. It must be open to educators to go on doing something that the recipient does not currently like if the long-term aims of education are to have any effect.

Different context of operation

Because of continuing government interest and because of the value-influenced nature of what they do, educational institutions are going to be affected in different ways from commercial organisations by the introduction of quality enhancement programmes. Once again, the concept of the 'customer' has a limited or at least different significance for educational institutions compared with commercial ones. There is also a longer-term commitment to an educational institution. In order to benefit from education one needs not only to follow the full course of study but to build up relationships with teachers and fellow-students and pupils in order for effective learning to take place. This means that there are limits on the extent to which the customer can take his custom elsewhere according to whim. The relationship between pupil and most forms of educational institution tends to be a long-term one.

The different context in which education operates also affects the system of quality assurance that is most appropriate. We have already noted state involvement and the value-oriented nature of education. But the long-term nature of education, both in its formal activity and in the fulfilment of aims, makes it difficult to see how all the most important aspects of what is worth while can be assessed in quality assurance systems such as BS5750 and TQM. The difficulty here is that the most valuable educational outcomes may make themselves manifest *outside* the time-scale in which quality assurance systems operate. QA systems are, above all, concerned with processes that go on within a factory, enterprise or institution. The assumption is that if the processes are got right then it is likely that the product will be got right as well. But there is a way of checking that this is so. For example, a TQM approach may design mechanisms for customer response into a factory's or restaurant's system. If short-term customer satisfaction is taken to be the criterion of success, then it can be measured fairly easily and in any case will show up in a tangible form in market share and profits. For education, a key indicator of worthwhileness will be the *long-term* gains that accumulate during progress through education, or which come to fruition once formal education is completed. This means that education requires commitment and trust on the part of the person being educated. Without trust in educational processes it is very difficult to see how individuals or their parents could make a *personal* commitment to seeking the intangible and long-term benefits that may come from education. It is desirable that the implementation of agreed values will be embodied in the aims of education and that these will have ramifications for the curriculum, for standards and for pedagogy. The long-term nature of education together with the fact that it embodies the implementation of an agreed set of values makes it a distinctive activity the assessment of whose worthwhileness demands a prior philosophical examination. Commercially based QA systems will find this almost impossible to assess and inspection-based systems will also find it difficult. Research is one possible answer but, as we shall see, it has its own drawbacks.

Interest groups and customers

The outcomes of education are neither products nor services in the sense in which those terms are used in commercial enterprises, for they are not just 'use values' for a customer in any straightforward sense. The exception to this is commercially provided, focused training, for example in the use of a new software package for a firm's employees. The outcomes of education considered more generally, however, are not use values like this which can be directly measured in terms of the productivity and profitability of a firm. This is because education is concerned with long-term gains of various kinds. These include values, standards of behaviour and the maintenance of culture as well as the economic benefits, direct and indirect, that result from a country having a well-educated workforce. This is not to say that there is no analogy between the production of goods and services and the outcomes of education: the positionality of education goods is a case in point. But there is more to educational outcomes than this, because of the diversity of aims that exists in a public system of education in a democratic society.

It was argued in Chapter 1 that the idea of government-sponsored non-accountable liberal education was unsustainable both morally and politically. But the connection between public education and outcomes is both looser and broader than in the case of the outcomes expected from a commercial production process. Because they are looser and broader, the introduction of commercially derived quality assurance systems will need to reflect this changed environment. Two questions then arise: are these quality assurance systems capable of being adapted in this way and are they in fact being adapted in appropriate ways?

State involvement in quality assurance systems is likely to mean that educational institutions will not have a completely free hand in choosing how to monitor the system as a whole or even operations *within* an institution. State, and hence political, involvement in quality will tend to mean that the choice will, to some extent, be a political one. Perhaps the most obvious manifestation of this will be the need to indicate to the general public that quality assurance mechanisms are in place and are working. So, for example, the decision by the UK government under the terms of the 1992 Education Act to set up a privatised inspection system for schools, with a four-year inspection cycle and publicly available reports, reflected a political preference for private agencies, for frequent inspection and for public accountability. To a considerable extent, therefore, the choice of quality assurance mechanism will be a political choice, dictated by wider political priorities than just a concern for the operation of the education system. This cannot be assumed to be the case with a private enterprise, whose main concern is with increasing market share and/or profitability. The second difference is that education systems are involved in the creation and transmission of values as one of their main aims, whether implicitly or explicitly. This too implies a longer time-scale for assessment of worthwhileness than is the case with a private enterprise.

Systems that rely heavily on documentation (like BS5750) or on customer satisfaction (like TQM) may find this point difficult to deal with, since it is not obvious that a concern with values can be properly grasped through extensive documentation or through satisfying the needs of the customer. If the customer is a young child, for example, it is not clear that he could have any appropriate values that could drive the organisation (although child-centred forms of education have tried to do this). Most people, both inside and outside education, would view the school's job as one of inculcating values into children, rather than the other way round. A preliminary discussion does, however, suggest that the currently fashionable approaches to quality assurance may be difficult to apply to at least some kinds of educational institutions.

The reason for this is that there is no ready definition of customer that is appropriate to the public sector, first because there is a purchaser (taxpayer, state)/consumer split and secondly because there is a consumer/consumer split (for example, in the case of education, between parent and child). The situation is further complicated because the same individual may belong to different interest groups (for example, parent/taxpayer/politician) and may act differently according to which role is predominant at any given time. This is one reason why inspection continues to be a favoured option of some governments. It is worth noting that, although some of the considerations brought to bear about public sector education are specific to education in this sector, there are similar points to be made about other areas of public service such as health care, where attempts have been made to tie TQM to such user concepts as the 'needs of the patient'.[15] As in education in relation to the needs of the pupil, there are problems in defining needs and the answers are quite likely to be different depending on the perspective from which they are being considered.

Both documentation systems and TQM are based on the requirements of the customer. We have already seen that the notion of a single client group for education is problematic, as indeed is the notion of 'customers' for education. Any system that takes one of the interest groups involved in education and gives that group priority over all the others needs to justify that choice quite strongly if it is to be accepted. Commercial QA systems define the customer as the consumer and purchaser of products and services. But in the case of education this involves at least two interest groups and probably more. At the very least, therefore, such QA systems need to be heavily modified to take account of the customer/purchaser split and its consequences if they are to be applied in education. If they do not, then they will simply not be doing the job which they were introduced to do, namely that of seeing whether or not the outcomes of education are 'fit for purpose'. When the consumer/customer defines the purpose this is not too much of a problem. When multiple influences go to make up educational aims, reflecting the interest of different groups who have an involvement in education, then assessing fitness for purpose is going to be more difficult, for the question 'Whose purpose?' has first got to be addressed.

Where the purpose/aim has been clearly defined and is, broadly speaking, accepted there need not be so much of a problem, but the point made above needs to be borne in mind, that the realisation of educational aims (which are the purpose) may only be possible in the long term. This point should not, perhaps, be exaggerated. Some educational aims, such as the development of literacy, numeracy or particular skills or items of knowledge, can be clearly stated as aims, and outcomes are relatively easy to measure (provided that the results of tests are accepted as valid). But assessing whether other educational aims have been achieved, particularly in the development of values, or autonomy or appreciation of cultural heritage, may not be as easy.

V PUBLIC CHOICE THEORY

One very important influence on conservative and neo-liberal thinking about the management of the public sector has been what is known as *public choice* theory.[16] Public choice theorists hold that the instrumentally rational *homo oeconomicus* model of human action, used in the model-building of economists and found, for example, in the theory of market functioning, is just as applicable to the action of individuals in organisations.[17] Where the institutions operate within a market, the desires of the individual become subordinated to the maximisation of utilities for the organisation. But where market disciplines do not apply, such as in a public-funded education system, then such individual 'rent-seeking' behaviour will not serve the ostensible purposes for which the organisation exists. In practice employees will work to aggrandise their own positions and to secure advantages for themselves and the bureaucracy for which they work.

There are two possible solutions to such a barrier to the efficient working of a public service or utility. The first is privatisation and the second is regulatory control. When a public service is transferred to the private sector, efficiency is guaranteed by the market as it is in the self-interest of individuals to make the organisation competitive. We will see in Chapter 9 what the limitations of the market for the provision of educational goods will be at the macro level: it cannot guarantee the matching of resources to needs in education. At the micro level the problem does not disappear because the self-interest of individuals within the firm is not guaranteed to make the firm function well by co-operative behaviour. The behaviour of purely self-interested individuals may be quite capricious, depending on their short-term goals.[18] For a firm to function effectively there must be a measure of non-self-interested behaviour allowing for long-term planning and mutual co-operation in a common endeavour. But to concede this is to attack the most basic assumption of public choice theory.

The alternative, control, suffers from the same problems, if the assumptions of public choice theory are taken seriously. For the controlling bodies will only be interested in maintaining quality to the extent that it serves their own self-interest. But this confluence of interest cannot be guaranteed. It may be, for example, that self-aggrandisement on the part of the quality assurance body demands the creation of a large bureaucracy with lots of paperwork, whether or not this serves the stated purposes of quality assurance. On the other hand, if non-self-interested behaviour is found within the quality assurance bureaucracy then this particular justification for policing education fails for precisely the reason that, by parity of reasoning, one cannot assume that education is a purely rent-seeking activity.

In any case, accountability can be justified without such extravagant and implausible assumptions about human nature. All that needs to be said is that accountability is a democratic requirement and that, if it is taken seriously, there need to be mechanisms to assure it. There is a particular need when the self-aggrandising *tendencies* that we all harbour within us are subject to no scrutiny whatsoever and when a particular section of society is not obliged to pay attention to the points of view of other sections. Either way, public choice theory, on its own assumptions, cannot justify the use of the market or of a bureaucratic control mechanism to ensure quality in education.

VI CONCLUSION

These considerations should lead us, not to reject commercially based systems of quality assurance in education outright, but to become aware of their possible shortcomings. It may well be the case that they are more effective in some parts of education than others. They will probably be useful in the following circumstances:

1. Where education/training organisations are operating in a genuine market environment with tangible consumer/purchaser-based short-term

outcomes available for assessment. In these cases the desired outcome can be specified quite precisely and it can be related primarily to the needs of the organisation that is providing the service. Highly specific short-term job training would be an example.

2. Where educational aims are agreed upon, are realisable on a relatively short time-scale and can be validly assessed in a fairly trouble-free manner. Examples of such kinds of activity would be intervention programmes such as reading remediation or behaviour modification programmes. Even here there are limits, for the aims, although explicitly short-term, are implicitly long-term (it is assumed to be undesirable that the result of the intervention should disappear or be negated in the long-term). Assessing the long-term quality of an intervention may entail the use of longitudinal research techniques.

3. Where activity and investment that is ancillary to education and which has the clearly defined purpose of assisting teaching and learning is being assessed. This includes the provision of management, administration, financial control, management of building stock and capital equipment. In such cases, there are two broad possibilities. One is to adopt the standards approach and set up detailed specifications for each function and an accompanying system of documentation and audit to ensure that specifications are met. Such an approach would appeal to many institutions as it would appear, at first sight, not to disturb traditional management hierarchies which rely on a non-collegial top-down approach to management and administration. TQM could start with a consideration of pupils/students and teachers/lecturers as the 'end users' of the services provided. The analogy with a commercial enterprise would still be far from complete, since there will not be any outside competitive pressures brought to bear on the quality of the services delivered (unless, that is, these services are put out to short-term contract). But the implications of using TQM from the end-user point of view could eventually lead to a questioning of management hierarchies. For it could actually result in downgrading the status of ancillary functions that are often thought to be more important than the activities of teaching and learning.

   The consequences of such an approach are, however, worth considering because they may have more impact on the working of an educational institution than is usually realised at first sight. But because of the important differences between the private and public sectors it is unlikely that the manufacturing model of quality assurance will ever predominate in education. What may happen is that the appearance of the manufacturing model may become prevalent without any serious consideration of its appropriateness to education.

4. Where administrative procedures directly affect teaching and learning. These include registration, assessment and pastoral care. In a complex institution whose main resource is people, there will always be a need for ways of keeping track of what is going on. Exams need to be set, marked and reported on; students need to be registered and their progress monitored; students with difficulties need to be identified and helped; proposals for theses have to be assessed and approved. It is not possible to

do this efficiently without the use of data-handling techniques and these need to be designed and then operated by knowledgeable personnel who will, at least in part, be the academic staff themselves. In the past schools and colleges have tended to rely on established personal relationships and fairly informal procedures to process these administrative tasks to a far greater extent than was wise. For example, one area where this tended to happen was in the running of research degree programmes. As a result, completion rates in the UK, especially in the arts and social sciences, were extremely low. Since so little was documented as to the role of research supervisors, there was a tremendous reliance on the quality and conscience of the individual supervisor to see that the student was properly treated. Since virtually everything depended on the supervisor, who himself was not very often clear about his role, there was plenty of scope for inefficiency and waste, particularly of the time of the research student. The use of documentation setting out timetables, deadlines, clear expectations and role descriptions, together with a committee system to monitor and oversee progress, can go some way towards ameliorating such problems.

One feature of some of the quality research that is less remarked upon when quality assurance techniques are being recommended to education, is that quality in the commercial sector is often associated with non-hierarchical, non-paper and non-committee driven procedures. It is also associated with letting unorthodox but talented invididuals have scope for trying out ideas, even if they prove to be initially disruptive. Such scope is particularly valuable for product design and improvement.[19] In fact, nearly all the quality assurance procedures that have been introduced into education in the last decade or so have tended to reinforce hierarchies and increase the amount of paper and committee work. In general, the contribution of awkward but original people who are relatively low in their institution's hierarchy has not been recognised even where it has not been positively discouraged.

This suggests that the lessons that can be learned from the commercial sector are quite complex and that the way in which they have been selected indicates that the real agenda that governments are pursuing with quality in the public sector is not so much product excellence as it is control over what is going on. In fact, as was remarked earlier, since governments still retain *responsibility* for what goes on in the public sector, even when they cede some of their *power* to the operation of the market, this urge to control is hardly surprising. The irony is that accountability is thus exercised not through the market but through cumbersome bureaucratic procedures.

What then are the lessons that can *usefully* be learned from commercial concerns with quality? Public choice theory is sterile as a way of describing both the behaviour of individuals within organisations and the organisations themselves. On the other hand, those elements of anarchy and individualism that are often valued in some sections of the private sector have always existed to a large degree in education and are valuable for much the same reason, namely that those individuals capable of innovation and originality will be most likely to produce it for the benefit of all if they are given the institutional space to do so. If anything, bureaucratic methods of assessing the quality of teaching, for example, are most likely to make teaching conformist and unoriginal.

However, the need for scrupulous documentation to ensure procedural justice and efficiency in educational institutions suggests that there is a need for bureaucratic procedures in certain areas, and it may be that schools and colleges need to pay far more attention, as businesses have long done, to certain specialist functions within the organisation. Registries, secretariats and bursar's offices, staffed by properly qualified professionals, should be able to support these clerical, administrative and managerial functions far better than hard-pressed academics and teachers will be able to do. Undoubtedly there is a cost to all this, but against this must be set the opportunity and other costs such as increase in ill-feeling and loss of reputation involved in giving these functions to personnel who are ill-trained and poorly motivated to undertake them.

If there is a distinctive approach to quality or worthwhileness in education, it should be concerned with the achievement of consensually negotiated and agreed aims within the context of an appropriate form of democratic accountability. And what can be learned from the commercial quality movement is only valuable to the extent that it serves that concern.[20]

NOTES

1. For these distinctions see Anna Coote and Naomi Pfeffer, *Is Quality Good For You?*, 1991.
2. Cf. T. Peters and R. Waterman, *In Search of Excellence*, 1982.
3. P. B. Crosby, *Quality is Free*, 1979.
4. Cf. J. Juran, *Quality Planning and Analysis*, 1993.
5. Associated with A. Feigenbaum, *Total Quality Control*, 1991. For a useful introduction to these distinctions, see C. Morgan, *A Practical Guide to Quality and Quality Systems*, 1994.
6. F. Taylor, *The Principles of Scientific Management*, 1911.
7. Simon Caulkin, Hezza's quality drive, *Observer*, 6 February 1994, B7.
8. Cf. Juran, *op. cit.*
9. See Peters and Waterman, *op. cit.*
10. Ibid., Ch. 10.
11. This is a different concern from the one examined in Chapter 9. Whether education is provided by the market or by government, international economic competition remains.
12. See Stretton and Orchard, *op. cit.*
13. Cf. R. Barnett, *Improving Higher Education: Total Quality Care*, 1992.
14. L. Merriman, *The Transition from Degree to Diploma in the Professions Allied to Medicine*, unpublished Ph.D. thesis, Nene College, forthcoming.
15. See, for example, Wendy Ranade (1994), *Future for the National Health Service? Health Care in the Nineteen Nineties*.
16. See Stretton and Orchard, *op. cit.*, for a good theoretical introduction to the main concepts of public choice theory.
17. Cf. G. Tullock, The welfare costs of tariffs, monopoly and theft, *Western Economic Journal*, 3 (1967), pp. 224–233; W. Niskanen, *Bureaucracy and Representative Government*, 1971.
18. 'A behaviourist economic science which looks only to people's actions without trying to understand their thoughts is defective even for its own purposes. So — by implication — are the versions of public choice theory which impute exclusively self-serving purposes to all behaviour. (From that axiom Sen deduces: "Can you direct me to the Railway Station?" asks the stranger. "Certainly", says the local, pointing in the opposite direction to the Post Office, "and would you post this letter for me on your way?" "Certainly", says the stranger, resolving to open it to see if it contains anything worth stealing.)' Stretton and Orchard, *op. cit.*, p. 51.
19. See, for example, Peters and Waterman, *op. cit.*
20. Cf. Pfeffer and Coote, *op. cit.*, pp. 22–29.

Chapter 3
Education: A Contested Concept

I PERSUASIVE DEFINITIONS OF 'EDUCATION'

Ever since Socrates' attempts to provide definitions of such concepts as *virtue* and *justice*, philosophy has been concerned with language and often with the provision of definitions of concepts of philosophical interest. In most cases, the definition offered is claimed to have at least a plausible relationship with the way in which the concept is used in everyday communication. More often, though, it is selective (drawing on a preferred subset of uses of the term which expresses the concept), and prescriptive, indicating how the philosopher offering the definition thinks that the term *should* be used.

Much recent philosophy of education, although it purports to base definition on the common usage of terms, in fact offers prescriptive definitions of education.[1] These have, in the main, tended to emphasise the *liberal* conception of education, that is, the conception of education that places priority of value on personal development as a desirable end in itself.[2] *Instrumental* definitions of education, which value education for the extrinsic purposes for which it may be used, are much less commonly developed.[3] Yet it is well enough documented that most people who are not educators do tend to adopt an instrumental view of the nature and value of education.[4] Perhaps the educational philosophers are right and most other people who use the term 'education' without reflecting on it philosophically are confused as to its proper meaning. But if the purported analysis of the term 'education' is based on its employment in non-philosophical contexts, then it is remarkable that these uses are so little recognised in the definitions that are produced by philosophers of education. For these are, in the main, selective, prescriptive and biased towards a liberal view.

There *are* alternative views about the nature of education, even if they do not receive the same hearing in the academic world. This does not, however, invalidate them. Instrumental views of education of differing sorts are held by children, parents, politicians and businessmen. If accountability is to be taken seriously, then their views of the nature and purpose of education will need to be taken account of as well. Perhaps they are just mistaken. But anyone who begins philosophical enquiry by at least paying lip service to the need to take account of ordinary usage would be wise to pay some attention to the ordinary use of the term 'education'. A further feature of its use also needs to be taken account of, namely that it is *political* in the two important senses identified in Chapter 1. First, education is implicated in the interests of different groups. Secondly, as a form of preparation for life, it is concerned with the values by which life should be lived. For both of these reasons, it is a proper concern of governments and one of government's major activities.

The fact that there are alternative ways of looking at education, each of which is plausibly related to the everyday employment of the term 'education', together with the fact that there is a political interest in education, has led some philosophers to take the view that it is part of the very nature of education that people should disagree about what it is or what it should be. Concepts about which there are such radical and seemingly intractable disputes are sometimes labelled 'essentially contestable'.[5] Much of the debate about this issue, although important, is not directly relevant to the questions at issue here. It is enough to note both that *education* is contested and that the contestation is political in nature.

II   THE PRIVILEGED POSITION OF THE LIBERAL VIEW

It was said earlier that the liberal view of education as a means of self-fulfilment is the dominant one, particularly in academic circles. Does this not undermine the case for saying that the concept of education is a contested, let alone an essentially contested, one, since the contest has been won by the liberal conception and its proponents? The fact that one conception is dominant does not undermine the claim that the concept is contested, because the political nature of contestability virtually ensures that different conceptions will enjoy varying fortunes according to historical epoch, culture and place. In fact, many who hold a liberal conception believe that it is far from dominant.[6] It is my view that the liberal conception is, however, dominant, particularly in the United Kingdom and English-speaking countries. The cultural dominance of a liberal view of life, concerned with self-fulfilment, has long been prominent in British life and has come to exercise a hold far beyond the gentry and aristocracy among whom it originated.[7] This outlook in turn goes back to the influence of classical antiquity on the educated and leisured classes in Western Europe.[8]

Since people from such a background came to dominate the universities, government and the civil service and since, in any case, the outlook of the gentry found its way into other parts of society, it is hardly surprising that the liberal conception has been politically dominant. This dominance also explains the surprising ambivalence of the industrial world to technical and vocational education in the United Kingdom, an ambivalence which is not shared by most of the countries in Western Europe. Despite the advantages of a vocationally well-educated workforce, the business community is so deeply affected by the liberal ideal that it sometimes finds it difficult to recognise the advantages that may come from vocational education.[9] The liberal conception has, nevertheless, come under pressure particularly from sections of the political élite and the business world which have been concerned with the economic consequences of the liberal ideal. Those interest groups which do not have the same degree of political influence within the society, such as children and parents from working-class families, find that their alternative conceptions often receive short shrift.

A further source of the dominance of the liberal conception, particularly in the United Kingdom, lies in the disaggregated nature of the education system. The devolution of the control of education to local authorities consequent on the 1944 Education Act meant in practice that control over pedagogy and the curriculum passed into the hands of the education service, with little influence from outside. Since the liberal conception, and particularly the progressivist version of that, was dominant in the education service, it is not surprising that it came to be, and continued to be, particularly influential.

I have argued in Chapter 1 that education is a political matter because different interest groups are implicated in education in different ways. The most natural way of modelling such a situation is in terms of the working out of such interests within the polity, so that a negotiation satisfactory to all parties is reached. It should be clear that for historical, political and cultural reasons only a pathological version of this model would adequately describe the situation in the United Kingdom, and in England and Wales in particular.[10] Once lost, a political balance is not always easy to regain, because those who have profited from the loss of balance have found it easy to consolidate their position in the meantime. A pathological state of disequilibrium is likely to be long-lasting, if not permanent. There is little doubt that much of the concern for accountability in the public service in general, and quality in education in particular, arises from a wish to end this pathological state and to restore a more politically healthy equilibrium. But, for the reasons just stated, this is likely to be a more difficult and protracted task than the neo-liberals who originated the project originally thought.

The liberal conception of education is dominant, but its dominance is under a long-term threat. The success of alternative conceptions in creating and maintaining an equilibrium which is a better reflection of the range of interests and outlooks involved in education depends, to a large extent, on the political acumen and influence of the representatives of those alternative conceptions at all levels where education is important, from the universities to governments, homes and staffrooms. The contest between alternative conceptions will go on because the interests and points of view that they represent are both substantial and intrinsic to modern societies and are likely to remain so for the foreseeable future.

III   EDUCATION, TRAINING AND SCHOOLING

One possible way of defusing the essential contestability account of education and restoring the liberal conception to an undisputed pride of place is to classify alternative conceptions as different, although related, concepts. Thus those forms of preparation that are concerned to develop good citizens and social cohesion can be redescribed as 'schooling', while the vocational side of preparation could be classified as 'training'.

There are two aspects to schooling. One is fairly easily distinguishable from education, namely the process of inculcation into the particular rules for the functioning of individual schools. These rules would deal with such matters as uniform, conduct in the corridors, punctuality and so on. All pupils would need to learn and to adopt these rules in order to enable the school to operate. The other aspect of schooling is much more closely related to education; indeed it is not really separable from it, certainly not from some kinds of education. Most schools have education as their principal activity. Schools exist because they are a cost-effective way of preparing large numbers of young people for adult life (compare the cost of giving everyone a private tutor), but they generally include among their educational aims the social and moral preparation of young people. Since this is largely a practical matter, to be learned through one's dealings with others, both children and adult, it might be said that schooling is the most appropriate way of carrying out this aim of education. If this is so, then schooling in this second sense is a necessary part of education, not just a contingent aspect of the practical arrangements for education.

A liberal educator who hoped to save the liberal conception by separating it sharply from schooling would then have done no more than to presuppose what he sought to establish, namely the primacy of the liberal conception. But this move would convince no-one who was not already persuaded of the liberal's own point of view. Indeed, those liberal educators who see moral formation as one of the primary aims of a liberal education might find it particularly difficult to separate education from schooling. For if they believe in the practical nature of moral education, then they would be hard put to it to find a more appropriate medium than a school to carry out a large part of that project, since it is in schools that children learn how to act morally in situations of increasing complexity under the guidance of moral exemplars in the form of teachers.

Generally speaking, it is only possible to separate some of the activities of schools and colleges (e.g. grounding in basic literacy, numeracy and factual knowledge, vocational preparation, physical education and socialisation) from education properly so called if one can advance a favoured concept of education that excludes these other things. But it is in doing this that philosophers of education have failed to be convincing. *Why* they have failed thus will become clearer in the next chapter.

Training is not just a different *sort* of preparation from education, it is a different, although related, concept. There are forms of activity called 'training' which are difficult to distinguish from others called 'education', but the difference is not always, or even most of the time, merely one of nomenclature. Training is concerned with the development of *technique*, rather than with preparation for adult life. All education relies on the inculcation of technique to a greater or lesser extent and so training in moral codes, or in the use of a pencil or logarithmic tables, are all parts of education, although they are not an education in themselves. If this is true then it is quite absurd to claim that education and training can be divorced from each other. Vocational training in the use of an occupation-specific technique is not necessarily part of education (although it may be). But it might be part of a form of education that prepares young people for adult life through a programme of vocationally oriented activities which includes an element of training; it would still be education. What is more, it might well share some aims and characteristics with more liberal forms of education.[11] Once again, it is not possible for the liberal educator to favour his own conception of education at the expense of others without presupposing what he seeks to establish.

IV EDUCATION, WORTHWHILENESS AND QUALITY

It has been argued that there is a loose conceptual connection between education and worthwhileness. In particular, if I recommend a form of education to someone I am claiming that it is a good preparation for life. It is possible that some particular forms of education (or even forms of some conception of education) might not be worthwhile, but not the whole enterprise of education itself. Traditionally, a highly worthwhile education was, and still is, one where there is a great deal of prestige attached to the school or university in which the education takes place, where there are teachers and scholars of outstanding ability and where the curriculum is thought to be both demanding and prestigious. Such an education is worthwhile partly because it conveys a strong positional advantage, that is, those who benefit from it do so at the expense of these who do not.[12]

In this sense Oxford and Cambridge, Eton and Harrow and some of the grammar schools have traditionally purveyed an education that was particularly sought after, for the reasons mentioned above. The concern with prestige and positional advantage is largely irrelevant to the concerns of a mass public education system and new ways of conceptualising and measuring worthwhileness have been tried. The Revised Code of the latter half of the nineteenth century attempted to measure and reward performance against a set of standards.[13] Subsequent attempts to measure worthwhileness have sought to ground their judgements on the perceived performance of teachers; this account of worthwhileness, with modifications, has persisted to the time of writing. The major difficulty with it, though, is that it makes over the power of judgement to educational experts, and thus to one particular interest group. Not only that, but the judgements that it demands of them are subjective ones: not judgements about performance against objective and publicly available standards, but judgements on *preferred* ways of teaching and organising classrooms. Whether or not it is useful at all to judge such standards independently of the judgement of standards of educational achievement will be discussed in more detail later in this book.[14]

This 'producer-led' way of assessing educational worthwhileness could not withstand the call from the neo-liberals and others outside the teaching profession for a measure of worthwhileness that took into account the point of view of the *consumer* of educational services. A new view of educational worthwhileness, particularly associated with the term 'quality' and the associations that had been built up around that term in industry and commerce, was introduced into the world of education, with a view to supplanting, or at least modifying, the old views of educational worthwhileness (see the previous chapter).

It has been argued that the term 'quality' covers different conceptions and four of these have been outlined: prestige or positional advantage, conformity to standards, customer satisfaction, and customer empowerment. In addition, it can be argued that, insofar as education is a public service providing public goods (in the strong sense meaning goods that are necessarily public, such as clean air), a further criterion of quality needs to be considered, namely the achievement of these public goods at reasonable cost.[15] In addition there is a definition of quality which has been around at least since the time of Plato and which is still in current use: something is of high quality if it is fit for the purpose for which it was designed and built.[16] The advantage of the 'fitness for purpose' criterion of quality is that it encompasses the *design* as well as the *manufacture* aspect of the creation of something.

Enough has already been said to suggest that the concept of quality is a complex one, embracing several different dimensions. Quality is also an evaluative term: to say that something is of quality is to approve of it. The use of the term has, therefore, a considerable rhetorical significance. No-one wishes to be seen to be against or indifferent to quality. They may protest that their conception of quality is not the same as someone else's but this may sound lame. If a politician praises a college which 'provides a good-quality education which satisfies the customer', it may be dangerous to say that one is opposed to that as it implies that one is also opposed to good-quality education. Therefore appropriation of the term 'quality' is of considerable rhetorical significance in political debate. Because *quality* embraces different conceptions, it has a further very useful property. The agendas of politicians are constantly changing, but there is an advantage in at least appearing to have a fixity of purpose. A catch-all term such as 'quality' can cover the change of agenda in a way that masks the real extent to which one conception has been exchanged for another to suit the political exigencies of the day. Thus, if excessive attention has been paid to customer satisfaction in such a way that performance against standards has dropped sharply, it may be useful to emphasise that quality is about maintaining performance against clear and recognisable standards. In this way a radical shift in emphasis will have taken place under the cloak of a continuing concern with quality.[17]

V CONCLUSION

This chapter has made out the case for taking a broadly based view of the concept of education which takes into account the various different *conceptions* of it that different interest groups have. This is necessary if the debate about educational quality is to be engaged with in a meaningful way, since that debate arises from a form of political contestation about educational worthwhileness, which is to a large extent concerned with the legitimacy of certain conceptions of education that have failed to secure a politically dominant role, despite their espousal by significant groups within society. Such political dispute is intrinsic to the concept of education as it occurs in any complex society, but the actual position of the different conceptions at any one time is contingent upon factors of history, culture and politics. This chapter has explored those factors as they relate to education in the developed world in general, and the English-speaking world in particular, in the last years of the twentieth century.

Different conceptions of the concept *quality* as it relates to education have also been outlined and it was argued that the term 'quality' is now becoming associated with a particular view of educational worthwhileness that is closely aligned with a commercial paradigm. This has occurred as a result of the particular nature of the contest between different conceptions of education described above.

NOTES

1. See, for example, Hamm's construal of Peters's account in *Philosophical Issues in Education*, 1989, pp. 38–39: 'Education is the achievement of a desirable state of mind characterised by knowledge and

understanding in breadth and depth with cognitive perspective and by corresponding appropriate emotions and attitudes, these brought about deliberately, in a manner not to infringe upon the voluntariness and wittingness of the part of the learner.'

2. In this book the term 'liberal' as it applies to education means the conception of education as primarily concerned *either* with personal fulfilment *or* with the achievement of an acquaintance with a cultural heritage. According to many liberal theorists, the achievement of the latter is a precondition for the achievement of the former. *Neo-liberalism* on the other hand refers to a set of political doctrines that advocate the minimum of state regulation and the maximum of exposure to market forces.

3. With the change from an oligarchal to a democratic society, it is natural that the significance of an education which should have as a result ability to make one's way economically in the world, and to manage economic resources usefully instead of for mere display and luxury, should receive emphasis. Cp. John Dewey, *Democracy and Education*, 1916, Chapter IX, p. 119.

4. National Commission on Education, *Learning to Succeed*, 1993, p. 151: 'The vast majority [*sc.* of children] believed that schools should help them to do as well as possible in their exams and teach them things that would be useful when they entered jobs.'

5. The term is originally due to W. B. Gallie, Essentially contested concepts, *Proceedings of the Aristotelian Society*, 1955–6, pp. 167–198. For a later account, see M. Naish, Education and essential contestability, *Journal of Philosophy of Education*, 18.2, 1984, pp. 141–154.

6. For example Gray, *op. cit.*, p. 27; P. Abbs, Training spells the death of education, *The Guardian*, 7 January 1987; James Muir, The Isocratic idea of education and the irrelevance of the state versus market debate, *Proceedings of the Philosophy of Education Society of Great Britain*, 1994, pp. 21–27.

7. See Ralf Dahrendorf, *On Britain*, 1982, Chapters 7 and 8.

8. The origins of the liberal conception of education can be found in the work of Socrates, Plato and Aristotle. There it was considered a suitable preparation for the kind of life of contemplative leisure favoured by those philosophers.

9. See M. Sanderson, *The Missing Stratum: Technical Education in England 1900–1990*, 1994, however, on the enthusiasm which the Junior Technical Schools excited among many employers, as well as among children and their parents.

10. Ibid., Chapters 5–8 in particular.

11. See H. Entwistle, *Education, Work and Leisure*, 1970; C. Winch, Vocational education: a liberal interpretation, *Studies in Philosophy of Education*, 1995, for developments of this theme.

12. See Anna Coote and Naomi Pfeffer, *op. cit.*

13. Coote and Pfeffer term this the 'scientific' or expert approach, *op. cit.* pp. 5–9. For a recent account of 'payment by results' see Harold Silver, *Good Schools, Effective Schools*, 1994, Chapter 3.

14. See, in particular, Chapters 8 and 11.

15. See Coote and Pfeffer, *op. cit.*, for a useful account of these definitions. For an account of different kinds of public goods, see Orchard and Stretton, *op. cit.*, pp. 54–55.

16. Plato, *The Republic*, Book IV; also Book X.

17. Something like this appears to have happened in 1994, in relation to British higher education, against a background of concern about 'falling standards' in the newer (ex-polytechnic) universities.

Chapter 4
The Aims of Education Revisited

I THE IMPORTANCE OF THE ISSUE

Any healthy public system of education needs to maintain accountability. An organisation is accountable if it is possible to determine whether or not it fulfils the purposes for which it was set up. So accountability can be exercised by checking to see whether it is fulfilling its purposes and *how well* it is fulfilling them. In order for accountability to operate, the purposes of the institution must be stated or at least agreed to by the interested parties as *aims*; otherwise it will be difficult to divine those purposes, thus threatening the whole exercise. It follows, therefore, that if public education is to be accountable, then either it must articulate its aims or its aims must be agreed to in a consensual way by all concerned.[1] Furthermore, in order to assess quality (in whatever sense) it is necessary to measure performance against agreed aims.

When the major aims of education are not clearly agreed upon, there is a danger that *covert* aims may become the most influential in determining the operation of a public education system. It is likely that these aims will be set by the most influential groups operating both within and outside the system. Because there will have been little or no public debate about aims, it is likely that the interests of some will receive scant attention and may even be harmed. If a society does not have clear and agreed aims for its education system, there will be a danger that not only will it fail to have a healthy system that is respected and functions well, but there will also be widespread and damaging discontent among those groups whose interests are not well served.

This seems simple enough and it ought to be possible to go ahead and institute accountability through the requirement of an articulation of aims. Unfortunately it is not as simple as that, particularly in a large and complex society. It is possible to do it, however, under certain conditions. But, unless these conditions are recognised, it is likely that the articulation of educational aims will remain incomplete or non-existent. Perhaps the most obvious way of articulating aims for education is to ask what education is required *for*. Having answered that question it should then be possible to formulate aims that articulate those purposes. Then the rest—institutions, curriculum, pedagogy and assessment—will be designed in order to serve those aims. The analogy here is with an individual who decides that he has a need, for example, to mow his lawn: he then formulates an aim, namely to get his lawn mowed, and then purchases a lawnmower which is fit to achieve his chosen aim. The quality of the lawnmower can then be assessed against the two criteria of whether or not it does mow the lawn and how well it does so.

Some social change can be described reasonably accurately according to this technical model. For example, the behaviour of car drivers can be affected by making alterations to the road surface, thus causing the drivers to go slowly.

But even this technical kind of change needs some kind of involvement on the part of those affected if it is to succeed fully. Otherwise individuals will fail to co-operate with change and all kinds of unforeseen circumstances may arise which thwart the aim of getting drivers to change their behaviour.

But in any case societies are not mechanisms composed of institutions that carry out discrete functions. They are interconnected sets of institutions with histories, cultures and networks of rules that affect all aspects of the lives of individual members. The different aspects of a society affect each other. Changes in one aspect are likely to affect the way in which another aspect carries on. Thus changes in education are likely to affect the way in which the economy or the judicial system works. Since educational change is likely to affect the whole or a large part of a society, it cannot be just a technical matter for a few experts in education to determine, but ought at least, if the change is going to be a healthy one, to involve the representatives of all those affected.

Any education system will have aims of some kind even if they are concealed and/or implicit. A society that fails to articulate or even to get clear about the aims of its education system will most likely enjoy a second-rate one, because some of the most substantial interests in society will not have a chance to articulate what they want from education, thus losing the chance that their interests will be represented, leading to a danger of disillusion and contempt for the institution of education itself. The formulation of aims for public education systems is, therefore, a vital task for any democratic society which aims to have an effective education system that commands the confidence of all sections of the population.

Furthermore, education is intrinsic to *any* society, since any society that has ever existed or will ever exist has to prepare the young for adult life. Education is a practice as ancient as the human race. This means that it carries with it an enormous cultural tradition which runs back to the roots of any society. Any change to education has enormous implications for the cultural identity of the society in which the change takes place. As an ancient institution in any society, education will have its own traditions, rituals and practices that will, to some extent, determine how it operates *whatever* the external influences on it might be. In the absence of externally determined aims, it will develop internal, sometimes *implicit* but often, and most damagingly, *covert* ones which will depend largely on tradition, on the interests of those involved in education and on influential individuals within the education system, as well as other influences from the wider society.

Any proposed large-scale change to a system of education has two different kinds of implication. The first is the effect that it will have on the rest of society. The second is the effect that it will have on the institution of education itself. Unless both of these are understood, it is likely that the changes made will have unexpected and possibly undesirable consequences. Setting out, clearly articulating or changing the aims of education are three of the most fundamental changes that could be made to any education system. There is, therefore, a great temptation on the part of politicians and indeed of society as a whole to avoid or to put off such a discussion. The temptation is made all the stronger where it is known or suspected that there will be widespread and substantial disagreement about what those aims should be. However, if they are not set through a process of discussion and negotiation then they will emerge by default, most likely in an implicit form within the education system itself. This need not be the result of malice or of a desire to avoid accountability but may stem from the natural desire of people working within an institution to develop a point of view, to make sense of what they are doing and to make their lives at work at least reasonably satisfying and congenial.

II HOW BEST CAN AIMS BE ARTICULATED?

There is no one answer to such a question: it depends on the nature of the polity itself. In societies in which there is strong implicit agreement and low levels of conflicting interest, little or no debate need be necessary. In such cases, implicit agreement on aims may be possible with little or nothing stated in official documentation. At the other extreme, widespread debate and protracted negotiation may be necessary before the careful drafting of aims that are reasonably congenial to everyone actually takes place. This is likely to be the case if a society is complex and if there are opposing interests at work between different groups, if for example there is a deep national or religious division within a society.

One problem suggests itself at the outset. Education is about the preparation of the young for adult life. It is therefore concerned with how human beings should live. Questions of ethical value are bound up with educational aims. Educational aims will partly articulate the values which a society considers important, whether these be religious or moral values or both. But to say that a person's or a social group's *values* could be the subject of negotiation is to commit a solecism. Values are not the *kinds of things* which it can make sense to say can be negotiated over. It is possible to negotiate about what should be the appropriate conventions of address, but not about whether people should be treated with respect. It is also possible to negotiate about the means by which one satisfies the values in which one believes. For example, two utilitarians may debate the likely consequences of a certain course of action. They both believe in the principle of promoting the greatest happiness of the greatest number, but they disagree on which course of action will best promote such an aim.

It seems, however, that the *values* that we hold are held unconditionally. However we arrive at them, they are so much a part of how we see ourselves and other people as well as how we see the world that they are part of our nature. To attempt to negotiate about them would therefore seem to be a case of acting in bad faith. If they are negotiable, then it is questionable whether we hold them sincerely. To say all this is not to be committed to an emotivist or intuitionist theory of ethics. Someone who believes that one's values are expressed through the exercise of virtues or who believes in the utilitarian position will be committed to the same thing. Neither could a Kantian hold the principle that rational beings should be treated as ends rather than as means, and simultaneously regard that principle as negotiable.[2]

This appears to pose a difficulty for the very basis on which the discussion of educational aims in terms of negotiation between different interest groups is being conducted. If educational aims are about values and values are non-negotiable then how could it be possible to *negotiate* about educational aims? The whole exercise seems to be doomed from the start. The objection is not, however, fatal to the political description of education that I have been advancing, although it certainly indicates that what is being proposed is something that could be quite difficult. The reason that the process of negotiation is not vitiated at the outset is that there is no requirement that anyone from any group should be required to negotiate their values. All that they are invited to do in any such process is to negotiate about the *implementation* of those values *in the public sphere*.

While this suggests that the exercise is perfectly possible, it also suggests that it may be difficult in certain circumstances, demanding a great deal of patience and tolerance, not to mention a willingness to settle issues by negotiation rather than by other means. There must also be sufficient common ground for dialogue within the society for negotiation to take place. If two groups are so out of sympathy with each other, with one for example not recognising the legitimacy of a negotiated settlement with the other group, then dialogue may not be possible. Certain conditions have to be met before negotiation about the implementation of values can take place. Where values are largely shared, then the problems of negotiation are lessened. There may be differences about which values should be given priority, but negotiation about this may not be too difficult if both parties are agreed that the same sets of values should be enshrined in educational aims and differ only about which should be given most prominence.

Again, when two sets of values differ but are not mutually contradictory, it should be possible to incorporate both to some degree at least within the overall aims of education. When two moral points of view are largely congruent but derive from differing and mutually contradictory religious standpoints it may not be too difficult to arrive at consensus either, so long as in the public sphere those values are promoted in a secular or religiously neutral idiom. The greatest problems arise when the moral values held by two groups are *mutually contradictory*. The problem is particularly acute when these values are of central importance to both groups.

This suggests that negotiation is not always possible. At the limit a society that cannot agree with itself on fundamental questions of value is not going to have much scope for negotiation. This discussion suggests that negotiation about the implementation of values can take place within a pluralistic and even a multicultural society provided that different groups with varying values are prepared to compromise on the implementation of those values and provided that they see the outcome of the negotiation as a reasonably fair one. The acceptance of a compromise does not merely presuppose a democratic and tolerant outlook on the part of the different groups, it also presupposes a willingness to submit to an external authority who can be trusted to put the compromise into effect and to see that its terms are adhered to. These conditions can be met by a modern society but it would be idle to pretend that they do not lead to strains and tensions and that they are not sometimes difficult to achieve. For some societies (the UK may be one of these) the effort may prove to be too much and a fundamental lack of clarity about the values embodied in and hence the aims of education may be the result.

III   AUTONOMY AS AN AIM OF EDUCATION

Education is primarily concerned with the preparation of young people for adult life. In most societies and certainly in one like our own this implies that young adults become *autonomous*, able to live an independent and productive life and to take responsibility for their own decisions. There are different senses in which one can talk about autonomy. In a minimal sense the term implies the ability to make one's way in the world with a reasonable degree of independence, but not in such a way that one is able to make the major decisions in life for oneself. Someone who is autonomous in this sense may be so in relation to *means* but not to ends. Most people in a democratic society would go further and say that at least some of the ends of life should be capable of selection by someone educated enough to make such choices sensibly. This sense of autonomy is sometimes known as 'weak autonomy'. Others would go further and argue that in order to be truly rational someone would need to be able critically to appraise the ends that society proposes as acceptable and to select those that are not necessarily society's own preferences in order for autonomy to be meaningful. This position is sometimes known as 'strong autonomy'.[3]

What do these various aims imply for education? At a minimum, *all* forms of education require young people to receive a *grounding*: that is, to gain an acquaintance with basic literacy and numeracy, a stock of historical, geographical and scientific facts about the culture, together with enough practical knowledge and skill to find one's way about.[4] In some societies such grounding might constitute a minimum threshold of autonomy in the sense of independence about choosing means, but this would not be the case in our own.

In a complex society, grounding needs to be extended beyond the primary stage into general secondary education, so that young people possess knowledge of the necessary breadth and depth in order to become productive members of society. Finally, children will need to acquire generic and specific vocational skills, knowledge and understanding in order to pursue their chosen occupation. These considerations imply that it is vocational education of a liberal temper, rather than liberal education as such, that is required to develop autonomy. And if autonomy is an intrinsic good, then vocational education of some form is one means to the achievement of that intrinsic good.

This is not to deny that liberal forms of education may legitimately have autonomy as their aim. Much of liberal education is concerned with the inculcation of knowledge in the breadth and depth that it is necessary to acquire if a young person is to find his or her way in our complex and changing society. But a liberal education that failed to make young people autonomous by making them productive members of society would have failed in its aims. If making them productive members of society requires an element of vocational preparation to a greater or lesser degree then it is an essential element in any form of education that chooses to call itself 'liberal'.

This could be achieved without much addition to liberal education as it has been traditionally conceived if knowledge in breadth and depth, together with the skills acquired in the course of acquiring that knowledge, was sufficient to hold down an occupation of some kind. Alternatively, if young people did not need to be productive members of society, for example if they possessed sufficient wealth to live without working and with no inclination to contribute to the political, domestic, social or economic life of the society, then a liberal education which did not have autonomy as one of its aims would be sufficient.[5] But this would be a fatal concession for the advocates of mass liberal education to make, for their proposals would not allow the great majority of young people to become autonomous, productive members of society, which is something that most of them want.[6]

Vocational education is concerned with the development of knowledge, skill and understanding insofar as these fit people for a particular kind of employment or range of employments. A vocational education can be one of a number of very different kinds of activity. In some cases it will look little different from liberal education. For example, a postgraduate degree in philosophy might be a necessary vocational qualification for someone who wishes to teach the subject at the level of higher education. But the curriculum and pedagogy of such a course need not, in any meaningful way, be distinguishable from the curriculum and pedagogy of such a course pursued with liberal aims. Yet the most common view of vocational education is that of *job training*. This is a very distorted view of what vocational education might be or actually is. It fails to take account of the wide variety of *occupations* that are available. These include vocations properly so called such as writing or the ministry, professions such as medicine or law, crafts such as cabinet making or metalworking and trades such as carpentry or plumbing. All of these require technical knowledge and skill, social ability and ethical commitment if they are to be pursued in an effective and worthwhile manner.[7] Making the choices associated with the pursuit of a vocation is in itself making choices about ends. Furthermore, there are values associated with the pursuit of an occupation such as diligence, persistence, honesty, pride in the craft and its traditions, which themselves are intrinsic values to be chosen along with the occupation itself. In this sense, vocational education is associated with 'weak autonomy' and not merely independence in relation to means.

There are various reasons why a particularly limited conception of vocational education has come to dominate lay and professional thinking about the matter in Britain and some other countries and it appears to be the case that different societies have different views of the purpose, value and nature of vocational education.[8]

Education for citizenship requires that a young person be prepared to play a positive and constructive role in society. Moral maturity and the achievement of weak autonomy appear to be prerequisites of this, as well as an ability to play a role in society through work, whether it be paid, voluntary or domestic. There is more to education for citizenship than this: for example, it may be necessary to learn the practical skills and knowledge necessary to be a parent, a voter or a local councillor. But it can hardly be maintained that there is no overlap between the aims of education for citizenship and the aims of vocational and liberal forms of education. Intrinsic and extrinsic aims need not be incompatible with each other either.

A liberal education that provided no preparation for work or life as a citizen would be intolerable to most people. Likewise, a vocational education that provided no intrinsic or social satisfaction would be bleak and unrewarding. A citizen with no cultural background and no ability to take part in the economic life of the society would be only partly a citizen.

These reflections all suggest that the degree of commonality between different forms of education is considerable and that they have some aims in common.

There will always be tensions in the degree of emphasis that ought to be placed on one set of aims rather than another, but diversity of aims need not lead to a loss of social cohesion if the aims complement each other and are arrived at through a process of negotiation. There is plenty of scope for negotiation as to which aims should receive priority and for the kinds of institutions that should accommodate them. The contested nature of *education* should, in a healthy polity, be about the *relative importance* that should be enjoyed by different conceptions rather than about which conception is exclusively the correct one.[9]

We have already seen how, although insofar as they are purposeful institutions schools and colleges have aims, it is not always clear either to outsiders or to participants what those aims actually are. It is difficult to avoid the idea that there needs to be a minimal threshold of being educated which defines the success of an educational system relative to the achievement of the pupils or students within it. This may vary from country to country or from culture to culture but there must be something like this for any education system that one cares to mention. If there is not, then it is difficult to see how one could begin to measure the success of the system as a whole. And if this were to be the case, then the problem of accountability arises. How can an education system that does not even set minimal standards of education justify itself to those who pay for it and to those who spend time in it?

Grounding in the sense in which Letwin (cp. n.4 above) uses the term, implying independence in the sense already described, seems to be indisputably an aim for any educational system. It would appear to be what Letwin calls an 'absolute duty' for schools to provide this for their pupils. Nevertheless, not all schools would recognise this as an absolute duty, holding perhaps that the achievement of grounding was to be a by-product of the achievement of other educational aims. Grounding pupils might be seen as a minimal aim, hardly one that would be worthy of inclusion in a set of educational aims. This is not just a theoretical issue; public awareness has been growing for some time of the fact that standards of literacy and numeracy may be on the decline in parts of America and Western Europe. This may in turn be connected with schools having aims which presuppose or even deny the desirability of other aims such as that of grounding pupils. It might, for example, be considered more important for pupils to be *creative* than to be competent in secretarial skills such as the ability to spell. The responsibility for grounding pupils is not clearly located in many educational systems, nor is it always clear what the proper limits of grounding are.

If grounding is an absolute duty of an education system, and liberal and many vocational educators generally mean by 'autonomy' something more than this, should weak autonomy be one of the major objectives of a publicly funded education system? White's answer would probably be 'no', for the reason that the achievement of autonomy involves the achievement of the ability to formulate a life plan and grounding may be a necessary, but is not a sufficient, condition for doing that.[10] Some might argue whether or not it is the business of education to provide the ability to formulate a life plan. Rasselas, Prince of Abyssinia in Samuel Johnson's novel, did not seem to be able to do this by the age of thirty, despite an extensive range of educational experiences.[11] There are difficulties as well in saying to what extent preparation for autonomy in the choosing of ends ought to be the proper business of education. Would it be proper for an education system to prepare young people to choose ends that had not been sanctioned in some way by the society in which they live?[12]

In a democratic society it is natural to suggest that preparation for life should include helping young people to gain the ability to make important decisions about how to live their lives within the framework accepted by society. In this context it might be objected that in such a society the framework should itself be the proper subject of critical appraisal. While a valid point, this does not imply that *no* values should remain immune from critical appraisal or revision; the framework of ends is arrived at through an established framework of negotiation. Undermining that framework compromises the basis on which that negotiation takes place. It could not be the role of a publicly funded education system in a democracy to encourage young people to question democratic values, although it could well encourage them not to take for granted all aspects of those values and the ways in which they are implemented.

While autonomy implies that people become independent in various ways, it cannot imply that they cease to be *interdependent* or able to function without the assistance of anyone else. Autonomy implies the ability to choose from a wide variety of socially sanctioned ends as well as the ability to make one's way in the various different spheres in life: economic, artistic, domestic, social and political, for example. But the ability to do any of these things implies that people are able to relate to each other and need to depend on each other in various ways. If education helps them to do this then it implies the provision of a great variety of curricula to make these choices meaningful ones. Such an education cannot be a purely technical one: it needs to include within itself a personal and social dimension if young people, whatever walk of life they choose, are to achieve the right balance of independence and interdependence which seems to be a precondition of autonomy in a complex and interdependent society.

IV   BRITAIN: A RADICAL LACK OF CLARITY

Britain is a good example of a society whose consideration of educational aims has been settled by default. The absence of national debate on substantive issues about the aims of education has been accompanied by a lack of consensus. This has led to a situation where the culturally dominant concept of education has set the aims of the system as a whole. Surprisingly, even the setting up of a national curriculum for the first time in the country's history failed to ignite a substantial debate. The near-absence of any thought on the question is reflected in the bland statement of aims at the beginning of the Act of 1988:

> The curriculum for a maintained school satisfies the requirements of this section if it is a balanced and broadly based curriculum which
> (a) promotes the spiritual, moral, cultural, mental and physical development of pupils at the school and of society; and
> (b) prepares such pupils for the opportunities, responsibilities and experiences of adult life.[13]

All that this statement does is to express a very general concept of education, giving no particular weight to any one conception. In relation to the controversial character of the concept of educaton (see Chapter 2), no issue is tackled. In practice this has meant that a liberal conception has dominated, although to some commentators this bias has not been liberal enough. For example, Gray writes of the National Curriculum,

> It overemphasises the vocational dimension of education at the expense of its role as an initiation into a cultural inheritance.[14]

Because there has been no consensus about aims and because aims have not been articulated, a general uncertainty pervades the whole system of education. The institutions that educate, the schools, colleges and universities, reflect this uncertainty. It takes two main forms: one about the place, if any, for vocational education; the other about the role of social, moral and religious education. The latter is a highly sensitive area in which there are competing views about what is appropriate. Some schools are allowed to have a specifically religious and moral ethos. These are the schools associated with particular religions. However, not all religions that would like schools associated with them are allowed to have them. In the secular schools the problem of what to do about religion, morality and the social side of education is also acute. To take an example, there is a requirement for a daily act of worship which should reflect the predominantly Christian nature of the society. But such an act of worship need not be conducted by believers and the majority of pupils may not be practising Christians, many belonging to different religions altogether. The aims of education in this area are not easy to ascertain at all. Christianity is allowed to retain a vestigial influence by default. Whether that is a good thing or not, the overall result is that religious, moral and social education lacks a clear focus.

The position of vocational education is equally unclear. The liberal conception remains dominant throughout the compulsory phases of schooling and the curriculum is a unitary one until the age of sixteen, although there are currently plans to introduce vocational variations after the age of fourteen. It is true that technology is now a compulsory subject but it is one that has been purged of its craft element and largely turned into an academic, liberal subject.[15] This lack of clarity is reflected in the institutional arrangements for education which predate the 1988 Act. In effect, Britain has an accumulation of institutional traditions in education with the liberal academic one being hegemonic. Now it is unavoidable and desirable that education should have traditions. But when the dominant one of these traditions does not accord with the abilities and aspirations of a majority of the population then the place of education is bound to suffer. The British are relatively uninterested in education and the state of the education system both contributes to and reflects that relative lack of interest.[16]

This lack of clarity of purpose ramifies throughout the system: each type of institution at each phase of education betrays a lack of clarity about its purposes, a lack of clarity which is usually resolved in some way in favour of the liberal hegemony.

Nursery education is neither compulsory nor universal in the United Kingdom. Its advocates point to the long-term beneficial effects that it is alleged to bring to children who attend and to its ability to compensate for the deficient cultural background (particularly linguistic background) of some families. It is also advocated as a form of child-minding although this cannot convincingly be put forward as an educational aim. Nurseries in Britain are largely dominated by the progressive tradition which sees the liberation of the child as the most important aim of education. Progressivism is in effect a branch of the liberal tradition, one which differs from traditionalism in its rejection of the role of authority in education. Despite the fact that those nurseries which are best at producing long-term effects have an ethos unlike the typical British nursery and despite the fact that there is convincing evidence that the alleged linguistic effects of nursery education do not exist, nursery education continues much as it has done in the progressive tradition while its advocates continue to claim effects for it which either it cannot deliver in its current form or it cannot deliver at all.[17]

Primary education in Britain has gone through many changes in the last 50 years, moving from the elementary schooling tradition of aiming for grounding, towards the progressive ideal of personal liberation, ending up by staying somewhat easily between these two traditions.[18] The advent of the National Curriculum has not really clarified the situation for these schools; if anything it has complicated the picture. In the first place, the government-sponsored struggle against progressivism has intensified. In the second place, there has been an attempt to move beyond the elementary grounding tradition to a range of liberal aims, stressing breadth and depth. Finally, a utilitarian pre-vocational element has been introduced into the curriculum through the addition of technology as a foundation subject. If primary schools were unclear about what their aims were before the reforms starting in 1988, they are certainly no clearer about them now.

The history of the aims of secondary education is equally chequered and unclear. There has been a grammar school tradition of liberal education preparing children for the professions. On the other hand, the central schools aspired to continue the process of grounding begun in the elementary schools. After 1900, a small number of Junior Technical Schools were created for the 14+ age group. After 1944, a tripartite system of grammar, secondary modern and technical schools was set up. The technical schools failed to compete against the grammar and secondary moderns. The secondary modern schools never had any clear aims, veering from liberal aims (the grammar school tradition), to extended grounding (the elementary and central school tradition), to technical education (the technical tradition) and pre-vocational education. It is not surprising that they were not popular with parents. With the advent of comprehensive schools, the dominant grammar school tradition with liberal aims re-asserted itself over the secondary system as a whole, allowing the other aims (pre-vocational, technical and grounding) a vestigial place in the school ethos.

Non-compulsory further education in Britain has, on the face of it, the aim of providing work-related vocational education and training in the post-compulsory phase. In some institutions the commitment to a particular craft or trade is strong: there are colleges of building, catering and engineering, for example. Other colleges are more generalist, training for a variety of occupations under the same roof: nursery nursing, catering, hairdressing, bakery, meat trades etc. Others again combine work-related training with a commitment to 16+ and 18+ academic education. Yet others have a substantial commitment to higher education and degree level work. This range of commitments makes it difficult not only to see what the generic aims of the further education sector are, but, in many cases, what the specific aims of particular colleges are as well. There is some evidence of academic drift from vocational to liberal arts subjects and from 16+ to 18+ education.[19]

Although higher education is a bastion of the liberal ideal, the universities originated in the need for professional education for lawyers, clerics and teachers. Professional education has always been an important part of the work of universities, in Britain and elsewhere. Unlike some of the continental countries, however, Britain has tended to shy away from providing specialist schools to serve particular professions or groups of professions, being inclined instead to provide the full range of liberal and professional education in one large institution. The technical and vocational sector of higher education was largely situated under local authority control until 1989 in the institutions known as polytechnics, whose main work lay in professionally and technically oriented higher education. Here also there has been a steady drift towards providing a more liberal form of education, a trend symbolised by the granting of university status to these institutions in 1992, thus allowing them to shed the vocational image that they had once been proud to bear. Even within the professional provision of these institutions, however, there has been a trend towards making the courses more liberal in orientation. This trend can be seen, for example, in the way in which courses in the professions allied to medicine have incorporated subjects such as sociology into their curricula and have diminished the amount of clinical practice necessary for professional qualification.[20]

All of this suggests that British education at all levels is affected by a radical uncertainty about aims, but is dominated, in the main, by the liberal tradition, either in a traditional or a more progressive form. This uncertainty does matter to the extent that it undermines the sense of purpose that sectors and particular institutions have. There is no reason in theory why a stratum of education or even a particular institution should not have a variety of aims. There *is* a problem when the different aims are seen, rightly or wrongly, to be mutually antagonistic. Then there is conflict and the dominant tradition tends to win out to the detriment of other traditions.

This has led to difficulties for technical, vocational and professional education. Not only is the ethos of the school or college rendered ambiguous, but liberal subjects tend to crowd out the vocational ones. The domination of liberal thinking, particularly in its progressive form, has led to a reduction of emphasis on grounding and training at the primary phase as well. In fact a healthy education system should have a variety of aims suited to the implementation of different, but not mutually incompatible, goals. The presence of antagonistic aims within one institution tends to sap the sense of purpose which that institution needs, and this tendency is more pronounced in fairly small, uncompartmentalised places such as schools than it is in large, department-oriented institutions such as universities, although it can be a problem at this level as well. The British have yet to work out the variety of aims which their public education system exists to support and the proper relationship between them at both the curricular and institutional level. As a result, a certain, historically dominant, tradition exercises undue sway over the system as a whole, to its considerable detriment. The process of political negotiation about aims has, despite many years of reform, barely started. James Callaghan called for a 'great debate' on the future of education in 1976; it has yet to occur in any substantial form.

NOTES

1. This latter proviso is necessary because there may be cases where a society's educational aims may be agreed and accepted by all without there being a written record of those aims. Conversely, they may be written down in an authoritative way yet fail to command the consent of all involved. Written aims are neither a necessary nor a sufficient condition to agreement; having them is a convenient way of making explicit the construction of a consensus which may have been arrived at implicitly.

2. None of this suggests that it is impossible for people to change their values or even to be persuaded to change them. One may see a particular point of view about how life should be lived as appealing and then, at a later date, perhaps as a result of a prolonged conversation with someone, come to see it as less appealing. But this is not the same thing as negotiating about values.

3. See, for example, J. P. White, *Education and the Good Life*, 1990; R. Norman, 'I did it my way': some reflections on autonomy, *Journal of Philosophy of Education*, 28.11, 1994, pp. 25–34.

4. Cf. Oliver Letwin, *Education: the importance of grounding*, 1988.

5. Indeed, if P. G. Wodehouse is to be believed, it is the valet of such a person, rather than the person himself, who would need such an education in order to steer the individual safely through society. Bertie Wooster does not need much of a liberal education in order to lead an exciting and full (if not productive) life.

6. See endnote 4, Chapter 3, and cf. M. Sanderson, *op. cit.*, Chapter 7 for evidence of how inadequate the grammar schools were in preparing many of the children who attended them for an autonomous life.

7. C. Winch, *op. cit.*, 1995.

8. In this regard, it is interesting to compare Germany with the UK. See HMI, *Aspects of Vocational Education in the Federal Republic of Germany*, 1990.

9. See Harold Entwistle, *op. cit.*

10. Cf. White, *op. cit.*, pp. 25–26.

11. Samuel Johnson, *Rasselas*. Available in Charles Peake (ed.), *'Rasselas' and Essays*, 1967.

12. See, for example, J. P. White, *op. cit.*; R. Norman, *op. cit.*

13. *Education Reform Act 1988*, 1988, p. 1.

14. Gray, *op. cit.*, p. 27.

15. See M. Sanderson, *op. cit.*

16. Cf. National Commission on Education, *op. cit.*, pp. 10–11; Richard Hoggart, *The Uses of Literacy*, 1957; E. A. Johns, *The Social Structure of Modern Britain*, 1979, Chapter 4, esp. pp. 167–180.

17. For evidence on those factors which are thought to promote long-term non-academic benefits, see M. Woodhead, Pre-school education has long-term effects: but can they be generalised? *Oxford Review of Education*, 11.2 1985, pp. 133–156. For evidence of the effectiveness of English teaching in British nurseries, see B. Tizard and M. Hughes, *Young Children Learning*, 1984.

18. See R. Alexander, *Primary Teaching*, 1984, *Policy and Practice in the Primary School*, 1992, and *Innocence and Experience*, 1994. See also P. Mortimore, P. Sammons, L. Stoll, D. Lewis and R. Ecob, *School Matters: the junior years*, 1988, Chapter 4, pp. 52–55 for the perceptions of teachers within the system as to what their aims are.

19. The evidence for this is to be found in the changing course profiles of the further education colleges: first in their involvement in A-level work, and secondly in their involvement in tertiary education, often of a not directly vocational kind.

20. L. Merriman, *op. cit.*

Chapter 5
Constructing Worthwhile Curricula

I WHAT IS THE CURRICULUM?

There are many different definitions of the curriculum available, ranging from 'all the experiences for learning which are planned and organised by the school', to a selection from the culture.[1] There are some writers who think that the idea that the curriculum should be something *prescribed* is a misunderstanding.[2] This view is mistaken, for the role that the curriculum plays in education is a *normative* rather than a descriptive one. The curriculum is what *ought* to be taking place in schools rather than what actually *is*, although ideally the two will coincide. Given that education needs to have aims if it is to be intelligible, then it must be possible to distinguish between those activities that are directed towards achieving those aims and those that are not. The curriculum is the *prescribed content* of education, that is, what ought to be taught in order to fulfil the aims of an educational practice or institution, irrespective of what actually goes on.

This distinction holds good even when aims are *implicit* rather than *explicit* for, although in such cases it may be more difficult in practice to identify the curriculum than in those cases where aims are explicit, it is still necessary to distinguish between what *ought* to be going on and what *is* actually going on. The curriculum relates to the knowledge, skill and understanding that are to be mastered (rather than to rules of conduct within the school, for example), and the sequence in which they are to be taught. In addition, it is related to a whole phase of education rather than to individual lessons, or even groups of lessons. The curriculum, then, could be defined as the prescribed content of knowledge, understanding and skill that fulfils the aims of education.

The character of the curriculum offered is of critical political importance in judging whether or not an educational activity is worthwhile. This is a consideration quite independent of the question of whether the prescribed content is actually followed.

It is political in the sense that different interest groups are concerned with the content and that some form of negotiation may be needed in order to determine it. Even when educational aims are agreed, there may be alternative means of achieving those aims. So the content of the curriculum is by no means settled by negotiation about aims, although specificiation of aims does narrow the range of curriculum options available. Very often the political nature of curriculum choices is obscured by the use of philosophical, ethical, psychological or sociological theories to justify certain choices, but the users of such theories cannot evade the need to acknowledge the political nature of the choices being made, since necessarily these affect the interests of different groups in different ways. These theories may influence curriculum planners to different degrees, but they can never be *sufficient* reason, in a pluralistic democratic society, for choosing one curriculum rather than another. It would not be going too far to suggest that a worthwhile curriculum would seek to accommodate the legitimate interest of each group, so that their needs were met in a way that benefited other groups as much as possible. There will, therefore, be no ideal curriculum, only one that is best at a particular time for a particular society.

But could not a philosopher or a psychologist make such a decision for a society in such a convincing way that all the interest groups agreed to his or her proposals? This is perfectly possible, if somewhat unlikely, but this is only the limiting case of a political decision; all the interested parties need to agree that their interests are best served by this particular proposal. There is no reason why curriculum construction should not be a co-ordination problem rather than a zero-sum game and therefore no reason *a priori* why some one person such as a philosopher could not come up with a solution that met the preferences of all better than any other possible solution could, however unlikely this might be. To put things in this way is to idealise the political process somewhat because, in reality, much of the negotiation may take place by default: if, for example, the accredited representatives of one of the interest groups are incompetent or have a mistaken view of the best interests of those whom they are representing, who, in turn, may find that there is a lack of an alternative to turn to for representing those interests.

Given that this is so, what does the curriculum tell us about the quality of the education being offered? Designers of curricula pick out and prescribe a particular range of subjects with a view to fulfilling educational aims. Some of these subjects exist as necessary conditions for studying other subjects which themselves, if learned, are thought to fulfil educational aims. Such subjects would include basic literacy and numeracy, for example. Other subjects are selected because mastering them is thought to fulfil educational aims. The subjects on the curriculum have, then, either a conditioned or an unconditioned value. They may be selected either explicitly by teachers working with other interested parties or implicitly by the way in which teachers organise their lives in classrooms, but either way they will reflect value judgements about what should be taught.[3]

II HOW IS THE CURRICULUM CHOSEN?

Given the vast range of possibilities, how are the choices actually arrived at? The subjects chosen are thought to be those that fulfil various educational aims. They may, for example, be chosen to reflect the important aspects of a society's cultural, literary and artistic heritage, if the aim of the curriculum is to transmit that heritage to future generations. They may be chosen to reflect the vocational skills that are thought to be particularly valuable for promoting economic growth, or they may be chosen as the best means of developing character attributes, such as autonomy or consideration for others. They may also be chosen because they are thought to develop particular intellectual skills whose application is potentially very wide and which thus serve a variety of aims (Philosophy and Mathematics have sometimes been thought of as belonging to this category).[4]

In practice, curriculum change and innovation tends to flow from a variety of pressures and to proceed in a way that does not always tally with the intentions of those who initiate the change. Some of these pressures are quite practical in kind and constitute constraints which limit the nature and degree of change. These include organisational, financial and legal factors. Important as these are, there are others that are no less significant. First are the political constraints that have already been discussed. Then there are cultural factors that predispose certain subjects to receive greater prestige than others. Then there are epistemological preconceptions about subjects that influence the way that people think about them.

All these factors affect the ways in which curriculum choices are made and they affect them in different ways, according to the interest group that one is looking at. What emerges from such a complex situation is, inevitably, a compromise. However, it is possible to extrapolate a few trends which can be seen as major influential factors. The first is the importance of deep-rooted cultural attitudes. These tend to work towards the selection of subjects that are thought to have prestige and subjects that are considered to be central to the cultural identity of the society and as such will appeal to all interest groups to some extent. The second is the perceived importance of *transferability*, but there is often confusion about what this means. The term can mean at least four things that are not always distinguished: technical transferability in numeracy and literacy; cultural literacy in Hirsch's sense, that is, propositional pre-requisities for further learning to take place;[5] higher-order intellectual skills; and cognitive breadth and depth. The notion of cognitive *breadth* in particular is important, as it is this that influences views about the appropriate spread of subjects, each with different cognitive characteristics, appearing on the curriculum. One does not have to accept the Hirst thesis of distinct forms of knowledge in its entirety to see that there are different cognitive and affective principles underlying different subjects and that knowledge of a range of subjects is necessary for the appreciation of these different cognitive styles. It is another matter whether acquaintance with these styles is sufficient to grasp the range of human cognitive and affective engagement. That is a much more disputable claim. The fact that Hirst was only concerned with the liberal curriculum is an implicit acknowledgement of this fact.

The third trend is that the imperative of economic growth and welfare (as opposed to personal prosperity and well-being) is fairly limited and is largely confined to three of the interest groups. Despite the overt and often loudly proclaimed need to make education systems meet the needs of economic growth, in practice this is often not so easy to secure; cultural factors may get in the way, or the development of certain kinds of transferable skills may work against the perceived requirements of the economy.[6] The deep-rooted dominance of one conception of education may be extremely difficult to dislodge, particularly when it is dominant both within the education system itself and within important sections of the political élite.[7]

A fourth trend reflects the changing demands of those who wish to be educated, together with the wish of teachers and lecturers to determine what they should teach. Where their expectations match up with each other, then, if there is some way of adjusting supply and demand (and a market mechanism seems to be the most obvious way of achieving this), it is possible for that subject to be offered and taught. The area of education in which subjects are most likely to rise and fall in this way is in the post-compulsory sector, where there is potentially a wide range of choice on offer for students wishing either to pursue a vocation or to increase their knowledge and understanding.

The ways in which these trends interact with each other in determining whether or not subjects should be offered can be illustrated with a couple of examples from the higher education sectors. The study of the Classics (Greek and Latin) and Philosophy was historically sanctioned as they were highly valued within the culture as a key to an understanding of the British and European cultural heritage. A major difference between the study of the Classics and the study of Philosophy lay in the necessity for students of the Classics to master Latin and Ancient Greek, languages that are no longer spoken.

The study of both Classics and Philosophy was also justified in terms of the *transferable skills* that they were said to cultivate. Both were believed to foster habits of mental discipline and clear thinking, which could then be applied in vocational contexts, particularly in government and administration. The claims of Classics fared less well in this regard, because knowledge of Latin and Greek was not obviously a transferable skill, although it was argued that learning these languages made the learning of other, classically based, languages easier. Philosophy, on the other hand, could plausibly lay claim to the development of logic and argumentation, as well as mental discipline, as important, vocationally relevant, transferable skills.[8] Both Classics and Philosophy have also been justified on purely non-instrumental grounds, as being necessary to the development of rationality, and this has, to some extent, accounted for the demand for them among students. However, neither subject was regarded by business or government as particularly important to economic growth and, in the 1980s, both suffered from contractions in the numbers of university departments that offered them. Despite this, Philosophy remained a popular subject, largely because of its novelty (hardly being offered at all in the secondary school), combined with its accessibility relative to Classics and its perceived transferability. Classics in particular suffered from a decline in the school curriculum and so very few school students were able to study it at university level. Even when offered in translation, however, it has not proved to be particularly popular, partly because its transferability is seen to be no greater and no less than that of the study of Literature or of History. In addition, the culture of ancient Greece and Rome has come to appear of less cultural significance to the society as a whole in the late twentieth century. A key feature, therefore, in the survival of Philosophy has been its perceived cultural significance and its perceived transferability, despite its lack of an immediate vocational relevance. A lack of these features led to a decline in the study of the Classics.

Other subjects, for example computer studies, flourish because of their perceived vocational relevance, but even here vocational relevance is not the only factor. The fact that the computer is seen as one of the major technologies of the late twentieth century and therefore has a certain mystique attached to it is also important. The fact that it is, in some sense, a cultural icon as well as a perceived engine of economic growth has allowed it to flourish in contrast to subjects such as engineering in its various branches, which although required for economic growth and hence a gateway to employment, do not share the same degree of cultural prestige, at least in Britain. Other subjects come into being because of political and social change, despite not being regarded as vocationally relevant, as developing transferable skills or as enjoying deep cultural prestige. The rise of Women's Studies, for example, can be traced to the changes in the sexual division of labour that have occurred in this century, together with the rise of feminism as a social movement.

There will not, therefore, be any one view as to what subjects should be selected for the curriculum. The selection will arise from negotiation against the background of changing fashions and preoccupations within society. This does not mean that the selection of curriculum content is inevitably going to be chaotic and arbitrary. Bearing in mind what I have already said about the non-binding nature of philosophical arguments about what should appear on the curriculum, it is, nevertheless, possible to produce philosophically based reasons for having a curriculum with a certain type of structure. These should be seen as producing *recommendations* that should inform, if not determine, curriculum structure and content and should be judged on nothing more than their own merits. The arguments are designed to show that a modern curriculum should have both a common core which all children should follow and also a significant element of diversification in the post-primary years, with the academic liberal route existing as one among several alternatives.

III AN ARGUMENT FOR THE COMMON CORE

The aims of grounding are to provide the *pre-requisites* of autonomy, personal fulfilment, economic growth and the achievement and preservation of a cultural heritage. The aims of grounding, then, should be presupposed by all other forms of education. There should thus be no serious dispute about whether or not there should be grounding, only about its *content* in terms of knowledge, skill and understanding. Surprisingly, however, argument about the desirability of a common core has been widespread. The reasons lie in the dominance of the curriculum by educators themselves and particularly by progressivist primary educators. There has also been opposition from English teachers and others who consider themselves to be political radicals. In some ways the argument for a common core has been seen as a conservative or even a reactionary one among liberals and socialists active in education. I hope to show that this perception demonstrates a misunderstanding of the need for a common core.

The arguments fall into two broad categories. The first is mainly a pedagogical one: it starts from a particular conception of *good practice* in schools (see Chapter 9). The contention is that learning takes place through discovery and that the traditional, didactic, methods of giving children a grounding are, in fact, not conducive to effective learning.[9] Although strictly this is not a repudiation of the case for grounding, that is what it amounts to in practice. For the proposal is, in effect, to hand over control of the curriculum to individual children. The argument for doing this is based on the view that the curriculum should correspond to children's interests and that the way in which to make it do so is to let children decide what they want to learn and when they want to learn it.

So much has been said about the inadequacies of this view that it is hardly worth repeating them here.[10] But I will make a point in relation to the demand for accountability that is a central theme of this book. Children are only one of the groups with an interest in education. Furthermore, they have an interest not only *qua* children, but also *qua* future adults who have to make their way in the world. In this respect, schools are accountable to children *via* their parents or guardians who safeguard those interests until maturity.[11] So the idea that children should control the curriculum is contrary to the interests of children, if we take interest to be connected to long term *need* rather than to short term *inclination*, as surely we must. If grounding is a prerequisite for autonomy and autonomy is in the best interests of the child *qua* future adult, then grounding is in the interests of the child and accountability demands it. Since no other interest group has a countervailing interest in not providing grounding for children, the argument from accountability works in relation to these other groups too.

The second argument stems from the view that it provides a cultural bias to children's outlooks that reinforces the hegemonic position of certain culturally dominant groups within society. In other words, grounding violates the legitimate interests of some to whom the education system should be accountable. Thus the imposition of standard English or of a literary canon or a particular set of historical and geographical knowledge favours the world-view and interests of the culturally dominant group in a society such as Britain, to the disadvantage of subordinate groups.[12] In the United States, arguments such as those of E. D. Hirsch have been attacked on similar grounds.[13] If grounding were a way of ensuring and enforcing a cultural hegemony that was oppressive and obnoxious to many of the population, then there would be a case to answer. The process of political negotiation would have failed to the extent that it did not allow certain significant groups to have their values recognised and implemented in the public sphere. But this is precisely what needs to be shown by the opponents of grounding. They very often fail to make the distinction between speaking on someone's behalf and actually *representing* them. Speaking on someone's behalf while failing properly to represent their views is also a way of silencing those views. There is no evidence that radical educationists who complain about grounding along these lines have actually bothered to take into account the views of those they claim to represent.

But there are two other reasons why grounding is important. The first is *epistemological*. It is not possible to understand what someone else is saying or writing without a certain amount of what Hirsch calls 'cultural literacy'. Effective speaking and, to a lesser extent, writing depends on the existence of a common stock of background suppositions and knowledge, which need to be communicated through a common language, intelligible to all. Since much communication makes use of common background knowledge, enthymematic argument or analogy and metaphor, possession of that knowledge is a necessary condition for effective communication and understanding. The second reason is *ethical*. In order for children to enjoy the opportunities that will become available to them as adults, and in order for them to make a contribution to the welfare of their fellow human beings, it is necessary for them all to have access to the knowledge and skill that is needed to do so. If this is a matter that is left to chance, then procedural justice may not be satisfied. Any society that claims to be based on fairness should be very concerned about the possibility of such an outcome.

IV AN ARGUMENT FOR POST-PRIMARY DIVERSITY

Grounding is necessary if young people are to be prepared for adult life. But the kind of life that someone will lead will depend on a great variety of factors, and it is desirable that many of those factors should be under the control of the individual concerned. It is particularly desirable that people should live a life that makes the best possible use of their abilities to enable both them and other people to flourish.[14] Given the variety of possible occupations and the variety of different abilities and interests that people have, it is most unlikely that they would all benefit from exactly the same preparation for adult life.

It has already been argued that a publicly funded system of education ought to be able to accommodate a variety of different aims. It ought therefore to be possible for it to accommodate a variety of different curricula. Given that grounding is a necessary pre-requisite of any further curricular progress and given the political arguments for the entertainment of a variety of aims, are there any other reasons why curricula should be diversified? The assumption usually made by liberal educators is that academic (and to a lesser extent, aesthetic) subjects should have a place on the curriculum. The arguments for this are framed in terms of acquaintance with the cultural heritage and with the development of rationality, which requires knowledge of a variety of academic subjects in breadth and depth.

Some liberal educators also value autonomy as an educational aim, because of the contribution that it makes to human flourishing at both the individual and the social level. But the aim of autonomy can be achieved in a variety of ways which go beyond the traditional academic curriculum. If we accept that academic ability (in the sense of ability to do well at a range of traditional school subjects: Literature, Mathematics, History, Languages and Science) is not the only kind that it is necessary to cultivate in order to ensure individual human flourishing, then the academic curriculum should not be the only one that is offered in the secondary years. There is a view that education should develop the intelligence and that this can only be done through an academic curriculum.[15] However, the concept of intelligence is deeply suspect and has been used to ill effect in the British educational system (see below). If it is rejected, then other possibilities are on offer.[16]

Ability is a 'transitive' concept. People are not just able or not able. They are able at various activities. For example, some people are able at academic activities while others are able at practical crafts. Some are able at cooking while others are able at sport. The factors affecting the growth of different abilities are similar to those affecting the development of traditional academic ability and it is likely that different people will develop a different range of abilities according to differing natural talent, motivation, interest and cultural background, all of which factors in any event interact with each other. These different abilities will be a source of intrinsic satisfaction to those who possess them, but they will also benefit any society which has a wide range of different requirements for welfare and economic growth. Development of them is, therefore, a source of both intrinsic personal and extrinsic social goods.

Some abilities presuppose others. For example, the ability to carry out archival research in history presupposes the ability to read and write. The contestable nature of the concept of education implies that different groups will value different types of abilities in different ways.[17] Different forms of education will be championed by different groups and some form of reconciliation of these different interest groups will have to be arrived at.[18]

The curriculum should, then, provide for a continuation of grounding into general secondary education where this is necessary, but it should also provide a variety of alternatives for those who wish to pursue different kinds of occupations. There should, therefore, be an *academic* strand to the curriculum for those of a scholarly disposition or for those who wish to enter teaching or administrative jobs. There should also be a variety of technical, aesthetic, commercial and physical strands for those who wish to pursue different kinds of careers. During the compulsory years of education these should not be direct job preparation, but a form of vocational education with what might be regarded as traditional liberal aims: autonomy, acquaintance with the culture, personal fulfilment, together with the more vocationally oriented aims of preparation for employment and the promotion of economic growth.

This kind of vocational education should continue general secondary education to complete the process of grounding but should also be *generic* in relation to the occupations that it seeks to prepare young people for. They should be taught general principles underlying occupations as well as generic and transferable skills and knowledge within particular occupations, which may well include a deepening of the numeracy and literacy curriculum.[19] The important point to bear in mind is that curricula need not be mutually exclusive, but should contain *common* elements as well as *different* emphases.

There are well-known arguments against secondary specialisation and these arguments have, on the whole, tended to prevail. But they have done so through default rather than through any intrinsic merits. It is now time to subject them to critical examination. The first concerns the alleged social divisions that would open up if different children were to follow different curricula. One curriculum stream (the academic) would have high prestige, the others (broadly speaking, vocational) would have less. In practice, curriculum selection would reflect and perpetuate social class divisions within society. Therefore all children should follow a liberal curriculum that will provide a general preparation for adulthood.

There is a question as to whether social divisions are necessarily a bad thing. Given that a modern society needs a degree of functional specialisation to prosper, it is not obvious that the social division associated with it is harmful. True, there are forms of social division that may be harmful and social division may be particularly oppressive when people wish to and cannot move from one kind of occupation and community to another. But the fact that this is so is often due to the perception that people of one class are poorly educated, ignorant and unskilled. This perception is due, in no small part, to the poor quality of the education that they receive. If they are already in receipt of an education that does not serve their interests, it is hard to see how the receipt of an education that was more suited to those interests could be more harmful to them than the one that they currently receive. The current generic liberal curriculum that has existed in the UK and the US from the beginning of universal, compulsory secondary education has, for a significant proportion of young people, been associated with failure. It is that failure, when combined with the offering of spurious academic theories as to why that failure has occurred (such as psychometric and verbal deficit theories), that has not only perpetuated social divisions but has embittered young people by seeking to demonstrate that those who do not benefit from an academic curriculum are *deficient* in some quite radical way.

A curriculum that was perceived to be beneficial, which engaged the interests and the ability of young people, and which led to satisfying and well-paid employment, would not have such negative effects and the class differentiation that occurred as a result of occupational specialisation would not carry a stigma. This is not a utopian vision. Some of the countries that do specialise the secondary curriculum and have well-established vocational routes succeed in combining economic prosperity with social cohesion. Germany is a particular example of this.[20]

Another argument, that was successfully deployed in the UK before and immediately after the Second World War, is that it is impossible to detect an aptitude for particular occupations during the years of adolescence.[21] Therefore it was thought impossible to have a specialised curriculum for the practically minded. Psychometrically inclined psychologists seem to have had an almost unbounded confidence that they could detect academic potential at the age of eleven, yet found themselves confounded by the task of detecting practical potential a few years later. This is not really as surprising as it seems when one considers the methods that they judged appropriate for the detection of potential. The ability to follow an academic curriculum was considered to be innate and detectable by measurement of the intelligence quotient. Those considered to have lower IQs were destined for skilled, semi-skilled and unskilled occupation in descending order of IQ score. So, in effect, psychometrists were very clear about how children could be selected for occupations that did not require academic ability. They assumed that the lower the IQ the less skill of any kind was required and that practical occupations could be managed by people who had less potential for developing high levels of skill.

But this way of thinking about potential is flawed because it is based on an untenable theory about the existence of something called 'intelligence'. If, as was argued earlier, ability is internally related to activity or to groups of activities, then it is not possible to say that one can detect *general* as opposed to some highly specific abilities through the administration of an IQ test. Instead of relying on pseudo-scientific accounts of intelligence and ability, educators would do better to keep records of the aptitudes and abilities of children, to test them periodically and more formally, and to keep in close touch with parents and thus arrive at a consensus with them about what range of interests and aptitudes an adolescent might have.[22] By the age of 14, if they are given encouragement to do so, children will be forming some idea of where their abilities and interests lie. Psychological testing may have a limited, subordinate role in double-checking on abilities and preferences but it should be there as a back-up rather than as a major tool of selection.[23] In any event, the argument is spurious on other grounds. It is not being suggested that secondary schools prepare children for specific occupations but for particular *kinds* of occupations, such as caring, engineering, dance and sport or commerce and trade.[24]

'But', it will be suggested, 'there is the possibility that mistakes will be made which it will prove impossible to rectify'. One can never be sure that a choice of which direction one's education should take will always be the right one. Yet there is no reason why such choices should be irrevocable. It should always be possible to re-orient oneself in an alternative curricular stream should this prove to be the best thing to do. The provision of *alternatives* for pupils is a condition for it being possible to rectify mistakes. It is the *absence* of alternatives that will inevitably lead to many children being left to follow courses for which they are unsuited. The important point is that there are clearly defined ways of reviewing one's choices and rectifying them where necessary.

The final objection to diversified curricula rests on the institutional implications of initiating such a move. Either the different curricula are taught in different institutions or they are taught in the same one. In the first instance, the risks of social divisiveness mentioned earlier appear in a particularly stark form. In the second case, the confusion of aims and of different kinds of ethos that was discussed in the previous chapter becomes a serious problem that undermines the sense of purpose that a school or college should have and, in practice, leads to the institutional dominance of the culturally prevalent educational tradition anyway—in this instance either the liberal academic or the liberal progressive tradition.

The second point is apparently persuasive in countries such as the UK, where a culturally dominant tradition tends to overcome attempts to diversify curricular provision within schools and colleges.[25] But the alternative, that of creating distinct institutions dedicated to different curricular routes, seems to make the problem of social division mentioned earlier even more intractable. However, the issue should not be shirked. There is no evidence to suggest that educating children in schools dedicated to different purposes is going to turn different elements of society against each other. That might be a problem if all that existed were schools of *differing* quality in terms of pupil ability, staffing and resources but otherwise offering much the same kind of education.[26]

When the question is considered in terms of whether or not it will lead to social divisions, then two factors need to be taken into account before a conclusion can sensibly be reached. First of all, there is no reason why vocationally oriented schools should not be invested with a certain amount of glamour, prestige and high-level resourcing if the political will is there. Secondly, it is a mistake to think that social cohesion requires *equality of treatment*. There is a confusion between the idea of *procedural justice* (that people in the same reference group are treated fairly) and of *social justice* (the principles according to which society is organised into different reference groups), and the idea that everyone should be treated in the same way, which may accord neither with procedural nor with social justice.[27] In a modern society dedicated to fulfilling the talents of all its members while promoting the prosperity of all in the context of a democratic polity, it does not depart from our ideals of social justice to say that at some stage in their educational careers children should follow different curricula in different institutions, particularly if it can be shown that this is the best way of achieving those aims.

V   CONCLUSION

There can be no single over-arching curriculum that is appropriate for all modern democratic societies. The curriculum is contingent on the negotiated outcomes of aims and while different curricula may support the same aims of education, precisely *how* those aims are to be served is a matter for further negotiation. Where negotiation fails or does not take place at all, then dominant cultural tendencies will set the curricular agenda.

There are, nevertheless, epistemological constraints on a curriculum which ought to determine its structure. Chief among these is the *progressive* nature of any accumulation of knowledge. Some knowledge and skill must be learned before more can successfully be learned. Secondly, certain *generic* skill and knowledge is required if learning is to continue, particularly learning that becomes progressively more independent. This suggests that, to be successful, it is likely that all curricula need to contain a common primary element of *grounding* that forms the prerequisite for future autonomy.

Having achieved the basic prerequisites of autonomy, the further aims of autonomy, self-fulfilment, economic growth and development of citizenship can be realised through a variety of curricular routes that build on a common grounding. There is no viable theory of general intelligence available to deny the proposition that ability is linked to activities. The argument of this chapter is that on philosophical grounds there is an overwhelming case for grounding at the primary level and a strong presumption of the desirability of curriculum diversity and, in some cases, of institutional diversity at the post-primary level. No philosophical argument in favour of a particular curriculum content can or should be compelling. Ultimately curriculum choice, like the choice of aims, is a political matter to be determined in accordance with a society's priorities. But any curriculum design that ignores the philosophical considerations developed here runs the risk of disadvantaging some, if not all, of those who have to follow it. The quality of the curriculum then is not and cannot be *determined* by philosophical considerations; it *can* be compromised by a failure to attend to them.

NOTES

1. For the first of these, see R. C. Whitfield (ed.), *Disciplines of the Curriculum*, 1971, p. 2; for the second, see D. Lawton, *Class, Culture and the Curriculum*, 1975, pp. 6–7.
2. Cf. I. F. Goodson, *Studying Curriculum*, 1994, in particular Chapter 8.
3. Where the curriculum is so informal and so implicit that it becomes difficult to see any significant subject differentiation or progression, it is arguable that a school in this situation is not providing a formal education in the sense in which that term is commonly understood. This is one reason why some forms of nursery schooling can only be called 'educational' in a limited sense.

4. Plato, *Republic*, Book VI.

5. E. D. Hirsch Jr., The primal scene of education, *New York Review of Books*, vol. XXXVI, no. 3, pp. 29–34.

6. Cf. Goodson, *op. cit.*

7. A point well illustrated in M. Sanderson, *op. cit.*

8. The case is more than merely plausible provided that one understands the claim to mean that study of other subjects is enhanced by the study of Philosophy, rather than that the study of Philosophy is a substitute for the study of other subjects.

9. There are psycholinguistic variants of this theory as well: see F. Smith, *Reading*, 1985; N. Hall, *The Emergence of Literacy*, 1988. For a critique, see M. Donaldson, *Sense and Sensibility*, 1989; C. Winch, Reading and the process of reading, *Journal of Philosophy of Education*, 23. 2, pp. 303–316, 1989.

10. See for example, R. Dearden, *The Philosophy of Primary Education*, 1969, Chapters 2 and 3; R. Barrow and R. Woods, *An Introduction to the Philosophy of Education*, 1974, Chapter 7.

11. See John Locke, *The Second Treatise of Government*.

12. Religious Education is not properly part of grounding and should be treated separately. Here I think that there is an overwhelming case for allowing confessional religious belief to be taught within the constraints of a national curriculum, if particular groups demand it. At the same time as their interests are attended to, however, so must they attend to the interests of others in receipt of publicly funded education. This is why religious education, if it is to be supported by the government, must take place within the context of a common curriculum.

13. See E. D. Hirsch, *op. cit.* For a recent criticism, see W. Feinberg, *Japan and the Pursuit of a New American Identity*, 1993. For a British example see D. Cameron and J. Bourne, No common ground: Kingman, grammar and the nation, *Language and Education*, 2.3, 1988, pp. 147–160.

14. I make no apology for talking about human flourishing in this connection. This is not just a matter of material prosperity but of ethical and spiritual fulfilment as well. I hope that this avoids the objections to talk of human flourishing that are raised, for example, by R. Gaita in *Good and Evil: An Absolute Conception*, 1991.

15. R. Barrow, *Intelligence and Education*, 1993.

16. The critique of the concept of intelligence is well known; see for example, Winch, 1990, *op. cit.*

17. The term 'intelligent' is used colloquially to denote not an innate property of mind, but ability at one thing or group of things. It is thus a concept that is dependent on the concept of ability, which is activity-related.

18. On the diversity of occupations required by a productive economy, see F. List, *op. cit.*, Chapter XII.

19. From the point of view of economic development, there are reasons for thinking that a society should play to its traditional strengths in its skill base. Thus for example there is an argument for maintaining and developing traditional craft skills within the West European economy. Schools can play their part through generic forms of craft and practical aesthetic education.

20. HMI, 1990, *op. cit.*

21. Sanderson, *op. cit.*

22. On the pseudo-scientific nature of IQ theory, see S. J. Gould, *The Mismeasure of Man*, 1981.

23. The Norwood Committee, which published its report in 1943, did suggest a form of secondary selection at the age of 13 on the lines that I have suggested, but its recommendations were largely ignored, with fateful consequences.

24. Even when, at the post-compulsory level, young people are preparing for particular occupations, there is a case for a continuing element of general education as in the German Berufschule system. See HMI, *op. cit.*, 1990.

25. Sanderson, *ibid.*, Chapter 7, documents the fate of technical education in the grammar and technical schools.

26. See David Cooper, *Illusions of Equality*, and the discussion in Chapter 10.

27. See the discussion in Chapter 10.

Chapter 6
A Defence of Educational Standards

I THE NEED FOR STANDARDS

In this chapter I will argue that it is possible to measure and to compare educational performances against standards and that it is also possible to compare standards of performance with each other in a number of cases.[1] It is most important to make this point in order to counter the kind of epistemic pessimism that asserts that it is not really possible to know whether and to what degree an educational performance has been successful. If this pretence is accepted then it is hard to see how education, understood as a purposive activity with more or less identifiable aims, is really possible. For if a teacher could not know, even approximately, the extent to which he was successful in what he set out to do with his pupils, then it becomes hard to see in what sense he would be teaching, since there will be no way of assessing the degree of learning that may or may not have been taking place.[2] Furthermore, the accountability of the educational enterprise will founder, leaving education vulnerable to the claim that it is a confederation of producer interests, unconcerned with whether or not resources are effectively deployed. This is not to say that learning may not take place without assessment, but if the aim of teaching is to induce learning, then the effectiveness of the teaching needs to be assessed. This is the point at which the neo-liberals come into the picture with market-led solutions which, in this case, will lead to a relativistic view of standards if any objective view of what they are disappears. All that will be left will be the opinions of those in the educational market place as to what constitute good performances and the standards against which those performances are to be judged. If performances against standards cannot be judged, then attempts to assess the performance of schools by such devices as value-added measures will also fail, since the point of such measures is that they compare performances against known standards at different points in a pupil's career.

II STANDARDS AND PERFORMANCE

It is necessary to distinguish between the standards by which an educational performance is measured and the nature of that performance itself.[3] The standard is the measuring stick against which the performance is assessed. So, for example, if the standard for a pass in mathematics is 50% correct scores on a test, then an individual performance can be assessed on the basis of whether or not it meets that requirement and the extent to which it does so.

Given a standard, therefore, it is possible to say whether or not a performance meets that standard. However, questions may be raised as to whether or not the standard is a valid one: that is, whether or not it does really indicate a level of knowledge, skill or understanding that could be put to use in conditions outside the examination hall or classroom. No test is going to be completely valid, but this does not mean that it is impossible ever to devise a workable form of testing. There is a trade-off between realism and comprehensiveness that always needs to be made in these situations. The more realistic and replicative of real-life situations a test is, the less likely is it to be generalisable to other non-examination contexts. On the other hand, the more context-free a test is, the less certain one can be that the knowledge or skill involved could be put to use in specific contexts. This illustrates, however, that the dilemma is a general one for any attempt at assessment and that the alternative is epistemic pessimism about whether it is possible to say that someone has learned something. Epistemic pessimism about the possibility of learning is not an option for the institution of education in *any* setting and so cannot reasonably be sustained.

So the aim ought to be to strive for forms of assessment of maximum validity consistent with a reasonable degree of context-dependence. It will always be difficult to justify the validity of tests and assessments and changing them will lay teachers open to the charge of compromising procedural justice. However, just because the goal is an ever-receding one of a generalisable and fully valid test, that does not mean that, within reasonable limits, systems cannot be operated, research cannot be carried out into their effectiveness and incremental improvements cannot be made at intervals. The best should not be allowed to be the enemy of the good.

Another significant objection to testing and assessment is that they cannot provide a good account of what a pupil *currently* knows since a pupil will always forget much of what he has learned for an assessment, so that the test will naturally be of poor validity for this reason.[4] This is an argument that proves too much, for it is also an argument against learning and teaching, making them look like futile activities because of a general scepticism about retention. There is an implicit confusion here about *memory* on the one hand and *recall* on the other. It is true that recall may be more difficult after the specific training undergone for a test has faded away, but it does not follow that what was learned has now been forgotten. The assessment sceptic has already claimed that we can only know what someone knows within a context-specific performance. The same point holds about memory. It is in specific contexts that memory will show itself to be effective, even after the ability to recall in examination conditions may have faded. Testing the ability to recall is a worthwhile and effective way of testing memory because it is relatively context-free.[5] It is also a good criterion of memory, since it involves a rigorous appeal to memory where all the usual supports of practical interest and involvement are not present. It is of itself not a necessary condition that something has been remembered, it is just a very good indicator and, in many circumstances, it is the best indicator that we have, even though it may be imperfect.

There are, then, no compelling reasons for dispensing with assessment of performance and there *are* compelling reasons why assessment of performance should be carried out if educators are to maintain any respect from the public. But it is also essential to the activity of teaching that it should include assessment. If teaching is a purposive activity, guided by aims relating to what a pupil should learn, then teachers, if they are serious about what they are doing, will wish to see whether and to what extent they are meeting those aims. Assessment is simply that activity, seeing whether and to what extent pupils are learning what the teacher intends that they should learn. Once this essential point has been conceded, then it becomes a question of what means will best fulfil such ends and validity and reliability will be a problem for any form of assessment; but the difficulties inherent in getting it right are to be found in most worthwhile activities. In the case of assessment, a balance has to be struck between the search for improvement and the need to provide a measure of stability within the system.

III SCEPTICISM ABOUT STANDARDS

It has been argued that assessment is a necessary aspect of teaching and that it must be possible to assess performance according to standards. Assessment is rarely a perfect record of a pupil's knowledge and ability, but it does not follow that an assessment, properly constructed and conducted, cannot tell us much that is valuable and useful about someone's level of achievement. What of the standards themselves: is it possible to compare them, so that one can, for example, find out whether or not we set the same standards for English as we did fifity years ago, or whether or not the Japanese set higher standards for mathematics for eleven-year-olds than the Americans?

The question is an important one since it concerns the expectations that people have about educational outcomes and whether it is right to question whether expectations are too high or too low or just about right. Having the right expectations is crucial, since without some view on what expectations it is reasonable to have it is difficult to have coherent educational aims and hence difficult to construct a coherent curriculum. It is not enough to be able to assess a performance against a standard if one does not know whether or not the standard is appropriate. Why should standards not be comparable? There are two reasons, one of them trivial and easily dismissed, the other more serious but also dismissable.

First, norm-referenced performance tables cannot be assessed against each other because the grading depends on the percentage of grades that are allowable at each level. So, for example, if a national assessment of reading gives a normal distribution of scores, it can be stipulated that the top ten percentile of scores merit an A pass, the top thirty percentile a B or above, and so on. However, from year to year the raw scores that yield the distribution may change, so that on some occasions, in order to achieve an A, a pupil would need to score higher than he would have needed on a previous occasion. But, provided that the raw scores were available and the same testing instrument was used on the two occasions, it would be possible to see at what level of performance a pupil merited an A in one year compared with another. It would then be possible to determine whether the standards for what counted as an A performance had changed from year to year. The process of norm-referencing presupposes that a raw performance score exists in the first place and that the comparison of performances can be used to determine what standards are being set in a norm-referenced test.

The second objection is that the idea that standards can be compared with each other rests on a logical confusion. This objection has been made by Pring and rests on the claim that any attempt to compare standards and to answer the question 'Have they gone up or down?' is confused.[6] The reason why it is confused, according to Pring, is that in order to compare one standard with another, one would need a standard against which to compare those standards. But then, in order to compare the new set of standards, one would need a further one and so on *ad infinitum*. But this objection is not tenable. In the first place, it does not follow from the fact that in order to compare, say, two standards, a further standard is needed and that this new standard needs to be compared with the first two. All that needs to happen is that the standard which is to compare the first two standards is accepted as a measuring rod for the original two standards. It follows from the requirement that two standards be compared that there should be a measure against which they should be compared. It does not follow that this measure should itself be compared with the first two. It is true that if one wanted to compare two or more of these second-order standards, then it would be necessary to have a further standard in order to compare *them*, but it would not follow that this third-order standard would need to be compared with the two second-order standards before a meaningful comparison could be made.

In case this argument does not convince, it may be helpful to take an example. Suppose that the standard of performance necessary to achieve a grade A in mathematics is 90% in 1993 and is 80% in 1994. Then it is possible to say that the standard necessary to acquire an A in 1994 is 10% lower than the standard required in 1993. The second-order standard needed to make this judgement is simply the calibration of mathematics scores on the assessment instrument running from 0% to 100%. By setting this measuring rod against the rods for 1993 and 1994, we can see that the standard has fallen over the two-year period. If we now wanted to compare the assessment instrument used to compare the two first-order standards with each other with an assessment instrument used in another country, then we would need another standard to do this. But this need not be a problem. It would be possible to construct a standard for mathematical performance that will take into account the differing aims, curricula, pedagogy and expectations in the two countries to be compared. It is not necessary to compare this third-order standard with the two seond-order standards against a fourth-order standard in order to make this comparison.

So it is perfectly possible to compare standards with each other according to another standard and there is no compelling logical objection to our doing so. It is true that there will be all sorts of practical objections that may arise in particular circumstances and these are particularly connected with the need for the second-order standard to be genuinely applicable to the first-order standards that it is comparing, or with situations where two first-order standards are sufficiently different from each other to make a meaningful comparison impossible. It is important, however, to see that the *principle* that standards are comparable is an important one and is readily intelligible. Were it not, educational accountability would be in real trouble.

IV MEASURING STANDARDS WITHIN SUBJECTS

The selection of subjects to appear on the curriculum is a complex matter, influenced by many factors. The question of the worthwhileness of different subjects is a matter of negotiation and compromise between different groups. At first sight, it would appear that the question of the integrity of standards *within* subjects would be far easier to resolve. There are two aspects to intra-subject measures. The first is the *diachronic* aspect and relates to whether or not performances and the standards used to measure them change over time. The second is the *synchronic* aspect and is to do with whether or not they vary from educational institution to institution. The former requires measuring rods that do not change over time. The latter requires that a degree of uniformity of either aims or content or both should be applicable to the same subject in each institution. A disaggregated market place is likely to discourage this, particularly if it is driven by the perceptions and wishes of prospective students. Such a market place is also likely, particularly in the further and higher education sectors, to throw up subjects the assessment of any of whose standards is likely to be problematic, particularly when it is already difficult to assess the standards of established subjects which may form some kind of reference point for the assessment of new subjects. For example, if it is difficult to say what are the national standards for a 2:1 performance in Philosophy, it will be even more difficult to say what the standards for a subject based on but not identifiable with philosophy, such as Medical Ethics, should be.

The measurement of standards of teaching is notoriously difficult to achieve, since the qualities that go to make up good teaching are often intangible and opinions as to what they are can be the subject of fashion and prejudice. Furthermore, there is a strong inclination, at least among non-educationists, to take the view that the proof of good teaching will be determined by the level of outcomes achieved, subject to some ethical constraints on what are and what are not acceptable teaching practices.

Determining whether or not performances or standards are falling over time is easier when short time-scales are being considered. There are still problems connected with the identification of secular trends when a year-on-year comparison is made, as there is always likely to be a random fluctuation in results from year to year. In principle, the problem of deciding whether or not a change in standards of achievement is anything more than a random occurrence can be determined by such techniques as the use of a rolling three-year average. The problems really begin when one tries to compare standards over longer periods of time, say over five or more years. One of the problems faced by researchers is the relative lack of information as one goes back over time, either because information has been lost or because it was not collected.

The other major difficulty, however, is that of obtaining a measuring instrument that will be *capable* of applying over historical periods of time. It is quite likely that different instruments will have been used in the past. As fashions change and techniques develop, so measuring instruments such as tests change as well. When testing methods change, then it is no longer possible to make the like-with-like comparisons that seem to be required for a proper judgement to be made as to whether or not standards have risen or fallen. An obvious example of this difficulty is the measurement of reading standards. Reading tests of any kind are a relatively recent innovation and so the assessment of reading standards before the invention of those tests is problematic. After the invention of tests, people became dissatisfied with particular tests, perhaps because of their perceived failings in terms of validity, for example, and so new tests were developed. But results obtained by the new tests cannot meaningfully be compared with results obtained by the old test as they are not necessarily measuring the same aspects of reading ability.

Even where the same test is being used, its own validity can deteriorate over time, particularly, for example, in relation to the fact that words will fall out of use and new ones will appear in the language (e.g. lorry, truck). Since many tests aim to achieve a normal distribution among the population to which they are applied they may need to be re-standardised periodically. In such cases, it may well be the case that the raw scores that result in a normal distribution have drifted upwards, in which case the test will no longer be a valid way of comparing either standards or performances over time. This does actually appear to be the case with reading, as the table below indicates.

The apparent difficulties should not, however, lead us into thinking that it is impossible to make meaningful diachronic comparisons of performance within a particular educational system, although the ease of doing so is considerably increased when there is a common yardstick applicable to the performances being reviewed, such as the Standardised Attainment Tests used in the English and Welsh educational systems and the American Scholastic Aptitude Test.

A good example of a short-term diachronic achievement evaluation study is that of Robin Alexander in the Leeds local education authority in the UK.[8] Although the Alexander study shows variations in short-term achievement in, for example, reading performance, he does not attempt to show that the variations are significant. The study, however, was an evaluation of an intervention, namely providing extensive extra resources for low-achieving pupils. In the absence of targets of achievement for these pupils given the provision of extra resources, it is difficult to see how judgements can be made as to the significance of the variations found given their relatively small size.[9]

Synchronic comparisons of performances, both nationally and internationally, are easier to achieve, particularly in certain areas of the curriculum. OECD measures of mathematical achievement are an example of this type of comparison being carried out successfully.[10] But there are limitations to such studies. First, they work most successfully in those instances where results are easily quantifiable and the curriculum is assumed to be broadly comparable across different countries, so that it is relatively easy to invoke a common standard. Mathematics is a clear example of such a subject. It will not be as easy to make cross-cultural and cross-national

Table 1 The average raw score of pupils on the Watts–Vernon reading test between 1948 and 1964[7]

Year of survey	1948	1952	1956	1964
Average raw score of 11-year-olds	11.6	12.4	13.3	15.0

comparisons for other subjects, because standards in them are much more subject to cultural and curricular variation. Thus, even though the principles of the natural sciences apply across the world, it does not follow that curricula are broadly comparable. History and Geography curricula are also likely to vary greatly between different countries. Standards and levels of achievement of literacy can be compared when the languages are the same — for example, the anglophone West Indies and Great Britain — but the exercise becomes more difficult when one seeks to compare the standards in different countries with different languages or different writing systems. For example, not only does the People's Republic of China have a different language from the United Kingdom, but writing is, to a large extent, organised on a *logographic* rather than an *alphabetic* basis.

Nevertheless, it would be unwise to conclude that these kinds of difficulties make it completely impossible to make synchronic international comparisons of standards. In these cases, one does need to construct a second-order standard against which the first-order standards can be compared. It will then *either* be possible to compare performances using the first-order standards and then adjusting for differences between those, *or* it may be possible to use the second-order standard to effect a direct comparison between performances. So, for example, if one wished to compare the reading performances of eleven-year-olds in China and the UK, it would be possible to do one of two things. One could first of all look at reading tests for the two countries (first-order standards) and determine which of these was the less demanding. Then one could adjust the scores achieved on the less demanding test to construct a second-order standard which would make a direct comparison between performances in the two countries possible. Alternatively, one could take the two tests, pick out salient criteria from each (say, measurement of size of vocabulary and sentence complexity) and construct a new measure incorporating the key elements in both the original tests (first-order standards). This measure could be used to compare the rigour of the original first-order standards (using it as a second-order standard) or it could be used directly to measure performance in a new set of tests (as a new first-order standard). In addition, it would be wise to devise weightings for the measurement of performances to take account, for example, of different ages of entry into school. But such adjustments are perfectly possible.

Even when it is granted that meaningful cross-national comparisons are possible in these areas, it is still necessary to enter the *caveat* that what they tell us is limited. Such cross-national comparisons are not as reliable or valid as national ones, for reasons that should be clear from the above. Neither can such comparisons by themselves yield like-for-like measures on other important aspects of educational performance. For example, such matters as the organisation of a national education system in terms of entry age, length of school day, per capita resourcing and value-added considerations cannot be taken into account on a pure comparison of standards at a given age-level. To make comparisons that take these kinds of factors into account, it will be necessary to look at the considerations discussed in Chapter 5.

V ASSESSMENT OF STANDARDS

So far, the discussion has been carried out on the assumption that any evaluation of standards and levels of performance is based on *achievement* rather than process. But the question asked at the beginning of this section related to standards of *teaching* as well as to standards of achievement. It might be objected to the comparison studies that have so far been mentioned that they concentrate on comparisons of performances against standards and that only levels of achievement rather than the quality of the teaching that takes place in educational settings have been considered. Even if we leave out the value-added side of achievement comparison, is it not the case that the quality of education cannot be assessed without some consideration of the quality of the teaching?

In one sense, such a suggestion seems to be unassailable. Not everything that promotes learning can be considered to be a legitimate educational experience. The use of intimidation and torture, for example, would not, in most cultures, be considered to be appropriate ways of getting young people to learn. But when one goes beyond this, the matter is not nearly as clear. First of all, the level of pressure that it is thought legitimate to exert on pupils in order to encourage them to learn does vary from culture to culture. Expectations also change over time within particular cultures. The parameters of what is ethically acceptable as teaching vary both diachronically and synchronically. They vary as educators, parents and other groups in society change their views as to what is the best way to promote learning, but they also vary in terms of different cultural views of what are the appropriate ways to bring up children.

Nevertheless, although this is true, it is not a point that should be exaggerated. The notion of educational standards is a fairly restricted one that does not encompass all aspects of educational achievement. In particular, it does not encompass a concern for values or long-term outcomes that some see as important aims of any worthwhile educational process. Very often educational thinkers who have been particularly concerned with the development of values have tended to regard an emphasis on standards of achievement as an excessively narrow preoccupation, one that could even hinder the achievement of more valuable educational aims.[11] Those who focus on the worthwhileness of education and, in so doing, tend to emphasise levels of achievement in fairly tangible forms such as the acquisition of skill, knowledge or understanding, will generally accept that there is a range of educational processes that are morally acceptable but will, within that range, advocate those that produce the highest educational performances. Those who make process rather than product the main focus of concern do not necessarily fall into the confusion of thinking that an educational process need not have an outcome, but will emphasise the intangible and long-term nature of educational outcomes and their process-dependence. The key points are that what *can* be assessed *should* be assessed, and it should be clearly indicated which aspects of education cannot be assessed so that the public understand the limitations of accountability and can make proper decisions on those forms of education which they wish to support.

VI ASSESSING STANDARDS

If the comparative assessment of standards is to stand any chance of carrying conviction it must satisfy two criteria. The first is that the mode of assessing standards really does measure what it seeks to measure, that is, knowledge, skill and understanding of the subject (sometimes known as the validity criterion). The second is that measurements should be consistent within and between different institutions. This is known as the reliability criterion. Whatever mode of assessment is used to measure educational standards in any particular performance, it must be both *valid* and *reliable*.

Reliability is fairly easy to achieve on formalised, quantitative techniques of assessment, such as the use of tests which can be standardised and arithmetically scored. Reliability rates of between 0.70 and 0.60 are normally expected on this kind of test.[12] Reliability is much less easy to quantify in other forms of assessment. To the extent that assessment involves an element of subjective judgement, reliability depends on the extent to which different individuals tend to arrive at the same judgement about a performance. The way in which to ensure reliability of intersubjective judgements is through internal and external moderation of them. This is a problem throughout all sectors of education and it is bound to arise whenever teachers are asked to make subjective judgements about the work that they assess. The practice of moderation is, then, an essential part of maintaining reliability in the judgement of standards. Moderation is, however, time-consuming and hence expensive and there is therefore a considerable implication for resources if it is used extensively. To give an example, the quality of the writing done by children in a primary school can be measured on an ordinal scale. Judgements can then be moderated by other teachers and a mean score arrived at. Such a system can be supported by criteria for making quality judgements such as fitness for purpose, appropriateness of style and overall organisation. This, in effect, was the kind of system devised by the Assessment of Performance Unit in the UK in the 1970s. It can also be extended to make international comparisons of the quality of writing.[13]

One of the objections raised to formal tests is that they may achieve reliability at the cost of poor validity. It is argued that they may test only a limited range of skill, knowledge and understanding and may do so in conditions which are unlikely to be representative of those in which those skills, knowledge and understanding would normally be exercised.[14]

VII HOW DO WE KNOW WHAT STANDARDS SHOULD BE?

Once a national system of assessment has been established, it can provide the data that allow everyone concerned to see what spread of achievement exists across an educational system. This makes it possible to construct *value-added* measures on the basis of such assessment. An alternative to a national testing system is the use of light sampling techniques to build up a picture of the spread of standards across an educational system, in the way that the Assessment of Performance Unit did in the United Kingdom before its abolition. A disadvantage of the national system of assessment as it operates in the UK is the fact that data are available only at ages 7, 11, 14 and 16. This does not provide a sufficiently detailed range of data to supply a national picture of performance. At the same time, its administration is thought to be too disruptive of education. This second objection ought to be treated with a degree of caution; if, as I have argued, the presence of assessment is a criterion of seriousness in teaching, then there ought to be some form of manageable assessment during each academic year. How simple or how complicated it is, is a matter for the finer detail of policy. But teachers cannot object on the one hand that simple tests are invalid and on the other that valid tests are too unwieldy. If assessment procedures and results are to be made transparent to the public, then a compromise must be found that both works and can be understood by people other than teachers and educational professionals.

An advantage of the light sampling technique is that it is cheaper and less disruptive of education and can build up just as representative a picture of the range of achievement in different contexts as a full national assessment. It would allow schools to compare themselves and others with the schools achieving the best performances in comparable circumstances. It is probable, though, that the climate of opinion, at least in the UK, is in favour of a national system of testing. But this will not be enough if performance is to be evaluated between and before the various assessment points. It might be said that inspections will ensure that this happens, but this is unlikely. Inspections are concerned above all with process and can only gain an impression of standards, except in relation to national norms and these will only by properly known for the assessment years. Rather than full inspections of every school, it might be worth while rather to spend some money on the light sampling of performance across the system and the building up of data for the purposes of comparison. It would then be possible to make a reasonable assessment of whether standards were being set high enough.

VIII   STANDARDS IN HIGHER EDUCATION AND THE FRAGMENTATION OF AIMS

A national education system may provide a strong guarantee that standards are consistent across a phase of education, by providing a common curriculum and means of assessment. Such a system can work well at primary and secondary level, where there can be clearly defined common strands in education. This is not so easy to maintain at the level of higher education, which is a non-compulsory phase and which is also, increasingly, market-driven in the sense that universities and colleges are allowed to run those courses for which they can attract students. Provided the teachers of these courses can satisfy validating boards that the courses are academically viable, then there is no reason why they should not be allowed to attract students. There will be a tendency to fragmentation as different institutions develop distinctive courses in order to establish a niche in the marketplace or to ensure that there is something distinctive about the course that they seek to provide. The result is that not only does it become difficult to talk intelligibly about standards across the higher education sector, but it also becomes difficult to maintain that the same subjects in different institutions have the same standards. Insofar as a *comparison* of quality between different institutions entails a comparison of *standards*, comparisons of quality will no longer be as easy, and may not be possible at all; hence the practice, in the United Kingdom, of assessing the quality of courses against the aims that course teams set themselves. The fragmentation of subject aims also means that the traditional method of ensuring comparability of standards in the same subject between different institutions through external examination is compromised. As the aims of courses in what was ostensibly the same subject become different from one another, so the base for comparability is narrowed until it may eventually disappear altogether, thus depriving the external examiner of his function, which is to ensure comparability of standards between different courses in different institutions. This is why the idea that there is a 'gold standard' of courses in well-respected institutions to which the others should aspire is no longer appropriate in such a situation.

One way of replying to this argument that standards are no longer comparable is to suggest that courses should have aims to develop generic skills such as that of becoming a 'reflective practitioner', which would ensure that, although there is a great deal of diversity within course aims and between different cognate courses, there is also an important element in common between them.[15] One would then be making *becoming a reflective practitioner* a second-order standard against which to judge the diverse first-order standards. Such a move can only be made if it is plausible to argue that there are such generic skills that are developed in different and diverse courses. Barnett's own solution of suggesting that the development of reflective practitioners should be a common course aim has the weakness that the concept of a reflective practitioner is itself highly fragmented, and subject to various interpretations, even in the form presented by its author, Donald Schon.[16]

Other attempts to suggest that education generally, and higher education in particular, should aim to develop generic thinking skills have all run into serious criticism from authors such as John McPeck. Even if McPeck's arguments, derived from Stephen Toulmin, are rejected for resting on an inadequate conception of logic, other objections can be made along the lines of suggesting that the ability to reason logically can only be applied in the context of particular subject knowledge, so that one could only reason logically within a particular subject if one had acquired a certain basis of knowledge within that subject.[17] All that the acquisition of a generic skill would be able to do, would be to assist the development of reasoning *within* a particular subject. Furthermore, since the development of reasoning skills *per se* could not be part of every subject, it would have to be taught within a particular subject such as, for example, Philosophy. This would mean that Philosophy might become a common component of a range of courses, but it would hardly show that *different* subjects could have common course aims. To a certain extent, professional education will be shielded from this fragmentation, as the professional bodies which have a significant role in validating and running courses which prepare for their professions will try to ensure a degree of commonality between them, but courses that are not attached to professional bodies will not be in this position. It is possible to conclude, then, that although national curricula will tend to maintain the synchronic comparison of standards in the primary and secondary phases of education, to the extent that market forces led by potential student demand have started to generate a greater diversity of courses with a diversity of aims, the comparison of standards across institutions will become increasingly difficult. Since the new course aims will tend to diverge from the aims of more traditional courses, the *diachronic* comparison of standards will become increasingly difficult as well.

The fragmentation of higher education, together with the increasing difficulties of setting and assessing intra-sectoral standards and performances, poses a threat to the idea of a unitary system of higher education. Inevitably, divergent standards will come to be recognised and a hierarchy of prestige for certain kinds of curricula will develop. There has always been a hierarchy of *institutional* prestige but this will be a new development which is not particularly welcome. Some of the higher education sector will be seen to be offering poor value in terms of *content* as well as in terms of the performances achieved. This raises questions about the worthwhileness of a mass higher education system which it is beyond the scope of this book to discuss.

IX CONCLUSION — PERFORMANCE, STANDARDS AND THE PUBLIC CULTURE OF EDUCATION

The standards that are set and the performance that is achieved in relation to them depend to a large extent on the efforts of pupils and teachers. But it would be a mistake to think that they are the only relevant factors. Almost as important are the culture and the expectations of the society in which the education takes place. Standards cannot move too far out of alignment with what society expects of education, whether its expectations are high or low. Here, the expectations of parents are a crucial factor, because if they do not match those of teachers, then there is likely to be resistance to teachers expecting high performance and to politicians and policy-makers who wish to set high standards. The question of raising standards then becomes one of political persuasion and social engineering, aimed at increasing the public's expectations. It is not clear how effective politicians could be in doing this directly; once the attempt is perceived to be taking place, it is likely to prove self-defeating. More promising would be an indirect approach, where, first of all, the public are made aware of the standards currently being expected and then invited to compare them with those of other nations. Something like this appears to have happened in the UK in relation to staying-on rates in education, where the example of the US and Europe seems to have affected the expectations of parents and children. Another approach would be to change the mix of aims and curricula so that the system appeared to be more inclusive of a wider range of interests.

This awareness of trends abroad has not yet been translated into an awareness of and concern about either the standards to be expected in schools or pupil performance in relation to peers in other education systems. If standards and expectations are low in comparison with those of other countries, then it is also likely that there is a mismatch between certain aspects of the prevailing culture and the education system.[18] We cannot conclude from the fact that a society has low expectations that it must be irredeemably slothful and unambitious. An alternative explanation is that one important group has been left out of the negotiation about aims and curricula and consequently feels disenfranchised by the system as it currently exists. This is an explanation that might well fit the UK, where even some of the leaders of the working class in the Labour Party and the trade unions have historically been either indifferent or actively hostile to training and to vocational education.[19] Expectations are likely to rise where people's desire for high-quality *vocational* as opposed to purely academic education is recognised and met. One cannot be surprised by the prevalence of low expectations, if those expectations are not linked to the prospect of personal fulfilment in adult life.

The standards that are expected of pupils and students are intimately related to the aims of education and the curricula that are designed to achieve those aims. Uncertainty about aims has direct implications for standards. If a social group finds itself unable to identify with an educational aim, then it will tend not to sympathise with the curricular provision that is made to achieve that aim and this will tend to lead to confusion about what standards are to be expected. There is no real alternative to a proper debate, or at least, consensus, about aims and curricula if all the significant groups in a society are to feel that they can expect high performance from those within an education system. This is particularly the case where the philosophical approach to the teaching of a subject has changed within the education system, as has happened, for example, with Mathematics and English in the United Kingdom. These changes have not been well explained to the lay public, and neither have their implications for standards of achievement. There may well be a justification for changes in the approach to the teaching of certain subjects, but all the relevant interest groups, not just the education professionals, need to be involved in decisions which lead to such changes.

Scepticism about the possibility of assessing standards and about measuring and comparing performances is a symbol of the resulting *malaise*. First of all, the arguments tend to have the self-interested effect of detaching educators from their side of the accountability obligation. Secondly, an argument that serves to fuel doubts as to whether meaningful standards can ever be set and compared with those of other societies makes it difficult, if not impossible, to have nationally recognised, reasonable expectations about what an education system can produce.

Nationally recognised, internationally comparable standards, which relate in an intelligible way to the aims of an education system and to the curricula that support it, are fundamental to the achievement of worthwhileness in education. In the modern idiom, they are also the cornerstone of quality.

NOTES

1. This latter claim is denied in R. Pring, Standards and quality in education, *British Journal of Educational Studies*, XXXX.3, 1992, p. 20.
2. See A. Flew, *Sociology, Equality and Education*, 1976, p. 89. This is not to say that some aspects of educational achievement are more measurable than others and that, therefore, a concern with quality may propel education in the direction of the measurable.
3. Pring, *op. cit.*
4. See, for example, A. Davis, *op. cit.*
5. For the distinction between memory and recall, see Norman Malcolm, *Memory and Mind*, 1977, pp. 69–70.
6. Pring, *op. cit.*, p. 20.
7. Taken from R. Beard, *Developing Reading 3–13*, 1987, p. 203.
8. R. Alexander, *Policy and Practice in the Primary School*, 1992.
9. Ibid., Chapters 8 and 9.
10. See, for example, S. J. Prais, Mathematical attainments: comparisons of Japanese and English schooling, in B. Moon (ed.), *Judging Standards and Effectiveness in Education*, 1990.

11. See, for example, Homer Lane, *Talks to Parents and Teachers*, 1954; A. S. Neill, *Summerhill: A Radical Approach to Education*, 1965.
12. D. Nuttall, Principles of measurement, in *Classification and Measurement*, 1981, pp. 72–73.
13. For the APU study, see Janet White, *The Assessment of Writing*, 1986; for a cross-cultural comparison using a similar technique, see C. Winch and J. Gingell, Dialect interference and children's difficulties with writing: an investigation in St. Lucian primary schools, *Language and Education*, 8.3 (1994), pp. 157–182.
14. A. Davis, *op. cit.*
15. This is the line taken by, for example, Ronald Barnett in *Improving Higher Education*, 1993.
16. Cf. D. Schon, *Educating the Reflective Practitioner*, 1987.
17. See J. McPeck, *Critical Thinking and Education*, 1984; S. Toulmin, *The Uses of Argument*, 1957; C. Winch, The curriculum and the study of reason, *Westminster Studies in Education*, 10, 1987, pp. 63–76.
18. Evidence on attainment in mathematics, for example, can be found in Prais, *op. cit.*
19. See, for example, the views of Ellen Wilkinson, Minister of Education 1945–7, in Sanderson, *op. cit.*, p. 132.

Chapter 7
Adding Educational Value

I INTRODUCTION

In the previous chapter we saw that meaningful assessment of learning is possible. However, standards achieved at one point of assessment do not tell us about *how much* knowledge has been gained, since that can only be measured in terms of a before/after comparison between the starting point of learning and its subsequent assessment. In the last ten years, the importance of this consideration for making comparative judgements of educational effectiveness has been increasingly recognised. One strategy that has been frequently advocated and often put into effect has been to measure the so-called 'value-added' by an educational process. The idea is that one can compare what the pupil knows at the start of a period of education with what he knows at the conclusion. Subtraction of the former from the latter will yield a measure of the educational value-added.

At first sight this looks very much like another attempt to introduce a manufacturing paradigm into educational assessment and the terminology used certainly suggests this. Materials of a certain value go into a production process in order to emerge as marketable products which can be sold at a certain value. The value added by the manufacturing process is the difference between the cost of the materials and the cost of the product at the end of the process, including the profit made on its sale. So far there is a similarity, but the analogy does not fully hold. The pupils' learning is not a marketable value or is so only when they seek a further place within the education system or when they seek employment. The difference in value in the educational case is a difference between pre-existing knowledge, skill and understanding and those attributes as they exist at the end of an educational process.

The use of value-added measures implies that, in assessing the value of an educational experience, relative rather than absolute learning is assumed to be decisive. An absolute measure of what is learned would indeed be a better indicator of the market value of an educational experience, since what admissions tutors and parents wish to know is how much the student or pupil *currently* knows rather than how much he has actually learned over a given period. This makes value-added measures more of a tool for administrators and policy-makers than for pupils and parents.

The reasons why value-added measures are thought to be a good alternative to measures of standards of achievement in the assessment of educational effectiveness are as follows. First, they are not a rival, but an alternative, form of measure to straightforward 'one-shot' measures of pupil achievement. One-shot measures, as we have seen, tell a prospective admissions tutor or employer what the pupil or student now knows, which is the main thing that he needs to establish in assessing suitability for admission or for employment. Value-added measures are designed to tell parents, governments, employers and others how *effective* a school is in raising levels of achievement.

Secondly, they are thought to be valuable because they give like-for-like comparisons by taking account of the various factors that may contribute to pupils learning or failing to learn. They do this in the first instance by controlling for what the pupil knows when he enters school. But, in their more sophisticated forms, they also take into account such matters as socio-economic status of the catchment area and resources available to the school.

Thirdly, they are popular, at least in some sectors, because they are thought to remove the stigma that may attach to low status or unpopular schools by showing that schools which are not favoured in a market or semi-market situation may nevertheless be effective in achieving what they seek to do, sometimes indeed proving to be more effective than schools which have higher outputs. In theory, neo-liberals should welcome value-added measures as they promise to provide more of the information needed for the effective operation of educational markets (see Chapter 9). The problem with them as a market tool is one that neo-liberal writers are quite well aware of: they are a sophisticated tool interpretable only by specialists and thus not accessible to parents and children. They threaten, therefore, to reinforce the power and knowledge of the educational expert at the expense of the amateur 'customer'.

II   HOW VALUE-ADDED MEASUREMENTS WORK

The basic idea of value-added measures is to provide an assessment of *progress* over a period of education, as opposed to an assessment of *achievement* at a particular point in time. Value-added measures are, then, logically dependent on measures of achievement because they measure the difference between two measures of achievement, the difference being the main component of the measure of added value. Institutions can then be compared with each other in terms of value-added by comparing the amount of progress made between two periods of assessment of achievement.

In order for it to be possible for value-added measures to work, there must be a degree of standardisation of measuring instruments used. If value added is measured by the difference between achievement at t1 and achievement at t2, then it must be possible to subtract the achievement at t1 from that at t2 in order to arrive at a measure of added value. The instruments used at t1 and t2 must, then, be in some way broadly comparable in order for a meaningful form of subtraction to be carried out on the two measures. This is the *diachronic* aspect of the assessment of value added and is necessary if a value-added measure is to be obtained for a particular course at a particular institution. But in order to be really useful, value-added measures ought to be obtained across a range of different institutions or courses. For such a *synchronic* comparison of value added to be measured, it is necessary that the measures used in the different institutions to be compared are either the same or are broadly comparable.

The measures of achievement used to obtain the data on which a value-added judgement is based are of various kinds. Usually they will take one of two forms: first, the use of public examination or test results taken at different times; second, some form of tailor-made test designed or adapted for the specific purpose of carrying out a value-added measure. The first type of instrument is most suitable in a system where there is a uniform kind of testing at different stages of education which would allow for comparisons within schools of achievement at different stages. Such a system will become possible in the UK as the assessment associated with the national curriculum becomes fully established and consistent in its operation. It has been used, for example, by Fitzgibbon in her analysis of the value added by Sixth Form studies.[1] The second approach is commonly adopted by researchers looking at added value in contexts where the requisite testing instruments are not already in place as part of an assessment system. Studies which have adopted this approach include Mortimore *et al.* 1988 and Tizard *et al.* 1988.[2]

Fitzgibbon's study is an attempt to use an algorithmic approach to adding value that will take into account variations in prior pupil achievement and also the actual grades that they achieve in public examinations, as opposed to just the raw pass-rate. Fitzgibbon's approach involves using a pupil's GCSE grade in a particular subject as base data, using a predictor such as 'the expected attainment for a pupil at A level is one grade lower than the grade achieved at GCSE in that subject' and then constructing a prediction equation such as:

$$\text{A-level grade} = \text{GCSE grade minus one}[3]$$

This equation can be used to predict the performance of individual pupils in a particular subject and, by averaging, it can be used to predict the performance of pupil cohorts within a school and to make comparisons between cohorts at different schools. It is possible, using this technique, Fitzgibbon argues, then to assign positive and negative points to schools depending on how they deviate from their mean predicted grades. Every grade that is greater than the predicted grade scores one positive point, while every grade less than the predicted grade scores one negative point.

> The difference between the actual grade a student gets and the grade predicted for the student is called a residual. Positive residuals indicate better than predicted performance. Negative residuals represent worse than predicted performance. By averaging the residuals for a school we can see if, on average, a school's results are better or worse than would have been predicted on the basis of the prior achievement of its candidates. The averaging should be done subject by subject.[4]

Fitzgibbon argues that such measures can be made more meaningful by controlling for other factors that may affect educational achievement such as home background, ability or other measures of prior achievement. The statistical technique known as *multiple regression* is usually used to provide this sort of analysis.

The second kind of data that is used, especially in research into educational value added, is tests either used or developed specifically for the purpose of obtaining measures of prior and subsequent achievement. An example is the study of Mortimore *et al.* into London junior schools.[5] This used a variety of measures, including a standardised reading test and a creative writing exercise, in order to obtain measures of achievement. In addition, various measures were taken of non-cognitive development, using such instruments as the 'Child at

School' questionnaire schedule, which class teachers had to complete.[6] A similar approach was used in the study of Tizard *et al.* into progress in London infant schools.[7] It was then possible to compute progress in various areas, both cognitive (connected with the curriculum) and non-cognitive (connected with behaviour and attitudes) between different assessment points. As with the Fitzgibbon study mentioned above, residuals (the differences between initial and final achievement) were computed.

III   ADDED VALUE AND SCHOOL EFFECTIVENESS

By taking into account differences in sex, ethnic group and social class background, the effect of these factors on progress in the school can be isolated and quantified, so it is argued. The virtues of such studies into school effectiveness correlate well with their drawbacks. Value-added studies rely heavily on a quantified judgement of value added. This seems to be unavoidable if subjectivity is to be eliminated from judgements about the effectiveness of schools. On the other hand, it places great reliance both on numerical assessments of achievement and progress, and on various highly sophisticated statistical models and manipulations of data in order to arrive at meaningful judgements about school effectiveness in terms of value added. One might ask why relatively simple equations such as the one provided for illustrative purposes by Fitzgibbon are not sufficient for the study of value added. The answer is that they might be if all that one were interested in was a measure of the 'raw' value added by a particular school in a particular subject. But, it can be argued, such a measure is not a true indicator of school effectiveness.

The reason is that the equation could not take into account factors affecting progress which were not within the control either of the school or of the teachers within the school. For example, if it were the case that, with all other relevant factors taken into account, girls made more progress than boys, then one would expect the value added by girls' schools to be greater than that added by boys' schools. But this difference would not necessarily by a reflection on the greater effectiveness of girls' as opposed to boys' schools. It might even be the case that the boys' schools were more effective with less promising material than were the girls' schools with more promising material, even though the *progress* made by the girls was greater. Pure value-added measures cannot, then, be valid measures of school effectiveness. This is not just a theoretical point: different interest groups will want to know how *effective* a school is, not just how much value it is adding, if appropriate judgements are going to be made about the quality of education provided. This amounts to saying that the value that a school adds cannot be the whole story about a school's effectiveness: in order to arrive at a fair assessment of effectiveness it is necessary to take into account those factors affecting progress for which the school cannot be held responsible.

An understanding of this point is quite critical to any successful attempt to measure the effectiveness of schools and, even then, the attempt may not be completely successful. It is generally accepted that a number of different factors affect people's learning, including their ability, their sexual, ethnic or cultural grouping and their interest and motivation. Furthermore, these factors interact with each other in various ways, many of which are poorly understood. To make matters worse, theoretical constructions such as the notion of *intelligence* are sometimes used to conceptualise such everyday concepts as *ability* and to give them an aura of scientific respectability. In addition there are theories which purport to show how it is possible for children to learn certain things at one stage in their lives which it is not possible for them to learn at an earlier stage.[8] There are, therefore, potentially many factors that will affect someone's ability to learn which are not within the direct control of a school or a college.

If we adopt the principle that someone should only be accountable for those acts for which they are responsible or for those factors which it is within their power to influence, then we must be cautious in making judgements about educational institutions when it is not entirely clear what is and what is not within their influence and to what extent. This implies that any jdugement about whether a school or college is doing a good or a bad job needs to be based on a distinction between those aspects of adding value that the school *can* influence and those it *cannot*. It should be possible, for example, for a school to have control over pedagogy, but it is far less clear that it can control for the background of its pupils or, more crucially, the effects that the pupils' backgrounds may have on their learning and on the way in which they can be taught.

Once this point is conceded, however, then the statistical modelling required to derive measures of effectiveness which put the value-added measures into context is bound to become quite complex. It will no longer be possible to be satisfied with the residual between prior and current achievement. Some way of separating out those factors for which the school is responsible and those for which it is not and which nevertheless may have an effect on learning will have to be found. This has two consequences that will be discussed below. The first is that judgements of effectiveness will have to be based on mathematical or statistical inference which can only give limited and probabilistic interpretations of cause and effect. The second is that the interpretation of such inferences requires expertise in mathematical or statistical inference, thus severely limiting the number of people who can make informed judgements about school effectiveness and thus also restricting the usefulness of such measures.

Nevertheless, if such factors are not taken into account the whole enterprise of judging school effectiveness on the basis of value-added measures is compromised. The usual way in which this is done is through the use of the statistical technique known as *multiple regression* on the assumption that there is a linear relationship between those factors responsible for achievement and educational outcomes. The use of multiple regression equations allows analysis to take account of such factors as social class background, resources, and the ethnic and sex composition of the school as well as the value added during attendance at the school in order to produce a measure of the effectiveness of the school.[9] It should be noted that the use of multiple regression models has been criticised on the grounds that the residuals (the plotted differences between initial and final achievement) may be due to random effects rather than to the effective operation of the school. It is argued that this is particularly likely when aggregated (i.e. non-pupil) data are used, rather than data derived directly from pupil performance.[10]

Multiple regression models of the factors affecting school effectiveness have been used for example by Tizard *et al.* (1988) and these are based on data gathered from samples of individual pupils in different schools; the data are not available for direct comparison of the performance of different schools. We shall look at the problems associated with the use of statistical techniques to measure school effectiveness below, but before doing so it is worth making several points about the interpretation of multiple regression models. First, multiple regression allows the researcher to define some variables as *independent* and others as *dependent*. Independent variables are said to influence the dependent variables. They might include any factor about pupils, their background or the schools which might have a significant influence on their educational achievement. Examples could be sex, position in family, date of birth, social class background and initial achievement. The dependent variable would usually be the final assessment. Multiple regression should measure the relative influence of each of these factors on the final outcome and should be able to predict an outcome given certain factors. It can also indicate what the likely outcome will be if adjustments are made to one or more of these factors. Care has to be taken when interpreting regression equations: they do not, of themselves, describe causal or any other kind of influential relationships; they can only indicate that such relationships may be found. Further investigation would be needed to establish just what those relationships might be and how strong they are if they exist.

Secondly, the inferences that can be drawn from a technique such as multiple regression are *probabilistic*, that is they indicate that the balance of probability is that such-and-such factors influence the outcomes; but there is always a possibility that this is a purely random effect. Thirdly, the variant of multiple regression that is most commonly used, namely *multi-level modelling*, places more stringent requirements on the possibility of excluding random effects than does conventional multiple regression, thus making refutation of the hypothesis that differences between initial and final measurements are due to statistical error more difficult.[11] Fourthly, multiple regression analysis does not tell the researcher what *could have been* achieved given the antecedent variables, only what *has* been achieved. Since the aim is to measure school effectiveness, then an analysis that fails to describe the difference between achievement and achievement possibility is seriously flawed, or so it is argued.[12] These points also apply to *multi-level* analyses which also make the assumption of linearity in the data. Jesson and Mayston, who are among the more prominent critics of the use of regression analysis, draw attention to its lack of a theoretical explanatory basis (a point which has been made above), to its inability to distinguish between achievement and achievement possibility and the assumption that the relationships modelled are in fact linear. They instead recommend a technique known as *Data Envelopment Analysis* (DEA), which is supposed to be able to define efficiency as a ratio. Jesson and Mayston's procedures have themselves been criticised by Woodhouse and Goldstein because it can be shown that their equations describe a situation where efficiency declines in proportion to increases in input, which, they claim, is an unrealistic assumption.[13]

Enough has been said to indicate that the development and interpretation of school effectiveness and efficiency measures is a highly technical and contentious discipline, whose findings are not readily accessible in any reliable form to anyone who is not well versed in mathematics and thus most of the public and a majority of politicians and administrators are also excluded. The people who can interpret the equations and the findings that result from them are the research community and educationists who can understand the techniques used.

IV   WHAT CAN BE INFERRED FROM VALUE-ADDED MEASURES?

We have seen what are the complexities involved in constructing value-added measures and the need for caution in interpreting them. What, then, can they tell us about the effectiveness of schools?

First of all, there is the 'raw' information about the residuals (representing the added value) which might in itself be sufficient to send 'market signals' in the appropriate direction. Given, however, that measures of value added do not by themselves necessarily give a fair picture of the effectiveness of a school, there is the danger that these measures, like raw scores in tests and examinations, will present a misleading picture of a school's performance. There are conflicting duties here for a school authority in charge of a number of schools and responsible for providing meaningful information about school performance. If there is a duty to provide information, then decisions need to be made about how much information should be supplied and what interpretation should be given in order to understand it. Too little information (such as percentage exam scores) may be easy to understand but may also give a misleading picture of a school's performance in comparison with other schools. On the other hand, the results of a regression analysis of school effectiveness may be difficult to understand and interpretation by experts may itself even be open to dispute.

The theory of markets suggests that buyers and sellers need relevant information before they can make purchasing or selling decisions. This requirement works well enough in a street market for vegetables, for example, where a prospective purchaser can compare the quality and price of goods available at different stalls and come to a decision based on his budget. Matters are more complex when it comes to trading in the shares of companies, and stockbrokers employ analysts who monitor the performance of firms and make judgements about future performance; analysts can help purchasers of shares to make decisions about whether or not certain shares represent value for money. But share price is not determined purely by analytical judgements: external factors such as political events may have an impact on share price and it is arguable that there is a strong element of crowd psychology in many decisions to buy and sell, based not upon information about quality and price but upon the way in which other people are behaving in the market.

The use of information is, then, only one of the ways in which buyers and sellers make decisions in markets. Very often, only imperfect information is available, which makes its use even more problematic. Both these points are relevant to attempts to describe the choosing of schools by parents in market terms. We have already seen that the information available is often problematic and difficult to interpret. It is also possible that parents may not make full use of such information or may even ignore it in favour of other factors in making decisions about where to send their children.

The information may, however, be of more use to policy-makers when they are trying to fulfil their objectives. They may, for example, wish to optimise school effectiveness within a given set of resources or to explore the extent to which a budgetary cut may affect a range of effectiveness variables or how intervention in an antecedent variable may have an effect on school performance. Effectiveness measures may be one important tool for policy-making decisions at the level of school management, local authority or national education authority. Used in this way, they are not information which may inform market decisions but information which may be used in policy-making on questions of resource allocation, curriculum planning or even pedagogy. A major problem with their use as a policy tool is the fact that they are difficult to interpret and may result in flawed decision-making. At best, they should only be used in conjunction with other information.

Correlation of process variables with value-added measures can be made, for example, to see whether or not pedagogy and the curriculum have an effect. Once valid and reliable school effectiveness measures have been obtained, then it is possible to investigate those features of resources, staffing, curriculum and pedagogy that may be contributing to effectiveness or lack of it. This was one of the major research questions for Mortimore *et al.* Quantitative measures may be obtained for such associations as well, if that is required. By correlating effectiveness measures with certain features of a school, it may be possible to identify certain factors which are within a school's control, which, in turn, may contribute or fail to contribute to that school's effectiveness. For example, Mortimore *et al.* identified the length of service of the head, staff involvement in decision-making, the number of subjects being taught at any one time, the use of classroom-based questioning techniques and high expectations among teachers, as all contributing to the effectiveness of schools, irrespective of such contextual variables as social or ethnic background of pupils.[14] The building up of such correlations may contribute to an empirical base for judgements of what constitutes 'good practice', which is, as we shall see in Chapter 8, itself a problematic notion.

V   PROBLEMS WITH THE VALUE-ADDED IDEA

Although the idea of producing value-added and school effectiveness measures has obvious attractions, both for politicians and for policy-makers, the assumptions on which they rest and the technical difficulties that exist suggest a need for the greatest of caution in their interpretation. Very careful consideration should also be given to their practical effects. There is a great need for corroborative evidence of a non-value-added kind.

There are five main difficulties with value-added and effectiveness measures. The first concerns quantification. Difficulties begin when certain aspects of education and schooling are assessed on value-added scales. In order to derive a residual measure of added value, they have to be quantified in some way. These aspects include discipline, liking of subject, contentment with school and appearance of pupils. It is possible to quantify such aspects using, for example, attitudinal scales, but once one takes this path then a new departure has been made. Quantifying educational achievement in the cognitive areas is at best an inexact science but one which, provided certain reasonable safeguards concerning reliability and validity have been met, gives as good a picture of raw educational achievement as any other that has been devised. However, the importation of other techniques of psychological and sociological research is different.

In order to measure non-cognitive aspects of schooling, the assumption has to be made that they can be graded in some way and that they can be assigned numerical values. This approach suggests that human factors such as attitude are entities that can be numerically measured. The problem is even more daunting when one comes to try to assess learning in such areas as morality, aesthetics or religion, where any assumptions about what is learned are likely to involve contentious philosophical assumptions about the nature of morality, religion or aesthetics. This would perhaps not be a problem in a society in which there was a high degree of consensus about the nature of these aspects of life, but, notoriously, this is not the kind of society that is to be found in the modern West.

Whatever one's views of the truth of this assumption, it cannot be denied that it is contentious. The problem with accepting measures for non-cognitive aspects of educational value is that they are meant to be *definitive*, if they are to be of use in the assessment of performance and in policy-making. They cannot fulfil this role if they contain contestable assumptions. Contestable assumptions cannot be used to make substantive judgements and decisions about the distribution of resources and about people's careers, since this is an obvious violation of procedural justice. An analogy could be drawn with a court of law: faulty evidential procedures cannot be used as the basis for decisions of the court, even if all cases rely on such a faulty evidential basis.

The second difficulty with these measures concerns relying on social science. The problem extends beyond the non-cognitive aspects of educational value, because the importation of contentious social scientific assumptions is necessary for formulating school effectiveness measures as well. A great deal of reliance is placed on the efficacy of the social sciences when one adopts such methods and there is little reason to have such confidence in them, since not only are methods and results criticised from without the social sciences, but they are criticised from within them as well and, even within particular subjects, methods and results are the subject of vigorous debate.

An example is the use of linear regression in relating initial achievement and other factors to the final achievement of pupils or schools. The basic assumption of linear regression is that a relationship between two or more variables can be described which has the characteristics of a straight line function. Deviations from the straight line are attributed to random effects.

The randomness of variation might be a plausible assumption in the case of a true experiment. It is then possible to explain away the deviation and choose the regression line as the best way to interpret the data. But school effectiveness studies, whether or not they use data collected by administrators or by researchers, are not true experiments and it follows that deviations are not so easily explained away as random effects; in a non-experimental situation it is not possible to control for a whole range of factors that may be relevant to the results but which are not incorporated into the theoretical model being used to study school effectiveness.

> Extraneous systematic effects cannot be eliminated from studies of examination results because these studies are not experiments. Nor can they be incorporated into the models because the data are not available. The device adopted instead is to apply linear regression on the assumption that the model is correct and then interpret the residuals, not as reflections of random disturbances or inadequacies in the model, but as measures of effectiveness.[15]

Woodhouse is able to show that, if aggregated data are interpreted according to different models, some of which make assumptions that the best way to interpret the data is *non-linear*, meaning that the line showing the best fit to the data is a curve of some sort rather than a straight line, then very different results can be achieved for the same set of Local Education Authorities, resulting in very different rank orderings of them according to the model used to interpret the data.[16] These disputes between educational statisticians indicate that value-added measures have to be treated with a great deal of caution, particularly when the data are derived not directly from pupil achievement but from aggregated school and LEA records.

This does not mean that statistical analysis of pupil progress should be ignored, but it does suggest that such analysis should be treated with the greatest of care, and a minimal requirement for accepting its accuracy should be that a variety of plausible interpretative models, some of which should be non-linear, should produce consistent results in the rankings of schools, LEAs or other educational bodies. A further requirement is that the mathematical model used to analyse the data should be *multi-level*: it should include allowance for the effects of particular class and particular school as well as for LEA or locality. If this is not done, then the particular contribution that class teachers or schools are making to progress is not going to be taken account of. The main problem here is one that has already been alluded to, namely the dangers of importing contentious assumptions and methodologies from the social sciences when practical decisions have to be made. The use of multiple regression is only one example of such a contentious methodology: one could also criticise the use of scaling techniques for assessing attitudes, or the use of production functions. Because the social sciences are very far from being exact or even reliable disciplines, the dangers of using their assumptions and techniques cannot be ignored.

The third difficulty with value-added and effectiveness measures concerns the need to measure *sustained* performance. Value-added data are based on measures of progress between one assessment point and another. If the data are based ultimately on individual pupil performance (and it was argued above that they should be), then there is some likelihood that measures will vary from year to year, a value-added measure for one cohort of pupils being essentially a snapshot of achievement for a school. In order to build up an accurate picture, the aggregated data should reflect *sustained* performance which can be done through the use of a rolling three-year average. As this takes time to build up, the political value of such measures declines as they are not available for comparison within a time scale which would be considered feasible for an elected politician who has made commitments to the electorate about putting such measures in place. Once again, the danger is that such measures will only be of much use to professionals within the education business.

A fourth difficulty is the question of who adds the value. The original idea of a value-added measure was that the *degree* of pupil progress was the proper way of judging the performance of schools. The next step was to make allowances for the type of pupils that the school taught, pupils whose attributes may well affect educational achievement, but for whom the school is not responsible. The need to take account of such factors led to the development of regression models in order to explain the different effects of different pupil attributes on pupil progress and to isolate the effect of the school. The assumption here is that some of the added value may be contributed by factors outside the school, the most obvious one being the parents themselves.

One of the problems here is that, although this is a plausible assumption, the introduction of factors such as social class and ethnic background into the explanatory equations does not tell anyone much about the ways in which these factors might influence pupil achievement. A couple of possibilities will illustrate the nature of the problem. Assessment that relies heavily on coursework relies on work that may be produced to a considerable degree outside the school itself (it may be produced in conjunction with a child's parents). A substantial parental contribution to pupil achievement is going to yield a measure of progress for which the school cannot claim responsibility. However, an explanatory variable such as social class will not be refined enough to take account of such a possibility as it cannot make allowances for significant within-class differences. Another example might be the attendance of pupils at parent-run Saturday schools to compensate for perceived inadequacies of the school. It is obvious that the school cannot take any credit for progress made in this way, but this will not be taken account of in the model, because it is very difficult to do so.

The fifth and final problem centres on the fact that correlation does not mean causation. Even when we look at within-school factors that might influence effectiveness, the results of regression show only what factors are associated with effectiveness; they do not indicate how such effects actually work. Some studies suggest that attempts to intervene, by associating the factors that are supposed to contribute to success in schools that do not already have them or which have them to a limited degree, are not effective.[17]

How does one tell by whom and how the value is added? This requires research into the fine-grained aspects of a school's work. One can associate certain features with high value-added and impute a direction of causality between factors. The need for value-added measures arose from the perceived inadequacy both of raw scores of achievement taken at one point in time and of subjective judgements as to what constitutes good practice. But all effectiveness measures can do is to associate certain 'input' factors with output factors. They cannot tell why and how the input factors work. In order to establish why and how there is such a connection, a study needs to be made of the actual teaching, learning, assessment, planning and administration that go on in a school or college that is associated with a high value-added or effectiveness measure. The need to look at practice is, in the end, necessary but then we encounter the problem of good practice (discussed in the next chapter).

VI CONCLUSION

Value-added and effectiveness measures need to be treated with a great deal of caution and a strong contextual interpretation if they are to be of much use. Even then their use is likely to be confined to educational professionals rather than the lay public. It is common to hear the argument that 'crude' performance results are misleading and should not be divulged to the public, while the more 'meaningful' value-added measures should. Of course, giving both is quite possible. The view that tables arranged in rank order should not be given because they are misleading is quite mistaken. Performance tables show how schools perform against nationally set standards. Most parents, for example, will want to know how good the performances are at a particular school and not how much value it has added. There is a tendency to become obsessed with the rank-ordering of performance tables but it is the statistics that they reveal which are of real importance. Schools may be unhappy about being low in a rank-ordering: they have every reason to be more unhappy about a *low pass rate* and have every incentive to strive to push it up. This information is also of vital importance to parents, who are concerned, not just with the ranking of their child's school, but with what his or her chances are of success in public examinations. In any event, the information is of great value as it gives a national picture of the spread of performance and allows for like-for-like comparisons of various kinds. The publication of performance tables heightens awareness of performance and so, arguably, drives performances up as schools try to improve.

Value-added measures rely on performance figures for their construction, so the latter are in any case an indispensable part of the information. Given the uncertain state of value-added measure construction, there is no guarantee that such measures would inspire universal confidence, nor would they deserve to do so. If value-added measures are still dubious and if they are constructed out of performance data which are far less dubious, and which give valuable information, it would be treating the public with contempt to fob them off with value-added measures while refusing to give the performance data out of which these measures were constructed in the first place.[18] If, ultimately, value-added measures are too unreliable and too subject to statistical error to afford effective comparisons, then the data on performance against standards (the raw data) should be provided and the value-added data made available on request with appropriate *caveats* about interpretation.

There is an alternative way of looking at achievement in more detail by building up a set of examples that can serve as norms, both diachronically and synchronically. We saw in the previous chapter that there are difficulties in obtaining comparisons of standards, particularly long-term diachronic ones. The major difficulties relate, however, to obtaining the necessary examples. There is no reason in principle why like-for-like comparisons cannot be made about pieces of work produced at different points in time, for pupils from similar backgrounds. There would be a need for a bank of achievement data together with relevant contextual information. This could even include data about classroom practice, thus showing a link between achievement and teaching. This bank could consist of test and exam results as well as work obtained under normal classroom conditions. While the bank would not of itself show added value, it could demonstrate what standards of work were being achieved under comparable circumstances. Such a bank would not give a measure of school effectiveness but it would show what was achievable by pupils with different characteristics. Schools could then be assessed against such achievement norms. The advantage of such an approach is that it would be relatively accessible to the lay public as well as to professionals, and it would provide an external standards reference point for schools. A further advantage would be that it would enable standards to be compared over time and across space and would help to provide answers in the seemingly endless debates as to whether or not standards and performance are falling.

There is no reason why school effectiveness measures could not be used in conjunction with such a bank. For example, measures can be taken between two assessment points, a residual derived and the result compared against the achievement norm for pupils with comparable characteristics. The ability of modern information technology to hold vast amounts of data — visual, diagrammatic, graphic and mathematical — and the ease with which such data can now be accessed would make such a bank relatively accessible. Confidentiality could easily be maintained by describing the data in terms of school and pupil characteristics rather than through naming them. One would also need a testing body to gather updated data. This could be a body along the lines of the one advocated in the previous chapter.

NOTES

1. C. T. Fitzgibbon, Analysing examination results, in C. T. Fitzgibbon (ed.), *Performance Indicators*, 1990.
2. P. Mortimore, P. Sammons, L. Stoll, D. Lewis and R. Ecob, *op. cit.*; B. Tizard, P. Blatchford, J. Burke, C. Farquhar and I. Plewis, *Young Children at School in the Inner City*, 1988.
3. Fitzgibbon, *op. cit.*, p. 61.
4. Fitzgibbon, *op. cit.*, p. 62.
5. P. Mortimore *et al.*, *op. cit.*
6. Ibid., p. 102.
7. Tizard *et al.*, *op. cit.*
8. See M. Donaldson, *Children's Minds*, 1978, for a critical account.
9. An illustration of the equations used in such a regression analysis can be found in Tizard *et al.*, 1988, Appendix 3.
10. G. Woodhouse, The need for pupil-level data, in Fitzgibbon (ed.), *op. cit.*
11. Cf. H. Goldstein, *Multilevel Models in Educational and Social Research*, 1987, Chapter 2.
12. This argument was made by D. Mayston and D. Jesson, Developing models of educational accountability, *Oxford Review of Education*, 14.3, 1988, pp. 321–340.
13. G. Woodhouse and H. Goldstein, Educational performance indicators and LEA league tables, *Oxford Review of Education*, 14.3, 1988, pp. 301–320.
14. Mortimore *et al.*, *op. cit.*, Chapters 11 and 12.
15. G. Woodhouse, *op. cit.*
16. Ibid.
17. D. Reynolds, School effectiveness and school improvement: a review of the British literature, in B. Moon, J. Powney and J. Isaac (eds), *Judging Standards and Effectiveness in Education*, 1990, pp. 152–169.
18. On the importance of prior achievement measures in the construction of value-added measures see J. Gray and B. Wilcox (1995), *Good School, Bad School*, Chapter 6, pp. 125–126.

Chapter 8
Practising Valuable Education

I

In the last chapter it was argued that, in order for measures of added value or effectiveness to tell us anything useful about how certain results were achieved, they need to be supplemented with an account of classroom and school practice. But if practice is itself related to certain values which are embodied in the aims of education then judgements about practice are unavoidably value-laden.[1] To say that a certain teaching activity, form of classroom organisation or pedagogic approach is 'good practice' is, then, not just to make an assertion about whether or not it is effective in relation to the standards which one wishes to achieve, it is also to make an assertion about effectiveness in relation to certain moral values, some of which will be incorporated in the aims of education.

At this point a danger looms. Given that we cannot specify desirable or good educational practices in purely technical and value-free terms, how can good practice be specified without a collapse into moral subjectivism, since there is no guarantee that one person's view of what the values of education are will correspond to that of someone else? We have already seen that it makes no sense to talk of negotiating about one's moral values; does this mean that a teacher or lecturer must teach solely according to the way that his or her moral values sanction or prescribe? If this were the case then moral subjectivism would be the order of the day in pedagogic practice, since any coincidence of values between teachers would occur by chance. On the other hand, if the accountability of teachers to other interested groups within a democracy is to be taken seriously, then it would be dereliction of duty on the part of a teacher not to take into account the interests of governments, governors, colleagues, parents, children and others in formulating pedagogic practice. There is a possibility of tension between the values of individual teachers and the values of those to whom they are accountable.

We saw in Chapters 4 and 5 how educational aims and curricula could be constructed from a consensus that took into account different values and points of view by negotiation of the extent to which such different perspectives can be implemented. The same kind of response can be given to the question as to whether certain pedagogic practices are admissible or to be recommended. The point of view of the teacher is but one (albeit an important one) among others that have to be taken into account in the construction of a set of forms of pedagogic practice that are to be sanctioned. Within a publicly funded education system in a democratic society whatever counts as good practice ought to be what is capable of being sustained at the conclusion of reasoned debate and negotiation between legitimate points of view.

It is perhaps inevitable that practice should arouse more controversy and passion than more abstract matters such as aims and the curriculum. Practice is what teachers, lecturers, pupils and students have direct experience of; it is practice that structures the character of teaching and learning and it is in the context of practice that enjoyment and success or the lack of it are encountered. It is, then, in the context of practice that we may expect to see some of the most impassioned debate about the implementation of values; of all the aspects of education, classroom experience is something that everyone has vivid memories of and some commitment to what values should prevail there. It is not, therefore, surprising to find that the question of what is good practice in education is not just a technical debate about which means are to be deployed to agreed ends, it is about the values embodied in the means as well.

Much of this chapter concerns controversies that have been most marked in primary education. There are two reasons for this: first, this is an area of topical interest and, secondly, it brings out quite clearly the point that debates about practice are value-laden. But this does not mean that the arguments are of any less relevance to other sectors of education; indeed, even in higher and adult education the kinds of debates about values encountered in the primary sector concerning the autonomy of pupils and the authority of the teacher are replicated in relation to students and lecturers.[2]

II DEFINING GOOD PRACTICE

One recent critic of the notion of 'good primary practice' has been Robin Alexander.[3] Alexander has shown himself to be well aware of the need to avoid specifying good practice in purely value-free terms, but he has been criticised by Carr for falling back on a technicist description of good practice by calling for evidence that practice is indeed effective in achieving what it seeks to achieve, before we can call it 'good practice'. Alexander is particularly aware of the dangers of what he calls value-driven and political definitions of good practice. By value-driven he means the defining of good practice in terms of a teacher's own personal beliefs about what it is right to do in the classroom. By political definitions of good practice he means definitions offered by those in power or those who wield authority. Such definitions are inadequate, he argues, because they do not address the question of what actually works in the classroom and so are prescriptions without justification.

Is, then, the only alternative a value-free conception of good practice which begs the question of values in education? I will try to show how a concern with values and a concern for effectiveness can be reconciled. If a practice is said to be effective in relation to certain ends and those ends incorporate certain values, then it follows that practice is effective to the extent that it furthers the realisation of those values. There are two possibilities: one is that there is only one way of fulfilling such values, in which case it follows that there is only one form of good practice in relation to those ends.[4] The other possibility is that there is more than one possible way of fulfilling educational aims and that it is not absolutely certain which is the most effective way of fulfilling those aims in all circumstances. There is also the question whether the means adopted to achieve those ends are congruent with the negotiated values as to what constitutes an acceptable practice. In the first case there is no problem about identifying what is good, or indeed best, practice. In the second case it would appear to be at least partly an empirical and partly a political matter.

So there is no contradiction between holding that good practice ought to be effective practice and holding that effective practice can relate to ends that embody certain values. What of the danger that educational values are essentially subjective and that the practices that flow from those values are, to a degree, also subjective? One of the major difficulties concerning education systems in modern democratic societies is that there is a real danger that there will be a lack of consensus about the values and aims that an education system ought to embody and to strive for. The problem is, perhaps, a particularly acute one where there is an explicit process of political and ideological contestation in favour of some such concept as 'quality' or 'good practice'. Given the existence of different and competing sets of values abroad within a society and its education system, the danger of education becoming a battlefield between competing subjectivities about value seems to be a grave one. So how can an education system embody values and yet seek at the same time to reconcile the sometimes competing values of different groups?

The answer to this question is, in general terms, the same answer as that given to the question of who determines the aims of education and the curricula that flow from those aims. First, practice will, to a considerable extent, be circumscribed by the outcome of negotiation over aims and the curriculum. Secondly, it should be possible to negotiate over pedagogy and classroom practice as to what are the most effective ways of implementing agreed aims and curricula within agreed moral parameters and, in this context, it should be possible to make use of empirical evidence as to what seem to be the most effective pedagogic and organisational methods. In principle, then, both Carr and Alexander are right. Carr is right in thinking that attention must be paid to fundamental values before practice can be determined. Alexander is right in thinking that what good practice is can be arrived at by examining the evidence for the employment of certain types of practice. What both leave out of their accounts is the fact that negotiation about the *implementation* of values has to precede determination of good practice.

Alexander's characterisation of the confusion and ambiguity surrounding the concept of good practice has much merit. The notion of good practice does embody values, but the values that inform the practice are the outcome of the negotiation about *whose* values are to be implemented and the extent to which they are going to be implemented. When such a consensus has been arrived at, it is possible to come to some kind of agreement on what is going to count as good practice in the technical sense, that is, what are the appropriate *means* to the negotiated *ends* — what is effective in educational terms.

It is now possible to look at Alexander's critique of the concept of good practice and to see how helpful it is. Enough has been said already to indicate that it needs to take account of the criticisms advanced by Carr but, given this discussion, it may be possible to strengthen Alexander's distinctions and to clarify the relationship between them. He distinguishes between four important senses of the phrase 'good practice' and argues that one of them should have priority; this is a position that I will, in broad terms, defend. Alexander categorises 'good practice' statements into four broad groupings: pragmatic (this is what works for me), value statements (this is what I value and believe in), political (what practices do others in power most approve of?) and empirical (what practices can be shown to be most effective in promoting learning?). Alexander leaves out, however, the notion of good practice as what is democratically and rationally defensible as a means of ensuring that agreed aims are effectively achieved. We have already offered a defence of the empirical notion of good practice by arguing that it can properly apply to the ways that are thought to be most effective in bringing about the implementation of values negotiated at a political level. This leaves a very important role for the value-related notion of good practice, but as a starting point for *negotiation* about what should actually occur in classrooms rather than as a starting point for *classroom practice*. Problems can arise when this essential political element is left out and the implementation of a value-laden sense of good practice is thought to be quite unproblematic.

Alexander has a somewhat limited idea of good practice in the political sense. Someone (administrator, politician, inspector, head) may well have power over the work, career and promotion prospects of individual teachers. He or she will probably have his or her own value-laden concept of good practice as well. It is in seeking to impose this personal value-laden concept, *irrespective* of the political negotiation of the implementation of values conducted beforehand, that this sense of political good practice comes into play. In the light of the foregoing discussion it is obvious that attempts to impose good practice in this sense are quite illegitimate except under certain special circumstances which we will discuss below.

The construal of 'good practice' as 'this is what works for me' is, on the face of it and in the light of the foregoing discussion, not one that could be supported, suggesting as it does that the teacher is the determinant of what should go on in the classroom. In the sense that other interested parties have a legitimate interest in what happens in schools and classrooms and thus that a teacher should not have the sole say, this is perfectly true. However, what works for an individual teacher is important and need not be just an expression of a self-interested desire to lead an easy life. In the sense that successful teaching involves the building of an affective bond between teacher and class, then the character, talents and interests of individual teachers are important in establishing that kind of individual relationship.[5] There is room for such individuality to be expressed within an agreed context of what can reasonably be established to be effective teaching methods and classroom organisation ('good practice' in the empirical sense), yet there is little or no such room allowed by those who press the idea of good practice in the value or authoritarian political sense. Alexander's account of good practice does, then, need to be supplemented by a reference to the ethico-political dimension which emerges *after* value-laden notions of good practice have been put into negotiation

Just as it is difficult to be against quality, so it is difficult to be against good practice. To be indifferent or even hostile to what is considered to be good practice would seem to be a major dereliction of duty on the part of teachers or even, worse still, a sign of moral turpitude. Therefore to commend a particular educational practice as 'good' is to achieve a rhetorical advantage which it is difficult for a sceptic to overcome. This is particularly the case when the sense of good practice appealed to is not the empirical one (where it is assumed that, in some sense, a prior negotiation about value implementation has been successfully concluded), but the value-laden one. To be sceptical about good practice is, then, in this sense, to be sceptical about the values of the person commending a particular practice as good and the issue then becomes one of moral disagreement. Not surprisingly, when the person commending good practice is also an authoritative figure such as an inspector or headteacher, serious disagreement is not a practical possibility for most teachers.

This is an extremely unhealthy situation and leads to manipulation and dishonesty on the part both of teachers and of those who seek to control them. It is, therefore, important to ask how such a situation might arise and how it might be remedied. The situation described suggests a pathological condition within the education system so described. It can arise through the failure of a political system to subject its public education service to democratic scrutiny and to arrive at a negotiated consensus on the range of values that are to be represented within the system and the extent of their implementation. In effect it means that, by default, powerful figures within the education service itself become the dominant political figures. In the United Kingdom the domination has come from a particular source, namely the progressivist tradition stemming from the work of Rousseau and, to a lesser extent, of Dewey.[6] By degrees, through the controlling influence of progressivist inspectors, administrators and teacher trainers, that influence slowly became the dominant one within the education system. Thus a particular value system, anti-authoritarian and liberationist in ethical and political tendency, came to be dominant within the education system itself rather than outside it, where it was not very well understood and certainly not very influential.

It was only when education became the subject of considerable public and political interest from the mid 1970s onwards that a debate about practice became possible and only in the 1990s that it became at all prominent.

III PRACTICE CANNOT BE IGNORED

The conclusion of the previous chapter was that effectiveness depended upon practice, and we have seen that practice embodies ethical and political considerations. It is now time to look at one of the more puzzling features of the long contest between progressivism and traditionalism, namely why there should be a conflict and why it should be carried out with the passion and intensity with which it very often is. Any political consensus about the ethical values which are to be nurtured in a modern democratic society would have to embrace at least three important facets of human life: how society is to be governed; the appropriate balance between individualist and collectivist values; and the proper relationship between religious belief and secular values.

In the case of the first, most people would state the need for adherence to democratic values as the principal political value which it should be one of the main duties of education to establish a love and respect for. However, democracy means different things to different people and, notoriously, both Rousseau and Dewey held controversial views on the nature of democracy.[7] But this diversity of views provides enough scope for the kind of negotiation that I have argued is necessary to achieve a satisfactory consensus. Much the same points go for the balance between individualist and collectivist outlooks and value-orientations. If anything, the distinction between these two is even more of a matter of *degree* rather than *kind* than is any debate about the nature and operation of democracy. The case of religion is somewhat different and here the compromise will largely have to be on questions as to whether or not some parties will have to agree to tolerate views with which they are in near total disagreement in certain important respects. This is one reason why education that has a specific religious affiliation is often to be found *outside* the State education system, as is the case in France and the United States. Even in the United Kingdom, where some kind of accommodation has been found within the state system for different forms of religious education, this accommodation has been largely made by providing different types of schools within the state sytem.

Given that these questions are, to a large extent, about aims rather than being in any obvious sense about *practice*, why should they impinge upon practice? If, for example, it is possible for the different interest groups to reach a consensus on the implementation of values concerned with democracy, the balance between individualism and collectivism and the balance between religious and secular values, why should it not be the case that a workable consensus cannot also be found concerning the type of practice within the classroom that could accommodate that consensus? Given that teachers are by and large democrats, and believe in a balance between individualist and collectivist and between secular and religious values, why was a relatively autonomous education system able to generate within it a view of 'good practice' that seemed to be so out of sympathy with the views of those parties who were not teachers or educationists?[8]

The answer to the first question lies in the way in which education was left, for many years, outside the normal political processes of democratic negotiation. The answer to the second seems to lie in the nature of progressivist ideology and in some of the assumptions that it shares with other ideologies and systems of belief. By and large, progressivists believe that if the values that are to be developed in children are not, in some sense, *pre-figured* in the practice of the classroom, then they will not be accepted or even recognised in the adult. Progressivists do not take the view that one can get a child to submit to authority, subject him to a programme of training and instruction and expect him to emerge as an autonomous being. Indeed, if Rousseau is to be believed, the child will emerge as a seriously damaged human being, exhibiting all the undesirable traits of someone whose *amour propre* is out of balance.[9] Dewey too takes the view that educational experience must be of such a nature that the child can see the purposes of the things that he or she is doing; otherwise, he holds, their value as learning experiences is lost.[10]

It follows from this kind of position that one cannot so arrange practice that it can aim at producing adherence to a certain kind of ethical, religious and political outlook, without at the same time incorporating that outlook into the work of the classroom. One cannot expect adults to be autonomous, to possess intellectual curiosity and to work harmoniously with others, if one does not allow them to do so in the classroom. Then, if most early education takes the form of submission to authority, programmes of training in routines and instruction in facts, this will not be possible and the aims of education will not be fulfilled. Progressive classroom practice becomes, therefore, a prerequisite of reaching the educational aims that are most widely agreed on.

How could one, for example, come to adhere to certain moral values without experiencing them in a practical way in childhood? It would seem to be absurd to say that a child could learn about reading and counting and little else and then come to understand what is at stake in the sphere of moral action and understanding. Or again, how could one come to make responsible choices as an adult without the experience of doing so during childhood? While both these points seem to be undeniably true, they are oversimplifications. Such devices are fine in rhetorical combat, but they rarely help to clarify the questions that are under discussion. The point at issue between progressivists and others is not whether or not there should be any form of prefiguration in classroom practice, but *how much* and *at what stage*?[11] A general agreement about the need for some form of prefigurative practice does not preclude the need for vigorous discussion of the detail of how, when and where. In particular, there would need to be a discussion about the balance between instruction, training and discovery that is necessary in each area of the curriculum and at each phase of education.

It is surprising in some respects that progressivists do not see this. It is one of the central tenets of progressivism from the time of Rousseau onwards that children's intellectual, moral and emotional development takes place in stages and that different forms of teaching and learning are appropriate at different stages. This doctrine of developmentalism should make such educators sympathetic to the idea that not all classroom practice can be prefigurative of practice in the adult world. Morality and religion too, it would seem, need to be introduced at an early stage if they are to be effective in engaging a child's sympathy and understanding, rather than being left to the autonomous choice of the adult or late adolescent. When one incorporates into this view the Rousseauian doctrine that the age of reason does not begin until around the chronological age of twelve, then we seem to have a case for using non-rational forms of teaching about religion and morality for youngsters in schools. In practice, as is well known, most progressivists prefer to introduce children to forms of moral and religious practice and leave them to make autonomous choices about religion and morality at a later stage, rather than to get them to *participate* in those practices.

The reason for this apparent contradiction and its resolution in the form of advocating radical forms of prefigurative practice outside the areas of morality and religion (but not outside art or aesthetics) is that the fundamental value of progressivism is a dislike of authority, particularly the exercise of authority on the part of adults towards children.[12] A close examination of *Emile* should make this unsurprising, since the whole of the Rousseauian educational enterprise represents an attempt to educate children in accordance with nature and away from the corruption of society, with its inequality and its imposition of one will upon another.[13] Progressivists might well reply that it is *authoritarianism* rather than authority as such that they are opposed to, but since authoritarianism is the *excessive* use of authority this leaves open the question of what level of authority *is* excessive. The answer that comes from Rousseau is that all forms not based on some kind of social contract are.

The fundamental feature of progressivism, then, that above all determines its notions of good practice, lies not in developmentalist doctrines, but rather in its radical rejection of authority, which in turn derives from the Rousseauian doctrine of innate goodness and the virtues of the natural.[14] Developmentalism is not deployed to justify special forms of teaching and instruction for young children, but as a way of freeing children from the pressures associated with learning, by stressing their individualism and self-motivation. This is particularly the case in the Piagetian tradition, which has had a long association with progressivism in British primary schools. Progressivists, it could be argued, have been quite eclectic in their search for reasons why one should have low expectations for children, ranging from the enthusiastic embracing of the theories of restricted and elaborated codes of Basil Bernstein in the 1960s and 1970s, to the more covert acceptance of IQ theory. In the 1970s and 1980s, psycholinguistics was appealed to as another source for denying that authoritarian methods should be imposed on children learning to read and write.[15]

Progressivism, then, insofar as it is thought through by its adherents as a coherent doctrine, is part of a radical political project to change and perhaps dismantle the power structures that prevail in most societies, based as they are on inequalities of power. As such, when it is practised within a polity not committed to such ends, there are bound to be tensions between a body of teachers and educationists committed, even if only partially, to such doctrines, and most of the rest of the society. It is partly for this reason that the dispute over progressivism has been so sharp politically; the other reason is the concern over standards (see Chapter 4).

The doctrines of progressivism regarding classroom practice cannot be supported by evidence that it produces work of a high standard, because the value-orientation of progressivist thinkers is towards an ideal of individual development rather than to standards of academic attainment in the sense understood by most lay people. It might be said in their defence that they are profoundly concerned to develop the creative abilities of children, but closer inspection of this claim suggests that the concern is not so much with standards as with self-expression and, perhaps, originality. Creativity is re-interpreted as self-expression rather than as the achievement of competence in a genre or of high standards within a discipline.[16] Given their views about the imposition of authority on children, it becomes extremely difficult for them to see that the ideal can be realised at the *end* of the process, rather than directly from the beginning. Progressivist educators and educationists, especially those of a radical stamp, will only come to accept the debate about good practice on the terms suggested by Alexander if they can be brought into a consensus with the other interest groups about the aims of education, and this would involve a negotiated compromise on the implementation of values.

IV TRADITIONALISM AND PROGRESSIVISM: NOT NECESSARILY A FIGHT BETWEEN LEFT AND RIGHT

So far, I have looked at the political and ethical dimension of the good practice debate and have tried to situate the question of research within that debate. However, the dispute about progressivism versus various forms of traditionalism is not merely a dispute about values: it is also a dispute over philosophical assumptions about human nature and the nature of learning. If progressivist doctrine can be shown to rest on mistaken philosophical assumptions of an epistemological nature, then there would be an independent reason for doubting the practices that flow from it. This would not necessarily convince progressivists, but it would serve to show that the dispute about classroom practice is not just one about politics but one that needs to be handled in a way that goes beyond the political.

Progressivism, as we have seen, is based upon a rejection of authority. However, authority is implied by any rule-governed system. A system of rules governing action implies that there are right and wrong ways of acting and that there are certain people who have a right to point out what are the right and wrong ways of acting; these people are parents and relatives in the early years of life and, later on, teachers and other adults. If human society is rule-governed, then authority has a necessary place in any human society and learning how to act in society involves learning to follow rules and hence involves a submission to authority to a certain extent, in order for someone to be able to act autonomously. This is not an empirical observation, but one that follows from reflection on the nature of human social life. If human life is rule-governed, then successful education must involve getting children to follow rules; and if they follow rules they do, in a sense, submit to authority. So, no matter how they are taught to act, if they learn to take part successfully in normal human activity then they submit to authority. The question of good primary practice thus becomes one of asking what kind of teaching and learning methods are most appropriate to achieving such a result, given a certain consensus about democracy and individualism.

Once this is admitted, questions about the efficacy of discovery methods versus training and instruction can be asked, together with questions about the degree of discipline necessary to maintain order in classrooms. The question as to whether didactic methods are necessary or not is then not a straightforward political matter. It becomes a series of questions about the characteristics of humans that allow teachers to take advantage of certain types of teaching methods, about how methods may change as a child matures and about the evidence available concerning the most effective methods at different phases of education. There is no consensus about these questions which has a necessary association with either the political right or left. Someone of an extreme neo-liberal persuasion might find the individualistic and anti-authoritarian doctrines of progressivism very much to his or her taste, while a socialist might be attracted by the collectivist nature of more traditional forms of teaching and learning. Indeed, like the Italian Marxist Gramsci, a socialist may see the early years of schooling as concerned with the inculcation of habits which will allow for autonomy in adulthood.

In education one is dealing with children in whom one has to inculcate certain habits of diligence, precision, poise (even physical poise), ability to concentrate on specific subjects, which cannot be acquired without the mechanical repetition of disciplined and methodical acts. Would a scholar at the age of forty be able to sit for sixteen hours on end at his work-table if he had not, as a child compulsorily, through mechanical coercion, acquired the appropriate psycho-physical habits?[17]

The point that Gramsci is making is that academic education requires training in certain habits and disciplines. But the point could equally well be made about vocational education. There is an important sense in which progressivism is as subversive of the basis on which this can be conducted as it is for academic and traditional liberal forms of education. Superficially this would not appear to be the case, for the idea of 'learning by doing' is one of the central tenets of progressivism and also one of the central requirements of vocational education and training.[18] In particular, a student needs to experience the tools and materials that he is working with, to explore their capacities and properties and to get a feel for what is possible and what is not possible with them. Surely this can only be achieved through *exploration*.

There is a strand in progressivism, particularly associated with Dewey, which takes this idea very seriously indeed. Dewey was opposed to practical and aesthetic education that did not allow children to use and experiment with materials and to experience at first hand what they could and could not be used to do. But for Deweyan technological education, just as for other aspects of progressivism, the prefigurative fallacy applies just as well. This fallacy consists in moving from the truth that competence requires successful performance to the false proposition that it can only be achieved by attempting performance in the first and subsequent instances.

To conclude, debates about good practice cannot become debates about empirical matters until they have been resolved at the level of compromises about the implementation of values. A teaching profession and corps of educationists cannot move too far away from the dominant outlook in civil society without provoking a reaction that will reduce its autonomy. Progressivism as a radical doctrine has shown signs of doing this and of provoking a reaction in the spheres of politics, culture and civil society which to a large extent transcends the conventional debates between right and left. Furthermore, there are reasons for thinking that progressivism may rest on deep philosophical errors that may undermine its claim to be a serious political alternative to more established ways of thinking about human learning.

There is still room for much reflection and debate on what constitutes the most effective ways of teaching and learning for different subjects and for different ages. But although such questions become empirical ones at some stage, they cannot become such until questions about *what* should be taught and *what* are ethically and politically acceptable ways of teaching it have been settled. But it needs to be recognised that negotiation about the nature of an education system needs to incorporate, not just aims and the curriculum, but also the kind of educational practices that are most appropriate in the classroom.

Many different voices need to be heard here, not just those of teachers and educators. The fact that they were not heard for so many years in the United Kingdom suggests a low level of political interest in education which has not been helped by the disengagement from publicly funded education of so many in the political élite, particularly in the governing party which has, even now, left it with both an effective disengagement from state education and a lack of appreciation of the detail of educational negotiation and reform. One long-term remedy for the state of affairs described in this chapter is precisely an engagement on the part of the political élite with the state education system through sending their own children to state schools. However, such a remedy is unlikely to be effected in the foreseeable future.

NOTES

1. David Carr, Wise men and clever tricks, *Cambridge Journal of Education*, 24.1, 1994, pp. 89–106. See also R. Alexander, Wise men and clever tricks: a response, *Cambridge Journal of Education*, 24.1, 1994, pp. 107–112.
2. See, for example, R. L. Boot and V. E. Hodgson, Beyond distance teaching — towards open learning, in V. E. Hodgson, S. J. Mann and R. Snell (eds), *Open Learning: Meaning and Experience*, 1987.
3. R. Alexander, 1992, *op. cit.*, especially Chapter 11.
4. I am assuming that the curriculum serves those aims and values as well (see Chapters 4 and 5).
5. Alexander acknowledges the importance of the affective element in learning in his *Primary Teaching*, 1984, Chapter 2, pp. 44–45.
6. There are not many good accounts of this process but see J. Darling, *Child-Centred Education and its Critics*, 1994, for a sympathetic account of some aspects of this process and R. Alexander, *Innocence and Experience*, 1994, for a rather less sympathetic account. Alexander in particular draws attention to the intransigent nature of the progressive campaign. Alexander, 1992, *op. cit.* also draws attention to the gradual nature of the progressive advance and the resistance and compromises of many individual teachers along the way.
7. Cf. Rousseau, *The Social Contract*; Dewey, *op. cit.*, 1916; Flew in Peters, *op. cit.*, 1977.
8. It needs to be borne in mind that such views were originally held by an élite within the profession and slowly moved into classrooms where even now they still encounter much resistance. However, progressivism succeeded in many respects: in influencing classroom organisation, selection and mixed ability teaching, in aspects of the curriculum and in the aims that teachers have themselves articulated, they have made their influence felt greatly. See, for example, R. J. W. Selleck, *English Primary Education and the Progressives, 1914–1939*, 1972.
9. See *Emile* for an account of the appropriate kind of upbringing that will avoid such psychological damage to the child. See N. Dent, *Rousseau*, 1988, for an account of Rousseau's moral psychology and its relationship with upbringing.
10. Cf. Dewey, *op. cit.*, Chapter 15.
11. This is not to imply that progressives are the only kinds of educators who fail to appreciate nuances in the discussion of pedagogical issues, but to take account of the fact that *in this particular situation* they have been relatively unwilling to compromise.
12. It has been remarked by more than one commentator that this anti-authoritarianism does not extend in practice to adult-adult relations, particularly for example, inspector-teacher or tutor-trainee teacher relationships (see Alexander 1992 and 1994, *op. cit.*).
13. Rousseau does not appear to distinguish between different forms of power, regarding them as all undesirable, although there are many contradictions to this in the pedagogical detail of *Emile* as well as in the larger political theory. See Joseph de Maistre, who remarked on this trait in the thinking of the Enlightenment; see his *On Sovereignty*.
14. See Rousseau, *op. cit.*, in particular.
15. The link between psycholinguistics and Rousseau is made explicitly by Jessica Reid, Reading and spoken language: the nature of the links, in R. Beard (ed.), *Teaching Literacy, Balancing Perspectives*, 1993, pp. 22–34.

16. See R. Barrow and R. Woods, *Introduction to the Philosophy of Education*, 1975, Chapter 8 for a discussion of the nature of creativity; I. Reid (ed.), *The Place of Genre in Learning: Current Debates*, 1987, for further discussions in the area of English teaching relating to this issue.

17. A. Gramsci, *Selections from the Prison Notebooks* (eds Quintin Hoare and Geoffrey Nowell Smith), 1971, p. 37. I have no large-scale evidence for the view that the progressive-traditional debate does not neatly follow left-right political lines, but careful study of the sayings of left-wing politicians and of the different teaching unions suggests a far more varied range of opinion on the political left than stereotypes would suggest. See, for example, Paul Boateng M. P. at a meeting of the Commission on Citizenship in April 1989, reported in *The Independent*, 15 April 1989, p. 6, entitled 'Black Children "betrayed by education fads"'.

18. Cf. H. Entwistle, *Child Centred Education*, 1970.

Chapter 9
Satisfying the Customer: Education in the Marketplace

I ACCOUNTABILITY AND THE MARKET

In this chapter the idea that education could or should be provided by a form of market mechanism will be considered. We have already seen that the commercial paradigm that has been introduced into education, largely through the influence of the neo-liberals, has been responsible for much of the current concern with quality in education. The economist's concept of a market has an important role to play in neo-liberal thinking about the provision of public goods such as education and health. One of the functions of markets is to provide buyers with information about the relationship between the quality and the price of goods. The question arises, therefore, whether some form of market mechanism could provide information about quality to the various interested parties involved in education.

Before we investigate this, it is necessary to establish that it is indeed a relevant question. There are two important points to note. First, different forms of education may each have different aims. Second, whoever provides the resources for education is entitled to some say in how they are allocated and used. It follows from these two points that *whatever* the aims of education are, if resources are provided to allow education to take place then the resource providers are entitled to have an account rendered to them as to how those resources have been employed (resources are understood here not as a gift but a payment for services to be rendered). Thus even if the aims of education are set in a way that does not refer to any non-educational normative structure, this point still holds. In this case resource providers will wish to know to what extent and how well such aims of education have been fulfilled.

It might be replied to this that only *schooling* rather than *education* can legitimately be the object of such a requirement for accountability, but even given the validity of the distinction between education and schooling this point would seem to be very difficult to sustain. The point about accountability is a moral one. If the resources provided for education are not donated either as a gift or as a form of exaction or penalty, then custom and practice suggest that accountability is a right. It is in the interests of the donor to know how the resources have been used, and custom and practice in democratic societies has been that the providers have made use of their right of review even if it is taken in nothing more than periodic elections. The slogan of the American War of Independence, 'No taxation without representation', is an expression of this principle. Although derivable from social contract theory, it need not be: interest, together with custom and practice, establish a *prima facie* right in common parlance. Since the resources provided by, for example, the State allow for education as well as schooling to take place, then the education provided falls under the accountability requirement, whether it be an instrumental or a non-instrumental form of education. It may be possible to distance the state from educational provision and still maintain the accountability requirement by disaggregating expenditure and giving it directly back to the taxpayer as a form of hypothecated grant: voucher systems operate on this principle. Accountability is preserved by making the schools responsible for their performance to the grant- or voucher-holder.

Given that accountability is a moral requirement, what is the best way to ensure that mass forms of education are accountable? There are two broad answers to this question: (1) the state provides and is accountable ultimately through the electoral process; and (2) private individuals and groups provide and accountability is secured through the operation of supply and demand in some form of market for education. There is also a third possibility that a limited form of market mechanism can be introduced into the system of state-funded education in order to provide market disciplines while an element of planning is retained. Broadly speaking, the neo-liberal proponents of quality in education favour some form of the third, hybrid, approach but in order to consider it properly we need to examine how economists view the operation of the market and then see if education can be truly said to be a marketable good.

II   THE MARKET IN ECONOMIC THEORY

The simplest version of a market is the village market, where farm produce is exchanged. When goods, sellers and buyers are brought into physical proximity it is possible for buyers to compare prices of like goods or to make trade-offs between price and quality in their purchases. The crucial point is that the relevant information for purchasing decisions is available to buyers: in a *perfect* market all the relevant information is available to them, while in an *imperfect* market it is not. There are two further points of importance for the successful operation of a simple market model: the customer must bring the relevant knowledge to the marketplace that will enable him to make rational purchasing judgements and there must be an infrastructure of space, organisation, safety and transport. Although in economic theory perfect markets exist when the relevant information is available in the marketplace, it is still possible for the market not to function in the instrumentally rational way described by economists without the relevant customer background knowledge.[1]

For example, a buyer in a horse market might be able to inspect the horses on their condition and compare them on condition and price with other horses for sale, but if he is not able to make proper judgements about the condition of horses because of ignorance about factors affecting their health, for example, he can neither ensure that he pays the cheapest price for the commodity nor that he can make a meaningful trade-off between type of commodity and price.[2] We would normally assume, therefore, that customers in markets would have the relevant knowledge, but that assumption cannot be made in every case and in those cases where it does not apply a theoretically perfect market might still allow for purchasing behaviour that was sub-optimally rational. Although the primary and simplest sense of the term 'market' is undoubtedly the kind of example given above, markets do not have to be a spatial unity: provided the abstract requirements are met that all the potential buyers and sellers can be made promptly aware of the prices at which transactions take place, that each buyer and seller can compare the offers made by other buyers and sellers and that any buyer can make an offer to any seller, then one has a perfect market.

In some cases, the lack of customer and vendor knowledge is remedied by middlemen. For example, a representative of a motoring organisation might accompany a customer to a car showroom in order to make an inspection of vehicles considered for purchase. Another example is the use by dealers on the stock market of specialists called *analysts*, whose job it is to research the likely future performance of companies and of their equities in order to help the dealers to fix prices. Given the difficulties that we have already noted concerning standards, effectiveness and practice, the requirement that educational customers have the relevant knowledge available to them to make purchasing decisions is likely to be hard to fulfil in practice.

There is, however, a further complication in the case of education. In most markets a range of different commodities will be offered for sale. There is also a tendency for markets to specialise: if too many commodities are on offer in the same market, then not enough choice of each commodity will be available to the customer and other sellers may be crowded out. At the limit, if enough of the goods available in the market are actually separate commodities, then there is no market as there is little or no meaningful choice: each supplier is in effect a monopolist or near-monopolist. In relation to education this is not merely an abstract consideration. Consider the factors relevant to possible purchase of an educational good. The *locality* of a school may be a key purchasing factor, both for physical availability and for social reasons. In addition, the aims, standards and practices, not to mention the teachers, may all be relevant factors. This means that, as commodities, schools may differ even when they are of the same type, since as far as the customer is concerned they fall into different purchasing categories. For example, two secondary schools alike in all respects except that one is twenty miles further away from a parent's home than another, are, to all intents and purposes, distinct commodities, since the cost and inconvenience of twice-daily travelling make the distant school an undesirable purchase from the point of view of a parent living in a particular locality.

Cultural, ethnic and class factors are frequently important. Parents often wish to send their children to schools which have a particular social make-up with which they identify, or to which they aspire on behalf of their children. Such wishes often take priority over whatever data may be available on the performance, practice and standards that prevail at a school.

As a result of the lack of customer knowledge of potentially relevant purchasing factors and the proliferation of educational commodities, the operation of an educational marketplace is likely to differ from the perfect markets described by economists. This is not to say that market forces cannot operate in the provision and purchase of education: it is to say that educational marketplaces are likely to be *sui generis* and that their operations are difficult to describe in strictly economic terms. In certain circumstances the proliferation of commodities may be restricted, for example in the private boarding school sector where distance from parental home becomes a less important factor in purchasing decisions. Likewise, if the real object of the purchase is to gain *prestige* and social standing associated with attendance at a particular school, then the relevant knowledge of which institutions are most prestigious may be readily available to the customer and so some form of market may exist. In this case, the quality of the education becomes of secondary importance and it is questionable whether the purchase is of education *per se* or of education together with attendance at a particular institution.

There are two other important features of education which make it resistant to conventional economic descriptions in terms of the marketplace. First of all, popular schools are not rationed by price: even within the independent sector, the pricing of education is relatively inelastic in relation to demand. The reason for this is that the quality of pupils is as important as the price that parents are prepared to pay for their education. If the quality is allowed to decline then, even if the price charged for education is very high, the standards of education achieved at the school will decline as well, making the school a less desirable commodity and reducing market value. Secondly, schools cannot simply expand to meet demand without compromising those features which led to the demand in the first place.[3] All these factors—the lack of accurate information on school effectiveness, the non-commodity nature of education, the way in which culture and class influence educational choice, and price and supply inelasticity—mean that, even without state intervention of any kind, a private market in education would not be likely to behave like a conventional market in economic theory. Attempts to treat education as just another market commodity may lead to a grave misunderstanding of its nature as a private, public and positional good. This point is discussed further below.

In the case of popular or sought-after educational institutions, it is the *supplier* rather than the buyer who is in a position to regulate access to the product and it is common for this to occur through an assessment of the ability and suitability of the candidate rather than his or her ability to pay a demand-led price for the service. There are two, possibly three, good reasons why this is the case. The first is that most educational institutions have an ethical mission which is part of their educational mission, even if they are independent of the state: they wish to take pupils who can benefit from the education they provide, as well as those who are able and willing to pay a fee. Secondly, there is a measure of self-interest in this. An educational institution's reputation is based partly, at least, on the perceived ability and commitment of its students or pupils. It is therefore in the interests of schools, colleges and universities to obtain the best possible candidates at the time of admission in order to help maintain the institution's reputation. Finally, schools, colleges and universities are very often anxious to show that they do not prefer candidates from a particular class, sex, cultural or ethnic grouping, thus making them less vulnerable to charges of élitism and discrimination. This too makes them less anxious always to accept the highest bidder in price terms.

III   CUSTOMERS OF EDUCATION

In the vegetable market there are buyers and sellers. It is clear who are the customers. In education a different situation operates. This is not just because of the split between purchaser and user (e.g. parent and child), but because it is not obvious that the clients of education (pupils and students) are *consumers* in the sense that the purchaser of a hamburger or a massage is. Education is something much more complex than a product or service of the kind that is usually considered in economic theory. The client is often in a poor position to make a judgement of the quality of what he is receiving as it is only loosely, if at all, related to his immediate satisfaction. The most uncomfortable experiences may be the most valuable for him from an educational point of view, but he may not realise this until some time later. In addition, the paying client is very often not the user of the service and so has a potential problem in obtaining the information necessary to deciding whether the service is being properly provided.

The second reason is that there are *various* interest groups which can legitimately be concerned with the nature of educational provision. The third is that some of these interest groups make a direct financial contribution to the maintenance of the education system. In an independent system, fully financed by parents, one may safely say that the parents are the primary clients and, because of their parental rights, they exercise purchasing power on behalf of their children, subject to a general regulatory framework. But even here, for reasons given above, they are not customers in the usual sense of that term.

In a state-financed system of education the situation is different. Resource providers will include citizens who are not parents, together with corporate entities such as businesses. On the accountability criterion mentioned earlier, they too could be considered to be purchasers of educational services. Even though they do not provide resources for education at the time of use, children are the prime users of educational services in the schools and they are also future citizens and taxpayers. They too are clients of education in more than one sense, as users and as future parents. Parental taxpayers are the most obvious example of a potential educational customer and they are the principal choosers of educational services for their children. But they are not the users of the service and may have little knowledge of the worthwhileness of what is being provided.

Finally, in the classical economic marketplace the customer has the exit option: he can refuse to continue to buy the product or service on offer if he no longer likes it or the price it is offered at. Alternatively, he has the voice option. He can complain or he can negotiate about the price: if he is still dissatisfied he can exit. But because education is not a true market, voice is only backed up by the exit option to a limited degree, giving the educational 'customer' a much smaller degree of autonomy than the economic customer. In most countries exit is not possible from the service itself. If society undertakes to protect the interests of children, even a privatised education system cannot allow that an element of compulsion on irresponsible parents should completely disappear.

These considerations show that the notion of an educational customer is not a straightforward one but, in state-provided education, is highly problematic.[4]

IV STATE OR MARKET PROVISION: NEO-LIBERAL AND CONSERVATIVE ARGUMENTS

Within a state system there is a loose accountability link between resource provision and service. Because it is a link with intermediaries (who may also have their own, self-serving interests) and because of the relative difficulty of establishing the worthwhileness of what is happening in schools, particularly when intermediaries might make this difficult, there are those, particularly on the neo-liberal and neo-conservative right, who think that the state should to a large extent withdraw from the provision of education.[5]

The dominant reason why various thinkers on the right adopt this position is that they think the state is a malign influence on educational provision. They believe that this is so for one or more reasons. Following Mill, some think that State control of education is inimical to personal and political liberty.[6] Secondly, it has a tendency to introduce a vocational bias into education at the expense of maintaining a common cultural heritage.[7] Thirdly, it entrenches producer power, allowing what are seen as the prejudices of ideologically motivated teachers and officials to dominate the educational agenda.[8] Fourthly and finally, it generates wasteful and expensive bureaucracies that fail to provide a cost-effective service.[9]

Three families of solutions have been proposed. The first involves opening up the marketplace of education by making schools open to access from all pupils. Secondly, it has been proposed that educational vouchers should be issued to all children and students, to be cashed at any institution of choice that will accept the voucher. Finally, the privatisation of the education system has been proposed.

The first solution is one that has been put into effect in the United Kingdom in the 1980s and 1990s. It was coupled with other changes to promote accountability and to provide information on which market decisions could be made. These included devolution of financial and managerial power to school and college level, the increased representation of parents on the governing bodies of schools (and of employers on the governing bodies of colleges) and the introduction of a mandatory system of inspection for schools and colleges, with the results publicly available. The problem with this system from the neo-liberal point of view is that it does not address the shortcomings of the putative educational marketplace that have already been discussed, namely its non-commodity nature and the inelasticity of supply.

The introduction of a voucher system would permit greater diversity than at present exists. In particular, it would allow for the development of schools that reflect the cultural and religious diversity of Britain (and of other countries that share such a diversity) the lack of which is currently unjust to those sections of the population who pay their taxes and do not see their ethical and religious beliefs, as well as other cultural practices, reflected in their education and that of their children, even though *some* groups *do* enjoy such benefits.

Despite this advantage, according to Gray the *disadvantages* of vouchers are twofold. First of all, they do not take the provision of education away from the state, thus leaving the problem much as it was before, and secondly they make the independent sector reliant on funding from the voucher scheme, thus *increasing* the dependence on the state of that sector. The introduction in the United Kingdom of a national curriculum, the teaching of which is required by institutions in receipt of government funding, would accentuate the risks inherent in dependence on government. In addition to these problems, seen from a conservative point of view, there are the further problems, already noted, of the non-market nature of educational supply and demand. Gray's preferred solution, following the radical thinker Ivan Illich, is to detach educational provision from the state altogether.[10]

The result would be a lower tax rate which would release disposable income for the purchase of education. For the less well-off, educational credits that could be used at different times in the life of an individual could be provided. They could be used at any accredited educational or training centre (not necessarily a school) and their take-up would be ensured by the compulsory testing of children at various ages to ensure minimum standards of literacy and numeracy in the first instance and other areas of knowledge, skill and understanding at a later stage. Such a system would ensure maximal choice, and would free education from the vocationalist bias of the national curriculum and the dead hand of the educational bureaucracies and in particular from their tyrannical pressure to introduce outmoded forms of progressivism into the schools. In addition, like voucher schemes, cultural diversity could be allowed to flourish. There are two further features of Gray's proposals which should be noted. The first is that educational credits supply a minimum of resources for education: there is no ceiling on potential expenditure by individuals or families. Secondly, the able and educationally ambitious poor are permitted to compete for additional credits to allow them to attend schools and colleges for the academically gifted.

V A CRITIQUE OF THE MARKET SOLUTION: THE PRISONER'S DILEMMA AND EDUCATIONAL PROVISION

Market solutions to the problem of educational provision, such as the one advocated by Gray, have been widely criticised by the political left on the grounds that rational self-interested behaviour in the marketplace leads to sub-optimal results for all under certain conditions. It is sometimes argued that the State should confine itself to activity that resolves such situations. Defence is a good example. It is not in the interest of any one person to provide resources for the defence of the realm if no-one else is prepared to do so. On the other hand, it is not in the interests of anyone to fail to provide such resources, since internal disorder and external assault are likely to be the outcome. The individual providing for himself could not avoid such an outcome on his own and would lose the resources he put into a futile attempt at defence as well. On the other hand, it is most unlikely that, in these circumstances, anyone could hope to be a 'free rider', expecting everyone else to provide the resources for effective defence. The solution to such a situation is to levy taxes on all to provide defence for all. For any individual calculating on the basis of rational self-interest this solution is worse than the free rider outcome, but better than the other two possibilities of internal and external disorder and internal and external disorder with personal cost of defence.

This kind of problem is known as the Prisoner's Dilemma. The solution to it which avoids the free rider solution (the optimal for any given individual) and the 'sucker's payoff' (the worst option), is to levy taxation on all in order to provide defence for all. In game theory such situations are known as *co-ordination problems* and, according to Lewis, characteristic recurrent solutions can be regarded as conventions.[11] The easiest way to illustrate the Prisoner's

Dilemma is through the two-player version, although in fact $n+2$ player games are perfectly possible and indeed are required if the Prisoner's Dilemma is ever to be applicable to a wide range of political situations.

Two prisoners, Tom and Bill, are held pending their trial for bank robbery. The only way that they can be convicted is by one of them confessing and implicating the other. A confession would reduce the sentence of the confessor. The sentence tariff they are likely to encounter in court is as follows: no conviction, 0 years; conviction without confession, 10 years; conviction with confession, 3 years. The options facing both can be represented on a grid as follows:

Table 1

		Tom's choices	
		confess	don't confess
Bill's choices	confess	3,3	3,10
	don't confess	10,3	0,0

Each number in the grid represents years of sentence each would receive.

In these circumstances, confessing would ensure a short prison sentence for either, and not confessing would lead to either a ten-year sentence or freedom. The dilemma for the prisoners is that non-confession could give both their freedom while it could also yield the maximum sentence for one of them. If we accept the years of a prison sentence as a unit of negative utility, and define rationality in this situation as *loss minimisation* then it is rational for both Tom and Bill to adopt a strategy that *minimises* their negative utilities. The 'confess' strategy yields a value of 6 years, the 'don't confess' strategy yields a value of 10. The 'confess' strategy is therefore best for both and is consequently the dominant strategy.

Coleman writes:

> The Prisoner's dilemma provides the most vivid illustration of the way in which rational self-interested behaviour may lead to stable inefficiencies. In the prisoner's dilemma, inefficiency results from an inability among the parties to reach agreement to co-operate.[12]

On the face of it, such problems are comparatively rare and can be used to justify certain minimal forms of state intervention, such as the provision of defence. As such, an account and justification of the state in terms of its ability to resolve these types of situation ought to appeal to conservatives and neo-liberals.[13] At the same time it becomes important to advocates of the small state to show that these sorts of situation are relatively rare, or else the prisoner's dilemma could be brought in as a justification for all kinds of state intervention. Theorists such as Gray need to show that the question of eductional provision is not a prisoner's dilemma situation. Coleman's point, however, is that such situations arise through the operation of the market, and the question quite naturally occurs whether a market in education could be modelled along the lines of the prisoner's dilemma.

One important point needs to be made about the Prisoner's Dilemma as it applies to n-player situations where n is a large number. For one individual among, say, a million, to adopt the non-dominant strategy when everyone else is adopting the dominant one could lead to large individual gains. So if everyone else is limiting his or her wage increases in order to restrain inflation, in return for a moderate increase in real wages, it becomes rational for one person not to do so as his wage increase will be greater but will not raise the rate of inflation. He, therefore, will be a *free rider*, benefiting from the restraint of everyone else. However, since everyone else will also reason in the same way, it will be rational for everyone to become a free rider. The result would be that all would suffer from inflation and a low real wage increase, whereas all could have benefited from low inflation and a moderate wage increase if all had decided to co-operate.[14] This situation suggests that for the best solution to be arrived at, some form of external constraint such as an incomes policy with an element of compulsion needs to be put in place in order to make the solution happen. Prisoner's dilemmas thus point to solutions where state or collective action becomes necessary in order to achieve the most desirable result for all. This means intervention in the market.

For example, Tooley has attempted to show that the provision of education cannot be modelled as a prisoner's dilemma and that, therefore, it is possible to leave the provision of education to market forces. The argument is made by using a number of different scenarios and showing that they do not conform to the requirements for the prisoner's dilemma.[15] Tooley's first scenario supposes that, in a two-player game, there are two schools, A and B, and that A is the better school. Child 1 is more able than Child 2 and the parents of each wish their child to go to school A, which is nearly full and has a place left for only one pupil. The benefits from attending A for each child will be say, 10 units of utility and the benefits from attending B will be 3. The situation now looks like this.

Table Two

		Child 2	
		Send to A	Send to B
Child 1	Send to A	10,3	10,3
	Send to B	3,10	3,3

Child 2 is no more disadvantaged if Child 1 goes to school A than if he does not: there is no sucker's payoff, where a worst outcome arises as a result of the decision of someone else. Child 1 has nothing to lose by choosing school A. So this kind of situation, which is supposed to model the allocation of scarce educational goods, is not a genuine prisoner's dilemma.[16]

The next situation posed by Tooley is supposed to model the *positional* nature of educational goods, that is, the fact that the possession of education by someone affects the well-being of someone else. Once again, Child 1 is more able than Child 2. Both children have the choice of working hard or of not working hard. Will Child 2 be disadvantaged by working hard if Child 1 works hard? Tooley thinks not. For Child 2, the outcome is the same if Child 1 works as if he had not worked but no worse than if he had not worked. It is still in his interests to work in the hope that Child 1 is lazy.

Table Three

		Child 2	
		High Effort	Low Effort
Child 1	High Effort	10,3	10,3
	Low Effort	3,10	3,3

Tooley then goes on to examine the public benefits of education, such as economic growth and law and order, to individuals. Suppose the cost of education for a group of people (say anything from 1 to 30) is £1000 to cover the salary of a teacher, equipment and facilities. Let us also suppose that the public benefit of one educated person is £700. Then the education of one person would lead to a cost of £300. However, if two were educated the public benefit would be £400 ((£700 + £700)–£1000). The situation would look like this:

Table Four

		Child 2	
		Educate	Don't Educate
Child 1	Educate	400,400	− 300,700
	Don't Educate	700, − 300	0,0

This situation is a prisoner's dilemma as there is a 'sucker's payoff' for the educating parent if the other parent is a non-educator. In effect the non-educator is enjoying the benefits brought about by the educator and incurring none of the costs. Addition of the utilities along each line of choice suggests that **don't educate** is the dominant strategy, yielding 700, while **educate** yields 100 irrespective of which player is considered. The most likely result is, then, that neither educates, with zero utility for both. Tooley, however, dismisses this model as a true reflection of the situation as parents will not simply calculate costs and benefits in this way, but will act out of a sense of moral obligation to their offspring. There are two points to be made about this. If markets are supposed to work on the basis of self-interested instrumental rationality and the prisoner's dilemma is a model of the situation in education then one would say that it models self-interested individuals. Otherwise one is saying it is not possible to model the provision of education on a cost-benefit basis in this way. For the model to work, it presupposes pure acquisitive individualism on the part of parents. In effect, one is modelling a 'worse case scenario', but it might be replied that this is just what policy-makers ought to do in order to see how it can be avoided.

Tooley points out that these previous models ignore the private benefits that may accrue from education. Let us suppose that these amount to £400, so that the total benefits from education come to £800. Then the matrix of possibilities is:

Table Five

		Child 2	
		Educate	Don't Educate
Child 1	Educate	800,800	100,700
	Don't Educate	700,100	0,0

Tooley argues that the best stratagem for each party is to educate, since even educating while the other party does not educate is going to yield benefits, while non-education is likely to yield no benefit.

None of these models really captures the complexity of the issue of educational provision. The parent–child relationship and the payer–consumer split have already been mentioned. But there is a further important point which relates to the *positionality* of educational goods. Tooley appeared to account for this in the second of his models but, in reality, this model does a poor job of that. To see this, let us first take the *personal* value of education. This might plausibly be represented as non-positional in the sense that one person's spiritual enrichment does not affect the spiritual quality of another. Personal enrichment is a valuable and sought-after end of education, but once we move to the more instrumental ends of education and, particularly, the necessity of education in order to gain employment, then the positional character of educational goods becomes self-evident and its nature is such that it cannot be accommodated to Tooley's model.

The market for jobs is a competitive one, even in conditions of full employment, because competition will still exist for the better paid and more congenial jobs. If education and training are prerequisites for jobs, then failure to educate will remove an important competitive advantage for a starter in the labour market. Education for all will intensify the competition for jobs but there will still be relative gains for those who have been educated more successfully than others. Those who have not been educated at all in a society where the great majority have received some sort of education will be at a real disadvantage in getting *any* kind of employment. A more suitable model for this situation would be if the net gain for Child 1 being educated when Child 2 is also educated were £200 while it becomes £300 when Child 2 is not educated (through increased competitive edge in the labour market). Child 2 loses out when he is not educated and Child 1 is educated, by not being able to gain any employment at all—he actually loses income as a result of the choice made for him. Let us put this loss at £300, since a lifetime's unemployment will lead to a great loss of potential earnings, far greater than the gain in earnings of belonging to an educated as opposed to an uneducated workforce. So the situation could be modelled as follows:

Table Six

		Child 2	
		Educate	Don't Educate
Child 1	Educate	200,200	300, − 300
	Don't Educate	− 300,300	0,0

Unlike the other situations, there is no genuine 'free-rider' option for the educatee as failure to educate when the others do does not lead to any real gain at their expense. The question is, 'Is this a realistic model?' There is every reason to think that, in a situation where nearly all forms of employment require numeracy, literacy and the various habits of organisation and self-discipline demanded by a modern technological economy, a failure to educate some of the population will lead to their becoming a class of unemployables.

Even in a society where compulsory schooling exists, many children fail to achieve any educational qualifications. This occurs largely because those children and, in many cases, their parents, lack the foresight and application to ensure that education is completed successfully. They are thus unable to see their own personal situations in the ways outlined by policy makers and so the significance of modelling their situation on the basis of the prisoner's dilemma is lost on them.

So far, the personal instrumental goods of education have been discussed in terms of a game-theoretic model. But it is also the non-personal and public goods such as economic growth, internal and external security and improved overall standards of living that are likely to flow from education, that need to be considered. Seen from this point of view, failure to educate leads to losses for everyone if the failure is widespread. It is true that where there are a few 'free riders' they will be able to enjoy the public goods that arise from the education of most of the population. Whenever there are a significant number of these free riders, however, the output of public goods will be compromised. The situation would then look like this in relation to public goods:

Table Seven

		Educate	Child 2 Don't Educate
Child 1	Educate	200,200	50,50
	Don't Educate	50,50	0,0[18]

The dominant strategy for both players should be **educate**. But for someone who really does not wish to be educated unless he is compelled to be, there is a reasonable chance that non-education will lead to some payoff, which might be an acceptable risk for him. The person who wishes to be educated, on the other hand, risks the loss of considerable public goods if the other does not wish to be educated. There is thus a potential conflict of interest in such a situation.

An advocate of market provision of education might want to reply that these models are simply not realistic models of the options available in an open market for education because parents would work out the situation and ensure that their children received an education. In addition, the state could ensure that parents whose children failed tests were fined. This would ensure that all children received an education at least at a minimal level.[19] The desirability of providing a market for education had a great deal to do with removing the dead hand of the state from educational provision and replacing it with the hidden hand of the market. A purely market-led approach would also undermine the monopoly of schools, since education could be bought at any accredited training or learning centre and the purchasing power of the poor could be topped up through a system of educational credits which could be used with any accredited agency. But the market would have to be regulated, to ensure both against irresponsible parents and against 'cowboy' education and training agencies providing low quality educational services. It is arguable that this happens already in the state-run system, with the emergence of an uneducated, unemployable underclass. It is far from clear, however, that the proposals of Gray and Illich are realistic. They need to show both that the current system is unreformable and that their solution would lead to a more effective and more equitable result. There are grounds for thinking that neither is the case.

Under Gray's proposals, the education element in taxation would largely disappear, to be replaced by a low-tax regime. This, he claims, would set the conditions for an educational market and remove the inequity for parents who choose their children to be educated independently having to pay twice for the privilege: once through taxation and once through fees. In return for the reduction in tax, parents would incur an obligation to ensure that their children met certain educational standards. There would also be a scholarship system for the able children of poor parents. One does not have to be a radical egalitarian to see how unfair these proposals are. Their naivety is also quite extraordinary.

Irresponsible parents do not suffer any direct losses from failure to educate their children. It is true that they will be punished if their children fail to pass tests, but a feckless parent may well wish to postpone the day of reckoning by using the increased income available for personal consumption. The fact that the parent is then punished is no consolation whatsoever to a child who has lost his education. Gray's proposals also release further resources for well-off parents to buy their children more education relative to the rest of the population than they would already have. Not only would this allow them to buy more education for their children, but they would also be able to buy more of those quasi-educational goods such as accent, manner and good connections that are very often associated with certain types of school and which provide an entrée into the best positions in society. Neither would there be any guarantee that a child would receive an education that best suited his talents. It would be up to the parent to provide resources at least to a bare minimum level of education, but beyond that he or she might not wish to spend any more money, or might wish to spend it on forms of education which do not suit the child best. Since parents do not have the close knowledge of the child at work that most teachers have, the possibilities of error could well be increased.

VI THE ALTERNATIVE TO THE MARKET: IS STATE EDUCATION REFORMABLE?

The advocates of market provision in education think that the state system of education, and indeed the school system generally, is unreformable, in the grip of producer special interests, too vocationally oriented and, potentially, a threat to liberty and democracy. These criticisms are not all consistent with each other: for instance the producer groups within education are nearly all hostile to vocationalism despite the Deweyan origin of many of their ideas and practices.

Advocates of market-based educational provision are quite right to reject the prisoner's dilemma model for the provision of *non-instrumental* personal education. The prisoner's dilemma does, though, supply a plausible model for the provision of personal *instrumental* education, but not for the provision of *public goods oriented* instrumental education. The model for the provision of this last aim of education should, however, give them little comfort, as it shows that rational self-interested behaviour on the part of some can lead to the loss of provision of public goods desired by all (see Table 7), which again suggests that public provision will benefit all.

Splitting up education in this way according to different aims is an artificial exercise. As was argued in Chapter 4, different aims exist alongside each other within an educational system and most systems are a kind of compromise between different aims. However, detaching them for the purposes of analysis can be useful, provided that one does not come away with an oversimplified idea of how education works, or how people think about it. The analysis provides little comfort for market theorists. Something like a market might work for non-instrumental personal education, but for the two kinds of instrumental education that we looked at there is a case for thinking that it would be dysfunctional. The kind of scheme advocated by Gray also has the disadvantage that the worst case is not adequately provided against, with the further disadvantage that it would have to rely on a quite extensive regulatory system in order to function without major failure and abuse. In the jargon favoured by neo-liberal thinkers, the control of quality within such a system would be largely left to market disciplines, together with the law and a certain amount of bureaucratic regulation and inspection. Given the potential for dysfunction, the need for regulation becomes correspondingly greater.

State control of education is one very natural solution to these problems. By ensuring that everyone receives an education, all three major aims of education can be achieved, to the mutual benefit of all and without the major costs associated with failure to educate. Nevertheless, some of the shortcomings of state provision of education identified by the New Right and by other conservative thinkers such as Gray should not necessarily be ignored. The claim that it is vocationally biased will sound odd to many who have long thought, and still do think, that a liberal rather than a vocational model dominates the system, particularly in Britain and the United States. Gray is here expressing his own personal predilections for liberal, non-instrumental forms of education, rather than voicing a real concern shared among many of the interest groups. We have seen that if personal fulfilment is the primary aim of education, then it need not be provided by the State as the social costs of not educating are not obvious. In this sense Gray could be right to claim that the private sector will do the job. But the discussion in Chapter 4 demonstrated that education serves a variety of aims at the same time and these include, and have to include, personal and social instrumental aims as well as personal non-instrumental aims. It is only in a situation where personal non-instrumental aims are being met in a totally unsatisfactory way within the state system that the question should arise of *supplementing* that system in some way.

Gray's other two objections seem to cancel each other out. On the one hand he argues that there is the danger of an excessive state control of education, while on the other hand he thinks that there is the danger that producer groups, particularly local education authorities and pressure groups of teachers, will influence pedagogy to accord with their own ideological prejudices. Excessive state control would mould pedagogy according to the ideas of politicians. Excessive producer power moulds pedagogy according to the desires of educators. It is only when those demands are in harmony that Gray's objection holds water. The history of recent politics in Britain suggests that the contrary is the case and that it is the producer point of view that holds sway. Gray's analysis is vitiated by a tendency of New Right thinking to fail to distinguish between the *public sector* of the economy on the one hand and the *government* on the other. The two are distinct groupings: although the public sector carries out one of the major functions of government, it is not to be identified with it.

The danger of party political bias over the curriculum is greatly exaggerated as the National Curriculum in Great Britain is subject to scrutiny and consultation from a variety of sources which severely limit the degree to which a party agenda could be imposed on the system. Most of the opposition to changes in the curriculum has not been party political but has come from teachers and others in education who have tried to resist challenges to their own positions. It is the influence of this last group on the curriculum, but especially on pedagogy, that is, perhaps, the most difficult and intractable one to change, as it is deeply rooted in a culture that has been allowed to flourish in conditions of near-autonomy for decades. But the problem need not be insoluble. The setting of norms of reasonable standards of performance, based both on historical and on comparative perspectives, can be effected reasonably easily. Whether or not performance meets acceptable standards can then be monitored using assessments and surveys of the kind carried out by the Assessment of Performance Unit. An alternative approach, which may be used in conjuction with the above, is the institution of regular inspections carried out in accordance with a nationally prescribed framework. The advantages and disadvantages of such a system will be considered more closely in Chapter 11; suffice it to say at this point that there is a problem about who is to staff the inspectorate without employing those whose influence the government is seeking to diminish.

Finally, the education of teachers needs to be addressed by any government seeking to change the culture and ideology of the teaching profession. The present British government seeks to do this by removing teacher education from higher education and locating it in schools, in the belief that the ideological influences that it seeks to combat will thereby be neutralised. Such an approach probably underestimates the degree to which those influences already permeate the schools themselves and ignores the practical difficulties of training large numbers of teachers within schools There are, in all likelihood, no quick solutions to a problem that has arisen because the consensual system of negotiation over educational policy making was allowed to break down over a period of decades, but the existence of a national curriculum, a concern over standards of performance, a degree of inspection and the reformation of teacher education to make sure that it matches the expectations generated by the other reforms, is the best way forward.

Teacher education needs to be reformed, not by emptying it of theory but by anchoring it firmly in the requirements of the national curriculum and by promoting a critical reflection on those parts of teachers' work that are inescapably political: aims, curriculum and practice. This suggests that the Philosophy of Education, so far from being marginalised in the professional formation of teachers, needs to play a prominent role in their education precisely so that they will not take ideological stances on trust but will be equipped to examine proposals on their merits. It is a kind of anti-intellectualism, reinforced by an ideology averse to rational persuasion, that has contributed to the problems that now beset the teaching profession. The results of such a process of reform will certainly not be instantaneous but they are the best that can be hoped for without inflicting severe and lasting disruption on education.

NOTES

1. J. Benham, *Economics*, 5th edition, London, Pitman, 1960, p. 167: 'A market is said to be *perfect* when all the potential sellers and buyers are promptly aware of the prices at which transactions take place and of all the offers made by other sellers and buyers and when any buyer can purchase from any seller, and conversely.'
2. Benham, *ibid.*, 'In short, each variety is, strictly speaking, a separate commodity for which there is a distinct demand and often a distinct supply.'
3. D. Hirsch, Lesson one: Hobson's choice, *The Independent*, 12 May 1994. See also the same author's *School: A Matter of Choice*, 1994.
4. For a further discussion, see J. White, Education and the limits of the market, in D. Bridges and T. McLaughlin (eds), *Education and the Market Place*, 1994, pp. 117–125.
5. The claim that producer interests are always self-serving needs to be treated with a strong degree of caution. The discovery of self-serving behaviour in some instances does not mean that it is necessarily a pervasive and inevitable trait of workers and institutions in the public sector. See Stretton and Orchard, *op. cit.*
6. J. S. Mill, *On Liberty*; see also Gray, *op. cit.*, p. 28.
7. Gray, *op. cit.*, p. 27.
8. Ibid, Chapters 1 and 4.
9. For an examination of this claim, see Stretton and Orchard, *op. cit.*
10. Gray, *op. cit.*, pp. 28–31, 162–166.
11. Cf. D. Lewis, *Convention*, 1969.
12. J. L. Coleman, *Markets, Morals and the Law*, 1988, p. 253.
13. Cf. Jonathan, 1990, pp. 116–132; N. Barry, *Introduction to Modern Political Theory*, 1981, Chapter 3, Section 3.
14. See Hollis, *The Philosophy of Social Science*, Chapter 6 for a fuller account of the relevance of game theory to social situations.
15. J. Tooley, The Prisoner's dilemma and educational provision, *British Journal of Educational Studies*, XL. 2, May 1992, pp. 118–133. This article is itself a reply to an earlier one on the same topic: Jonathan, *op. cit.*
16. Tooley, *op. cit.*, p. 122.
17. Ibid., p. 123.
18. The two-player situation is an artificial model as public goods would only be threatened if more than one player in a multi-player game decided not to be educated. The situation becomes more realistic if, instead of thinking of it as modelling individuals, we think instead of *groups* of individuals.
19. This is the solution proposed by Gray to the problem of parents failing to provide for their children, *op. cit.*, p. 165.

Chapter 10
Equality, Quality and Diversity

I PROCEDURAL JUSTICE AND EDUCATION

In Chapter 5 an argument was made for the view that a diversity of ability and talent is the natural human condition and that any society open to change and development should seek to take advantage of diversity and cater for it in the curriculum. In this chapter it will be argued that a concern for diversity implies a rejection of radical forms of egalitarianism. It does not, however, imply the kind of inegalitarianism proposed by writers such as Cooper, Jensen and the early Bernstein.[1]

II PROCEDURAL AND SOCIAL JUSTICE

If a group of individuals are alike in a relevant respect, then they should be treated as alike in that respect. For example, if two individuals have each been accused of a crime, then they should both be accorded the same investigative and legal procedures to determine innocence or guilt. An essential attribute of justice is that individuals alike in the relevant respect should have the same criteria of judgement applied to them. Notice that this does not mean that they should necessarily be given exactly the same *treatment*. We often say, for example, not just that a punishment should fit the crime but that it should be just to the individual, taking into account his circumstances and history. In many cases this will entail that the sentences given to different individuals for the same type of crime will differ. The principle under which they are sentenced, and to which all are subject, is that the punishment should fit the crime *taking into account the history and circumstances of the particular individual*. To take another example, if the principle operating in education is that all students should sit an examination in order to gain a qualification then it is a requirement of procedural justice that they all sit it under the same conditions of difficulty. In practice this will mean that most will sit the examination under the same conditions, but others, who are not well or who are disabled, for example, will sit it under different conditions in order to ensure that the degree of difficulty is not greater for them than for anyone else.

The examples above illustrate the distinction between what are sometimes called *procedural justice* and *social justice*.[2] Procedural justice is concerned with the fair treatment of individuals within a given reference group. Social justice, on the other hand, is concerned with *which* reference groups there should be. Procedural justice is a requirement in any society where resources and outcomes are allocated in a consistent and predictable way. Arguably, any society needs a measure of procedural justice if it is to conduct its affairs in a way that is capable of making sense to its members. Consistency in the application of rules is a fundamental feature of social life: where there is no consistency in the application of rules then there is no conception of the difference between the correct and the incorrect application of rules and hence no notion of rule-governedness either.

Some critics have objected to the notion of social justice as a radical egalitarian notion.[3] Although it has certainly been used by radicals to campaign for a change in the relevant reference groups for the allocation of goods and outcomes, it is, for analytical purposes, indifferent between radical, conservative, liberal and reactionary conceptions of what these reference groups should be. A reactionary, for example, might wish to reinstate differential pay for men and women doing the same job, on the grounds that a re-establishment of a firm sexual division of labour is in the best interests of maintaining the family unit and hence in the best interests of society as a whole. A radical, on the other hand, may wish to abolish pay differentials of any sort within a particular occupation, on the grounds that the same work demands equal pay, relying on a principle of equality of treatment as a desirable ethical principle.

While it is obvious that any society needs *some* concept of procedural justice, is it obvious that it needs a concept of social justice? This is a pressing issue for education, for if there are different reference groups in respect of educational provision, then the possibility arises that different kinds of education will be worthwhile for different kinds of people. In that case, it will not be possible to judge the worthwhileness of education according to one standard: a multiplicity of standards will be needed. It is my aim in this chapter to argue that there are very good grounds for thinking that this is exactly what is required and that it is a corollary of this that some forms of educational provision will be different for some groups as opposed to others. This view will be defended against critics from both egalitarian and inegalitarian points of view and will show that the distinction between egalitarianism and inegalitarianism in education is at the same time more complicated than is sometimes thought and is also, in many respects, irrelevant to the main points at issue. In developing this view it will be necessary to draw on the conclusions about the curriculum argued for in Chapter 5, but those conclusions will be extended to other aspects of educational provision such as control, pedagogy and resource allocation.

First of all, it is necessary to say something about these issues in relation to *quality*. There will be no one benchmark of quality of worthwhileness, either in terms of aims, standards, curriculum or practice. This assertion follows directly from the acceptance of a diversity of educational aims and the consequent diversity of curricula, standards and practices that follow.

III   DIFFERENT CONCEPTIONS OF EQUALITY

In the previous section, one important concept of equality was introduced, namely equality as impartiality or procedural justice.[4] Some writers, particularly of the neo-liberal persuasion, have taken this to be the only notion of equality that is intelligibly applicable without running the risk of unfairness or even confusion.[5]

As we saw, equality as procedural justice should not be confused with the notion of equality of treatment. On occasions, procedural justice may well require that the same members of the relevant reference group receive *different* treatments. The point of the principle is that they are treated *impartially* as far as the relevant aim of the social institution is concerned. The aim will vary according to the type of socio-political situation that is being considered. For example, a legal system will seek to administer justice to all who fall within its control. A health care system will seek to provide appropriate treatment to those who need it and an education system will aim to make the most of the abilities of the pupils. There is little difficulty in seeing that, in different circumstances and for different defendants, patients and pupils, the treatment appropriate to each under conditions of impartiality will vary greatly.

Sometimes impartiality will require that the treatments given are the same and in this case there will be a coincidence between the requirements of impartiality and equality of treatment. However, there is no necessary connection between the two. The principle of equality of treatment requires that goods and outcomes be allocated equally to all, regardless of factors of entitlement, need or desert. Given the difficulties of assessing how need and desert should determine allocation, and the difficulty of reconciling the requirements of need and desert, equality of treatment might seem to be the least difficult and least controversial way in which allocations can be made. However, many critics have pointed to the lack of intrinsic moral value that equality has as a principle in itself, and the pragmatic arguments for adopting it show a tendency to avoid some of the difficult moral and practical issues that attend the just distribution of goods and outcomes.[6]

Equality of outcome is a principle of equality that asserts that the endpoint of a process ought to be the same for everyone who goes through it. For example, the outcome of the work of a hospital after a year might be that all post-operational patients recovered after six weeks, irrespective of the seriousness of the surgical procedures applied to them. More to the point, perhaps, the outcome of an educational process might be that all pupils on a certain course gained the same grades in their examinations. The concept of *equality of opportunity* frequently arouses some confusion. This is because it is susceptible of different interpretations. There are those who adhere to a *liberal* interpretation whereby it is thought of as no more than procedural justice. Radical interpretations of the concept, however, see it as more concerned with equality of outcome.[7] So, for example, it might be maintained that a certain outcome, whereby one group receives proportionally less of a certain good, say, higher education, than another, means that the opportunities of its members to take part in higher education must have been fewer than those applying in groups with a higher proportion of entrants.

It is not difficult to show that there are tensions between the different notions of equality, which make it hard to be an egalitarian in more than once sense of the term. It has already been noted that equality as procedural justice and equality as equal treatment are only related to each other contingently and may have requirements that frequently, if not on most occasions, contradict each other. The same is true of procedural justice and equality of outcome on the one hand and equality of outcome and equality of treatment on the other. Take the latter pair: given that individual people have different abilities from one another and that they employ these abilities in different ways, it is highly unlikely that, even if they start out with the same resources, they will each achieve the same outcome. Even if they are treated in the same way throughout a process, it is still unlikely that they will all end with the same outcome, since they will continue to have different abilities and to make different use of those abilities. This makes equality of treatment and equality of outcome difficult to reconcile in practice.[8]

Procedural justice and equality of outcome are difficult to reconcile with each other for much the same reasons. If, for example, an entrance examination is a requirement for entry to a course and, as a result of this examination, some groups of candidates do better than others, discrimination in favour of the less successful groups in order to ensure equal outcomes among all the groups will necessitate a violation of supposedly impartial procedures for candidate selection. It is important to note that there are no *a priori* reasons why following the different senses of equality should not produce compatible results, but the reason why they do not is not hard to find either: it is locatable in the fact of human diversity. Egalitarians do, therefore, need to come to some view of what sense of equality they are in fact committed to. Either that or they can view equality as an ideal, never to be reached but always to be striven for, using policy as a means of reconciling the applications of the different senses of the concept to produce a result that best satisfies the currently preferred notion of equality.

IV   THE EGALITARIAN CASE

There are two aspects to the egalitarian case for educational provision. The first is that all should receive the same education. The second is that the outcome of education should be the same for all.[9] One of the original impulses behind the drive for comprehensive education was the expectation that equality of treatment would lead to greater equality of outcome without too much difficulty.

The egalitarian case for education requires the view that, as far as social justice is concerned, there are no special reference groups for ability, with the exception of those who have some form of handicap, either mental or physical. Egalitarians generally accept that educational goods are positional and that the outcome for each will affect the outcome for all. They are, therefore, most concerned to ensure that no group is advantaged through receiving a special form of education or schooling that will enable its members to improve their competitive position in the struggle for positional goods.

It is easy to see that egalitarians might be led to reject independent schooling on these grounds, because the superior resources and social prestige that accrue to those who enjoy private schooling give pupils who attend such institutions a degree of competitive advantage that comes close to making a mockery of formal equality of opportunity. The solution could come in the form of universal state schooling, but this alone would be unlikely to satisfy a more radical egalitarian, since he would note that similar advantages accrue to people within a state system, citing the grammar schools in Britain as an example of how some groups are allowed to dominate access to a positional good, even under formal conditions of equality of opportunity.[10] Those of a still more radical persuasion might observe that even streaming and setting according to ability within the comprehensive school leads to the perpetuation of such competitive advantages, and they would therefore be drawn towards a policy of equality of treatment *within* the school by abolishing any distinctions between classes within a year-cohort.

The agenda of those who follow such a line seems to be to espouse a policy of equality of outcome through the pursual of a policy of equality of treatment. But such a strategy, as opposed to one that sought to reduce the domination of certain groups or to ameliorate the differences between groups, is doomed to failure. The differences between individual human endowments, the way in which people make use of their endowments and the way in which these factors interact with each other, make outcomes almost certain to be different. Identity of outcome for all individuals would also mean that competitive examinations for access to scarce educational resources would have to be abolished since such contests are, by their nature, a zero-sum game in which there are winners and losers. In order to counteract the possibility that equality of achievement would lead to inequality of outcome, the radical egalitarian would be driven to interfering with procedural justice by rigging tests and examinations or to altering his policy on equality of treatment, so that the less able and the less motivated received preferential treatment in order to guarantee identical outcomes for all.

Enough has been said to indicate that radical egalitarianism is not only impractical but is also internally incoherent given the highly plausible assumption of human diversity. The argument set out here does not, however, necessarily entail the contrary position known as *inegalitarianism*, whereby those who are more able or deserving, or who have merely already got more, receive better treatment than those less well endowed. More specifically, it entails that those who are more able, better motivated or both should receive a better schooling. All that the preceding argument shows is that it would be very difficult to give everyone the same education and at the same time expect to get the same results. This is certainly a telling argument against egalitarianism, especially in its more radical and utopian forms, but it is not an argument for inegalitarianism in education. It could equally well form the basis for an argument for *diversity* in eductional provision.

There is also a much weaker position concerning the distribution of educational goods, one which is not, strictly speaking, egalitarian but which is, arguably, egalitarian in spirit.[11] This is a position adapted from the writings of John Rawls to the effect that a distribution of primary social goods should be egalitarian unless it can be shown that another distribution exists which favours the worst off more than any alternative distribution. This is known by Rawls as the difference principle.[12] An egalitarian distribution is thus the ideal under certain circumstances, which is where the worst off will get a better absolute deal than under any other distribution. In practice, however, an inegalitarian distribution would be the practical alternative in most cases. The difficulty that many people opposed to egalitarianism in its more radical forms would have with this particular position is that it is quite compatible with the view that the best off would become less well off under a distribution made according to the difference principle.

They could be made worse off in two different but compatible ways. To see this, we need to imagine a situation where selective schooling picks the more able children for one school, A, which gives better education (in the sense of achieving higher standards) than school B, which takes the less able pupils and educates them to a lower standard than the children in school A. The *type* of education given in each school does not, however, differ radically.[13] The schools are unequal in the treatment sense and are likely to produce inequalities in the outcome sense as well. A reorganisation of this system abolishes its selective element and all children are now sent to a large comprehensive school, C, where again they all receive the same kind of education. At C, those who were the lowest achievers at B now attain a higher absolute standard of achievement than they would have had they attended B, while those who would have been the highest achievers at A now reach lower standards in an absolute sense than do those who were formerly educated at A. The outcome, although not satisfactory to radical egalitarians, is nevertheless in the direction of egalitarianism.

Although Rawls does not see education as a primary social good, he does see it as having an extrinsic value in that it is both an instrumental means towards gaining genuine primary goods and also a means towards gaining a secure sense of self-worth, which he does regard as a primary good. Therefore, even if education does not affect the gaining of any other primary good, the difference principle ought to be applied to it nonetheless.[14] On the other hand, if the distribution of educational goods has other consequences for the distribution of such primary goods as income and health, then these will have to be taken account of in making eduational distributions. Either way, therefore, the difference principle applies to the distribution of educational goods. However, if it applies in the second way, it need not have the kind of egalitarian implications for education described above. For example, if a selective system leads to greater provision of primary goods for the least well-off through, for example, greater economic efficiency, then it would be preferable to the comprehensive one.

Rawls is only an egalitarian in the sense that his system is designed to attend to the interests of the least well-off. But the difference principle can only justify egalitarianism in education under certain conditions, most obviously in the case when equality of treatment is likely to lead to more primary goods for the least well off than any other educational arrangements. The case for that could not be made in any general sense, but would have to be argued for society by society.

The real difficulties with adopting the difference principle for either egalitarian or inegalitarian positions in education is that it is argued for in ways that have come under heavy and persuasive criticism which it is beyond the scope of this chapter to address in detail. In particular, Rawls has been criticised for relying on a device, the veil of ignorance, and a psychological mind-set—that of cautious loss-minimisation—which are so arranged that the difference principle follows trivially from them.[15] Further criticism relates to the implications for individuation of people behind the veil of ignorance, stripped as they are of all the attributes by which we individuate them, together with the attribution of an identical mind-set.[16] These unresolved difficulties make it imprudent to adopt the Rawlsian model as a basis for any educational arrangements, whether egalitarian or non-egalitarian.[17]

With this in mind the discussion of the arguments in favour of educational egalitarianism will be concluded by saying that there is no justification for radical egalitarian views on educational provision in *general* formal terms, although there may be specific arguments for greater equality of treatment in specific cases, for example where it can be demonstrated empirically that egalitarianism fulfils societal aims for education by boosting economic growth or where rectificatory justice suggests an egalitarian redistribution of resources.

V THE INEGALITARIAN CASE

One argument given for inegalitarianism is that there are differences in ability, either innate or acquired, that justify different forms of educational treatment. Such differences in treatment are justified because only through them will individuals with radically different capacities be able to fulfil their potential. The best-known of these accounts is that of the theory of intelligence quotient, which postulates innate and fixed intelligence. Another popular inegalitarian doctrine is that of verbal deficit, associated with the work of Basil Bernstein, particularly his early work.[18] The psychometric theory of intelligence has been criticised in various places and is flawed both conceptually and empirically. A similar case can be made against verbal deficit theory.[19]

It is important to note, however, that an inegalitarian is not compelled to rely on the truth of such theories about the distribution of ability in order to sustain his case. One way of doing so is to make four plausible or persuasive assumptions to construct a case for giving more able pupils a better education than less able pupils.[20] The first of these is that some pupils have a greater potential than others to succeed in academic achievement. The second is that high academic achievement is an intrinsic good which requires no further justification. The third is that as far as education is concerned the ability to succeed in traditional academic subjects is the only kind of ability that is worth taking into account. The fourth assumption is that pupils who deserve a better education through the way in which they have used their abilities should benefit from it if it is available. It follows from these four assumptions that a system where able pupils go to a better resourced School A, while the less able go to a less well resourced School B, is justified in contrast to a system where all go to the comprehensive school C where the least able to better than they would at B, but where the most able do less well than they would at A.

I want, first of all, to clarify a few points about this argument. It is more concerned with high achievement of academic standards as a criterion of quality than it is with the value that might be added by a school. This is a defensible position to hold given the second assumption, that high achievement has an intrinsic value. There is, however, some tension between the second and the third assumptions. If we take desert in this context to refer to the extent to which a pupil has educationally transformed himself before he is considered for admission to School A or School B, then it is perfectly possible that a pupil starting from a very low base of achievement succeeds in educationally transforming himself to a greater degree than another pupil starting from a higher base position. Nevertheless, in terms of achievement at the time of selection, the second pupil would be selected for school A, rather than the first pupil who had actually 'added more value' through his own efforts than the second. It would be odd to say that the second pupil deserved the place more than the first if we acknowledge that desert should be linked to past action.

It might be replied to this that the second pupil is nevertheless *entitled* to his place because his higher achievement at the time of selection places him in a better position for the future than the first pupil.[23] While this is a legitimate response, it is important to note that it entails a shift in the selection criteria from desert to *entitlement*. Although inegalitarians are generally favourable to desert considerations as a basis for selection, they might be better off relying on an entitlement theory.[22] There is nothing heinous about a concern with achieving the highest performance possible; indeed there is a case to be made out on Rawlsian lines for making this a priority as we have noted above. It would have to be granted that this case could be made more convincingly with instrumental or vocational education, but this point will be returned to.

However, there is a tension between this objective and the proposal that a good school educationally transforms pupils ('adds value') better than any other could. It is possible for a school to add more value to more pupils than another school without reaching the same absolute standards with any of them. This implies that the principle of selection and the type of education offered might differ radically in different inegalitarian systems, depending on which aim was adopted. Since the aims are potentially incompatible this is a problem within an inegalitarian orientation which has, to my knowledge, not been satisfactorily resolved.

So the better school in the inegalitarian framework might be the one that achieved the highest absolute performances for a specific number of pupils and the achievement of this objective would be ensured by the performance of the pupils on entry, by their ability to attain high academic standards in public examinations and by the quality of the resources put at their disposal.[23] Such a conception of education is a liberal one (which is arrived at through a prescriptive definition) and amounts to the provision of a certain range of goods,[24] these goods being those provided by a traditional liberal education. Cooper, for example, acknowledges that schools could provide processes other than education, for example training for specific jobs, but maintains that such activities are not education and so do not fall into the framework that he has set up for the distribution of educational goods.

The first assumption, that different pupils have different potentials to succeed in achieving high standards in traditional academic subjects, is unexceptionable and does not depend in any way for its truth on IQ or verbal deficit theory. Determining who these pupils are, particularly taking the long view, may be more difficult than is sometimes acknowledged. The model is inadequate in its assumption that ability can be tested in a once-and-for-all way through the administration of a single test at a particular age. The reason that it is an inadequate assumption for describing anything more than a highly simplified model for the distribution of educational goods is that ability, in the sense of potential for success in traditional academic subjects, is not merely fixed at an upper limit from one's genetic inheritance, but alters according to such factors as exposure to a stimulating educational environment, motivation, interest and cultural background. It is therefore not possible in reality to select accurately who will most benefit from a certain school by a one-off test. Greater flexibility would need to be built into the system in order to determine who would continue to benefit most. In particular, there would need to be something more than a simple reliance on absolute standards of achievement at the entry point for selection: this is not adequate even as a criterion of *entitlement* if *potential* is to be taken into acount. There would also need to be provisions for rectification of errors in selection.

The third assumption, that education is concerned with the provision of liberal academic goods and that other activities that occur in schools are not, strictly speaking, educational, is debatable. While there is no objection to adopting a prescriptive definition of education and then using it, it runs contrary to the approach adopted in this book to take such a position. In Chapter 3 the view was taken that *education* is a contested concept that arises from its inevitably political nature. The inegalitarian model for the distribution of educational goods is therefore inadequate because it presupposes an inadequate concept of education. In constructing a model of how educational goods might be equitably distributed, therefore, we need to take into acount both the way in which different parties conceive of education and the nature of the choices that need to be made by resource allocators (ultimately electorates and politicians in democratic societies). Even a society exclusively committed to liberal education in an inegalitarian framework would need to sort out the tensions between the achievement of the highest absolute standards for some and the greatest possible overall added value, if the system were to be properly accountable.

The model is one that is morally justifiable *provided* that certain assumptions are made about the aims and nature of education. But it is a simple one that relies on certain contestable assumptions and it cannot be a guide to the equitable allocation of educational resources in a complex society like our own. First, it relies on a particular view of the nature of education. We have seen that this is not a descriptively adequate definition if we are to take proper account of the variegated way in which the concept of education is employed. It is true that popular usage may be confused and therefore is not a sure guide to how a concept should be understood, but there is no reason to think that any one of the prescriptive definitions of education on offer is superior to any other or to the generality of ways in which education is understood within society.

If education is not solely concerned with the promotion of academic ability in the traditional subjects of the humanities and the natural sciences, then it will be concerned with the promotion of other sorts of ability as well (see Chapter 4, Section IV). But this does not alter the fact that an education system that seeks to cultivate a diverse range of abilities beyond the traditional academic ones will need to diversify its curriculum and almost certainly its schooling system in order to provide for that diversity. This means that the inegalitarian framework outlined above will no longer be helpful. Neither will the alternative model of an academically oriented comprehensive education of the kind developed in Britain over the last thirty years.

Both of these models presuppose that education should be concerned with the provision of a fairly narrow range of academic education to all pupils.[25] Yet this assumption is highly questionable. It represents the views of one, politically and culturally dominant, group as to what the nature of education should be. As such, it is quite properly open to challenge. Its predominance is a feature of Britain rather than of the major Continental European countries such as France and Germany, where the need to develop a diversity of ability has long been recognised. This recognition is reflected in the provision of different curricula and different kinds of school to teach them. The roots of these differences in attitude towards state-funded education go very deep and are beyond the scope of this chapter, but they can probably be traced to different views of the nature of work and economic activity in Britain on the one hand and in Western Europe on the other. The British view, which is well expressed in the work of Adam Smith, is that productive activity, as opposed to design, requires little more than trained, routine physical effort.[26] The Continental view, well expressed in the work of Friedrich List, is that an economy needs to develop its productive powers, which include the full mental as well as physical resources of the population.[27]

If it is the case that the wishes of interest groups should be respected in the provision of education, then the desire that most have to see education related, at least in some way, to their future employment should be reflected in aims and curricula that evince a desire to cater for a range and diversity of abilities and interests that cannot be encompassed within a traditional academic curriculum. Many would see it as desirable that the schools that teach vocationally and technically oriented curricula should receive the same amount of esteem as those that teach an academic curriculum. Of course, no-one can legislate for parity of esteem, even when it is considered to be a desirable objective. However, steps can be taken to foster greater respect for alternative forms of education, particularly through the provision of adequate resources for schools and by the use of ways of increasing the status of teachers working within that part of the education system. These things can be done without in any way seeking to denigrate academic education, whether that is conceived either instrumentally or non-instrumentally.

Acceptance of this diversity does not imply in any way that the procedural justice that can be secured by the implementation of a national curriculum need be compromised. It is most likely to mean that there will be a common curriculum in the years of primary or elementary education which will ensure a common cultural basis for mutual understanding and tolerance and literacy and numeracy among all pupils. This would be followed by branching curricula which would allow pupils to follow technical, craft, commercial and artistic interests and abilities. However, unlike the eleven-plus system that operated in Britain until the 1970s, this system would need to ensure that selection was made at an appropriate age and that there was sufficient flexibility to allow for mistakes to be corrected and changes of mind to be accommodated. It would also need to ensure that there were no arbitrary variations in the number of places available for sought-after schooling.[28] This requirement was not met in Britain during the time at which the eleven-plus system was in near-universal operation.

This important point needs to be related to the earlier discussion of the concept of *equality of opportunity*. In that discussion it was pointed out that *equality*, if it were to serve as a concept that could be put into coherent practice, would need to be interpreted as *procedural justice*. This means that the same opportunities would need to be available to all in the relevant selection group. This requirement would not be met in a system where some local authorities allowed 15% of an age cohort to go to grammar schools if they so wished and another authority made places available to 40%.

It is mistaken to think that the concept of equality of opportunity is inapplicable to educational situations.[29] It is both an undesirable and an unattainable ideal to equalise the abilities of individuals. It is both desirable and in most cases attainable to ensure both that individuals have the same opportunities to compete for desirable outcomes and that they have the same *chances* of success in that proportionately the same number of desirable outcomes is available to all. In this sense an inegalitarian system could well be run on the principle of equality of opportunity.[30]

Where an inegalitarian system is at fault is in its provision of a limited range of *kinds* of educational opportunity. This is connected with the view of education as a certain kind of good, namely one that excludes goods with an explicit vocational bias. We have already looked at the reasons for that assumption and found them wanting. It is worth noting, however, that the proposal to broaden the range of educational opportunities available to pupils need not compromise the principle that achievement of high academic performance is an intrinsic good. By sending pupils of different kinds of abilities to different kinds of schools where those abilities can best be catered for, one can strive to ensure that there is the highest possible achievement in all areas including the traditional academic ones. And, whatever one may think of the Rawlsian difference principle in relation to the distribution of educational goods with an intrinsic value, there are grounds for thinking that, at least, application of some form of competitive selection for places within the different sections of a schooling system that took account of different levels of potential for achievement could well lead to a greater raising of the standards of living of the worse-off through the economic prosperity and competitiveness secured by the pursuit of the highest possible performances against high standards in technical, commercial, craft and artistic forms of education.

It is difficult to see how *desert* rather than *need* or *entitlement* should be the principle of selection to whatever school or college a child goes to. The aims of education are generally concerned with fulfilling human potential in accordance with principles of justice. If entitlement does not confine itself to past performance but also includes future potential then it is the appropriate means of selection both for different types of schooling and for different schools within each category. If high performances are an absolute good for non-instrumental and instrumental forms of education, then selection should be concerned with the achievement and maintenance of the highest possible performance. So a selection procedure should be concerned with a child's potential for achieving the highest possible performance that he is capable of, rather than with whether or not he deserves a place because of his hard work, although his hard work may well have increased his potential.[31]

To conclude this section, some form of inegalitarianism in the provision of education is justified in societies like ours under the following conditions. First, that the kind of equality that is to be rejected is equality of *treatment*. Second, that diversity of ability be recognised in the provision of a range of opportunities for pupils of different abilities. Third, that principles of procedural justice operate strictly in the selection and allocation procedures that determine the schools and the kinds of schools that pupils attend. In addition, *entitlement* rather than *desert* will have to be the basis for selection procedures for school allocation, although rewards can be desert-based in other respects. But provided that the entitlement criterion is handled fairly it does not constitute a violation of procedural justice. The proposal advocated here is different in one very important respect from that offered by most inegalitarians in that it is based upon a much broader conception of education that recognises the contested nature of the concept and also recognises that different forms of education may have a value (both intrinsic and extrinsic) which makes it difficult, if not impossible, to say in general terms that one form is more valuable than another, although different people may value them differently.

Children should have the opportunity to attend the kind of school that is most likely to further their potential. This entails that there should be some form of selection. Pupils will be selected for different kinds of school according to an entitlement based on potential. Whether or not the different schools enjoy parity of esteem is not to the point: it is important that pupils receive the education that is in their best interests. In this respect, the scheme that I am proposing is non-egalitarian rather than inegalitarian. But in a large society there will be numerous schools of each different kind and some schools will be more attractive than others. So does this mean that selection should apply *within* sectors?

Recall that one of the inegalitarian's points was that a concern with high absolute achievement implied selection of the best pupils to work with the best teachers. He advocated this because high absolute achievement was thought to have intrinsic value. Now it is possible for a school to achieve the highest absolute performances with some pupils, yet fail to obtain as high a performance overall as another school. What should a diversified non-egalitarian system of public education go for? A high absolute level of achievement is important for research in particular. But, given that education, even on the liberal view, is a preparation for life, it is performances that best prepare the pupils to fulfil whatever aims are specified by education that should be sought after by the school, and these are not necessarily the highest possible absolute performances. A school concerned with preparing *as many as possible* of its pupils for future success will be concerned with maximising the overall performance of the pupils, even though they may not necessarily reach the highest absolute performance. However, taking a sector as a whole, it is quite likely that this could be best achieved by a degree of selection within the system, so that there was an appropriate matching pupil, pace of work and teaching ability. So selection according to potential can be justified even within a diverse system of education.

VI   EQUALITY AND PRIVATE SCHOOLING

The sense of entitlement defended above related to a pupil's abilities and potential for future achievement, not to the resources available to buy an education of high quality. The model above is not a justification for private schooling, since allocation is made on ability to learn, not on ability to pay. We now need to examine whether or not procedural justice can be used as an argument for restricting the right of parents to send children to schools of their own choosing that are not within the state-funded system of education.

Where the benefits of such an education are purely intrinsic, no-one else's material interests need be affected by the existence of a private schooling sector. However, some of the benefits are likely to be extrinsic, and since education in the extrinsic sense is a positional good the interests of others will most likely be affected. They will be affected in two ways. The first is through the way in which independent schooling affects overall economic prosperity, the second is through the way in which it may affect access to a limited range of scarce but desirable opportunities, particularly in employment.

Some of these latter effects will be due to schooling, rather than to the education (even conceived of in a broad sense) provided at an establishment. The prestige that attaches to a particular school and the social network provided by its alumni may well provide incalculable advantages in future life to those who pass through it. Similarly, the quasi-educational goods of poise, articulacy and confidence that a prestigious school may confer on its pupils may also place them at a considerable advantage. On the face of it, such advantages may violate equal opportunity considerations through allowing, and indeed encouraging, discrimination in favour of the alumni of certain schools in the market for jobs and influence.

As far as the educational benefits are concerned, these may contribute to the general good by contributing to overall prosperity or they may again ensure that scarce opportunities in employment and influence are monopolised by the alumni of certain schools. Should these features of an independent school system be allowed in a democratic society? In considering questions of this nature, one nearly always has to take into account the disadvantages as well as the advantages of a proposal. Merely to show that private or independent schooling has certain disadvantages for the operation of a prosperous and democratic society is not to make a case for its abolition, unless it can be shown that the disadvantages outweigh the advantages of its retention.

The radical egalitarian case against private education or private schooling can be rejected for the same reasons as it can be rejected for the abolition of selective schooling in general. The case against private schooling on the grounds that it gives access on the basis (at least partially) of the wrong kind of entitlement (wealth rather than ability) can be rejected on the grounds that to suppose that legitimately acquired wealth is not a proper basis to an entitlement would be to ban most transactions in any society, whether democratic or undemocratic. The accusation that private schooling violates considerations of procedural justice in the job market deserves to be taken seriously. It is a charge difficult to prove, but outcomes may well provide circumstantial evidence that such discrimination, whether conscious or unconscious, does exist. The question then arises, is this such a disadvantage to society that it can be remedied only by abolition and would the advantages of abolition outweigh its disadvantages?

The major problem that arises with the abolition or banning of private education or private schooling is the violation of parental rights that it would entail. These rights are fundamental to the protection of the interests of children and although the interests of children are not the only consideration that a society should have in making arrangements for the education of its future citizens, it is one of the most important.[32] Therefore, to seek to restrict this right in any way would be to undermine one of the more fundamental liberties on which any free society rests, namely the right of parents to interpret and act on the best interests of their children. In order to appreciate this, it is perhaps helpful to forget about the material and social privilege that private schooling can confer on an individual and to concentrate instead on some of the pupil's vital interests that may be served by the possibility of private education, whether conducted through private schools or through other means.

Parents may well interpret their children's interests in such a way that they come to believe that their moral and religious training and education can best be served through education in an environment which is dedicated to a particular system of values and beliefs that cannot and maybe should not be accommodated within the state-funded system of education. Alternatively, parents may be so dissatisfied with the quality of education and schooling that is on offer within the state system that they are prepared to pay in order to gain the aims, curriculum, standards and practice that they believe are in the best interests of their own children. In such cases the only alternatives are either to deny them such opportunities or to insist that they avail themselves of them outside the time set aside for compulsory schooling. Both these alternatives appear to discriminate unfairly against individuals whose beliefs and values do not conform to those of the majority of the population. Such a form of discrimination would undermine an objective of any democracy that does not wish to become a tyranny of majorities, namely the objective of protecting and respecting the wishes of minorities.

To summarise, the existence of independent schooling for the wealthy and influential may well contribute to unfair discrimination in the allocation of positional goods acquired through the possession of certain forms of education or schooling. Certainly thought needs to be given to lessening or eliminating such discrimination where it can be proved to exist. However, the disadvantages to the social and moral fabric of a democratic society that would be entailed by the banning of private education would far outweigh the advantages to be gained. There is, though, no reason why public sector education should be undermined by state support for the private sector. A case can be made out along these lines for the abolition of charitable status of independent schools. Likewise such initiatives as the assisted places scheme, which allows academically able children from poor families access to private education through the state sponsorship of their fees, should be discontinued, and certainly not expanded. Assisted places are particularly damaging to publicly run education as they are designed to select the most academically able children from the state system where their presence plays an important role in ensuring good performance. In this instance, therefore, public funds are employed for educational purposes, one of whose side-effects is to undermine the public education system on whose success a society depends. Such schemes should not be carried out with public funds, not because they violate a principle of equality of opportunity (which they do not), but because they threaten the provision of the public instrumental goods of education through a subversion of the state system of education.

Inegalitarianism is not an absolute value, any more than egalitarianism is. It is not a violation of principles of justice or liberty not to have an assisted places scheme; neither is it a requirement of the concern for high standards that inegalitarians profess, that the highest possible standards should always be achieved *irrespective* of any other socio-political considerations. In the light of the discussion in Chapter 9, there are overwhelming reasons for not damaging public education.

NOTES

1. D. Cooper, *Illusions of Equality*, 1980; B. Bernstein, Social structure, language and learning, *Educational Research*, 3, pp. 163–176: A Jensen, *Educability and Group Differences*, 1973; R. Herrnstein and A. Murray, *The Bell Curve: Intelligence and Class Structure in American Life*, 1994. Cooper's form of inegalitarianism can, however, be accommodated in a limited way in the argument presented below.
2. Barry, *op. cit.*, Chapter 6; Gray, *op. cit.*
3. Gray, *op. cit.*
4. Cf. Barry, *op. cit.*, Chapter 7.
5. Ibid., *Chapter 6.*
6. For a recent argument see J. White, The dishwasher's child: education and the end of egalitarianism, *Journal of Philosophy of Education*, 28.2, 1994, pp. 173–182.
7. Cf. Marie Stowell, Equal opportunities, access and admissions: tensions and issues for educational policy, *Journal of Access Studies*, 7, 1992, pp. 164–179.
8. Cf. K. Sharp and C. Winch, Equal opportunities and the use of language: a critique of the new orthodoxy, *Studies in Higher Education*, 19.2, 1994.
9. Cf. Cooper, *op. cit.* It is unusual for those who call themselves egalitarians to subscribe to equality as procedural justice. A case where they might, though, is when procedural justice requires rectification for wrongs done by x to y. In some cases this could involve a redistribution of resources from x to y. Attention has been drawn to the potentially radical implications of Nozick's version of neo-liberalism by, for example, Alan Brown, *Modern Political Philosophy*, 1986, Chapter 4.
10. This is not strictly true of the UK, since the number of grammar school places available varied according to local authorities giving children in some areas, such as South Wales, a much greater likelihood of going to a grammar school than others. It is arguable that these anomalies constituted a violation of procedural justice and may have contributed to the demise of the selective system of education in England and Wales. There is also evidence that girls were discriminated against in favour of boys.
11. Cf. Cooper, *op. cit.*, Chapter 2.
12. John Rawls, *A Theory of Justice*, 1971. See also Rawls, *Political Liberalism*, 1993, pp. 22 ff.
13. This example is worked out in some detail in Cooper, *op. cit.*, and is discussed further below.
14. Ibid., p. 30.
15. For criticism along these lines see, for example, Brown, *op. cit.*, Chapter 3.
16. See Cooper, *op. cit.*, and Robert Nozick, *Anarchy, State and Utopia*, 1974, for criticism along these lines.
17. Rawls attempts to meet these difficulties in his *Political Liberalism*, 1993, pp. 22–28. I do not regard these attempts as satisfactory.
18. See Basil Bernstein, *Class, Codes and Control*, Volumes 1 and 2, 1973, 1977.
19. For a critique of both these approaches see Winch, *op. cit.*, 1990.
20. By better education in this sense Cooper means better teachers and better resources. These equip the school to give its pupils a greater degree of educational transformation than any other school. Cooper, *op. cit.*, p. 33.
21. Whether or not this is true is an empirical matter. A particular type of intensive academic education at secondary level may lead some pupils to experience difficulties at the tertiary level and in adult life.
22. See, for example, Cooper, *op. cit.*, p. 24, where an example which is very favourable to the entitlement case is used.
23. *How many* pupils should achieve the highest standards is not just an academic question since there may need to be a compromise struck between high standards and overall added value.

24. Ibid., pp. 151–2.
25. This view requires some qualification since some inegalitarians believe that most children would require a modified or watered-down version of the academic curriculum if they were to profit at all from education. See, for example, Cooper, *op. cit.*, Chapter 5; G. H, Bantock, *Culture, Industrialisation and Education*, 1968.
26. Cf. Adam Smith, *The Wealth of Nations* (1776; 1970 edn), p. 226.
27. F. List, *op. cit.*, especially Chapters XII and VXII.
28. It does not, of course, follow from the requirement of distinct curricula that there should be distinct types of schools. This point requires further discussion and, in any case, is a difficult one to make *a priori*. What I do maintain is that anyone who thinks that distinct curricula are desirable has to take very seriously the possibility that the best way of operating those curricula is to provide distinct schools.
29. John Wilson, Equality revisited, *Journal of Philosophy of Education*, 27.1, 1993, pp. 113–114.
30. For a defence of the notion that equality of opportunity is centrally concerned with sameness of permission, see Sharp and Winch, *op. cit.*
31. It follows from this position that the highest standards possible will be safeguarded since the most able pupils will be selected to the schools most capable of fulfilling the highest possible standards, no matter what kinds of standards these are.
32. See John Locke, *Second Treatise of Government*; C. Winch, Should children's books be censored? *Westminster Studies in Education*, 16, 1993, pp. 41–52.

Chapter 11
Inspecting Educational Quality

I DEBATES ABOUT QUALITY ARE NOT JUST DEBATES ABOUT STANDARDS

In assessing the quality of what goes on in an educational institution, governments are concerned with making *judgements* about what goes on and whether, or to what extent, it is worthwhile. One way of doing this is through inspection. In this chapter, I will look at what inspection involves and what the alternatives are. Finally, I will attempt to reconcile the need for a credible system of accountability with the demands of fairness, justice and validity of judgement.

Unlike other forms of assessment, which can rely on a range of performance indicators, such as the achievement of standards and examination results, inspection tends to focus on the process of education, the teaching and learning that takes place within a school or, to put it another way, the *practice* of education, which, as was observed in Chapter 8, can very often be a highly contentious matter to make judgement about. Inspectorates can vary greatly in character. Usually, though, they range from being *advisory* or *consultative* to being solely charged with making judgements about the performance of educational institutions. In some cases, they are also charged with a research function.

It is also possible to employ academic researchers to make judgements about the effectiveness of educational institutions and, for certain purposes, auditors are also employed. There is also scope for peer review of performance and this tends to be a model employed most frequently within the higher education sector. For reasons that we shall examine shortly, advisory services, auditors, academic researchers and peers are not considered to be generally the most appropriate persons or bodies to make these kinds of judgement and, in practice, inspection has assumed a very important role in the making of judgements about educational quality within Britain and some other countries such as France.[1] Whether this role is justified and under what circumstances, is an issue that will occupy the bulk of this chapter. But first of all the alternatives and their shortcomings will be considered.

II ADVISORY SERVICES

Advisory services were, until recently, in Britain at least, considered to be the main regulatory arm of the Local Educational Authorities. Very often they combined advisory and inspectorial roles in varying degrees. In some cases, the roles of advisors and inspectors were kept separate by allocating the different kinds of job to different people. The job of an advisor is to give advice so as to enable teachers to improve their teaching and, more generally, their classroom practice. Giving advice involves various aspects of the inspectorial role. In particular it involves having the authority to state what is good and what is not good practice and it also involves having the authority to *recommend* practice to teachers. It does not, however, involve the making of *judgements* on the performance of teachers and schools and so, in the strict sense, does not fulfil the role of inspection. In practice, however, the role of advisors across the public sector has tended to move, at least to some extent, across the spectrum towards an inspectorial role and this movement has reflected the culture of the advisory unit, the political priorities of resource providers, the political ambitions of the advisors themselves and a need for finance through the securing of OFSTED inspection contracts (see below).

In the eyes of their critics, and recent British governments in particular, advisory services have had two serious shortcomings. The first is their inability to make sufficiently authoritative judgements, and the second is their tendency to develop their own culture and their own view of good practice. These perceived shortcomings have, in Britain at least, effectively disqualified them from the inspectorial role.

III   AUDIT

The idea of audit originates in a concern that is primarily financial, namely accounting for how money is spent and tracing the operation of financial control systems. To some extent financial audit has a role to play in the assessment of schools, particularly in ensuring that they are spending money and looking after their assets in a competent manner. The notion of audit can be extended to cover the wider brief of ensuring that what is supposed to be happening actually is happening, in the *academic* as well as the financial sense. For example, an academic audit can be carried out on a school in order to find out if it has a policy on the teaching of spelling and whether or not that policy is being put into effect. But even in these cases the role of audit is essentially *quantitative*: it is concerned with what is taking place, rather than with *qualitative* judgements as to *how well* it is taking place. For example, it is one thing to discover whether or not a school has a policy on spelling and whether or not it is carrying that policy out. It is another matter to judge the *quality* of the spelling policy and the *quality* of the teaching which is putting that policy into effect.

It might well be argued that in practice it is possible to combine the making of the quantitative with the qualitative judgements and, indeed, it could be argued that the making of the latter presupposes that the quantitative questions have been answered beforehand. But acknowledging this point merely serves to underline the way in which inspection is different from audit. However thorough an audit is, it is only going to provide answers to certain questions which are of a certain kind, namely whether or not something is happening which is supposed to be happening. If an audit is to answer questions about, for example, whether or not good practice is taking place in classrooms, then it could only be so against a pre-established benchmark of what constitutes good practice. In this respect, audit is quite different from inspection in the important sense that the judgement of what constitutes *good practice* is, in the end, left to the judgements of inspectors. As will become plain later, this remains the case even when rules for the carrying out of inspections are rigidly prescribed and copiously documented, as is the case with the English and Welsh OFSTED system of inspection.

Another example of an audit system of inspection can again be found in an earlier period of British education, namely the 'payment by results' system of allocating resources to schools on the basis of tests carried out by Her Majesty's Inspectors (HMI) which operated in England and Wales throughout most of the latter half of the nineteenth century.[2] The main objection to audit types of scrutiny into the workings of schools and colleges is precisely that they are mechanistic, concentrating on pre-established questions, and that they therefore stand in danger of missing out vital features of the ethos, and the teaching and learning experiences, that are offered by schools. Worse still, they encourage the schools to concentrate on those aspects of education and schooling that can readily be measured, to the neglect of those, such as school ethos, which cannot but which may, nevertheless, be of vital importance. Finally, they are not suitable for qualitative judgements as to how well something is taking place. For these reasons, the idea that state-funded education should give an account of itself solely through audit procedures is not thought to be appropriate. This is not to say, however, that audit may not have an important role to play within the context of inspection.

IV PEER GROUP REVIEW

Peer group review is a system of accountability which seeks to moderate, and render consistent, standards of achievement across an educational sector by involving peers from comparable institutions in the process of assessment. The role of these peers is not inspectorial as they are involved primarily in the assessment of *performance* and *standards* rather than *practices*.[3] The best known example of this system can be found in the practice of external examination as it is carried out in, for instance, the British system of higher education. In this system assessment involves moderation by one or more external markers who also comment on the overall standards of work seen and who sometimes, on this basis, make judgements about the quality of teaching and learning on the courses for which they are examiners.

It is not difficult to see why peer group review would find limited favour with any government bent on securing accountability. It is not that they would necessarily discount its value; few would deny that some such process of moderating standards across comparable courses confers considerable benefits on the assessment process. But peer group review is precisely that: it does not involve scrutiny by other interested parties or the representatives of other interested parties. This in itself is enough to disqualify it as the sole way of achieving accountability, but there are other objections. The first is that it is limited. Although external examiners can involve themselves in talking to teachers and students in making their judgements and although they can give advice about teaching and assessment, their main purpose is to ensure that standards are maintained and everything else that they do serves that purpose.

V   RESEARCH

Chapter 7 was devoted to an extensive discussion of school effectiveness research. It might be thought that academic research could provide much, if not all, of the information necessary to make judgements on the quality and effectiveness of education. Research is apparently disinterested; it is usually thorough (especially if properly resourced) and methodologically sophisticated. Why, then, cannot it be employed to answer questions about quality and effectiveness?

There are several reasons. The first constraint that a research-based quality assessment system will run up against is that of *expense*. It will cost a lot of money to operate because of the rigour that professional standards of research will require. Such rigour is needed, not because of the inherently virtuous character of academic researchers, but because their professional reputations depend on the production of research that will stand up to the scrutiny of critical peers.[4] The empirical work of inspectorates commands confidence only to the extent that they are immune from such scrutiny. It could be argued that they should not be immune and, indeed, the existence of a publicly available protocol for OFSTED will tend, in the long run, to undermine that immunity.

A second, connected reason is that educational researchers test hypotheses either through statistical inference, through some kind of ethnography-based methodology or through a combination of these two paradigms. They seek to make general assertions about a *population* on the basis of studying a *sample*. Population studies, especially on a national system of education, would be far too expensive to entertain. And yet a system of quality assessment based on research would have to consist of population studies. For accountability to be secured (and this is the object of a quality assessment exercise), it is necessary that the population be studied because what is at issue is not just the performance of the system taken as a whole (although this is important), but the performance of each individual part that is in receipt of state funding. A population study will save the costs associated with rigorous sampling and statistical inference, but these savings will be more than outweighed by the costs incurred through the collection of data from a population study. To gain some idea of what these might be, if research into English using a sample of 30 primary schools costs £50,000 for a decent piece of work (and this is likely to be an underestimate), research into a population of 3,000 (again an underestimate) will cost £5 million and that is for just one subject in one age phase.

Third, an educational research community is unlikely to speak with one voice on methodology or even on interpretation of data. Any quality assessment exercise that is based on academic empirical research will, then, be contested by other members of the research community. That is not a problem for a piece of work that is presented as academic research or even as practical policy research. It is, however, a major problem for any exercise which is used to assess the performance of a whole educational system. Finally, it is necessary to draw attention to the different nature of the jobs of a researcher and of one who assesses quality in an inspectorial role. It is true that many of the skills of researchers and quality assessors and the assumptions that they make may overlap, but this does not alter the fact that the jobs are different. The final consideration will make this clearer.[5]

An organisation which is called on to assess quality is being asked to make judgements about particular episodes of teaching and learning and on the effectiveness of educational institutions. It is being asked to make an authoritative judgement as to whether teaching and learning are good, whether they are satisfactory or unsatisfactory and whether or not standards are appropriate. Its judgements must be sufficiently authoritative that it cannot be challenged by teachers, headteachers and governing bodies and it must be taken seriously by the government and by the public. This means, at the least, that the government must have, and must be seen to have, vested it with institutional authority.[6] Second, those judgements must be made in such a way that they look and sound like definitive and unchallengeable statements about the quality of education. Academic researchers *qua* academic researchers cannot fulfil either of these roles. In order to remain believable as academics they need to be seen to be detached from the state to a certain extent and, in accordance with both the methodology and the generally accepted ethical stance of academic researchers, they must hedge their findings with an appropriate range of *caveats* about reliability.

A possible compromise role would be for the government directly to employ academic researchers. Some departments of government, such as the Home Office in Britain, do this and indeed the Department of Education and Science had a body, the Assessment of Performance Unit (APU), which was, in some ways, like a government research arm looking into education. Such bodies, however, might be seen to have the worst of both worlds. They are completely dependent financially on money from the government on the one hand, and, as academic researchers, they cannot make authoritative judgements about the quality of education. On the other hand, this conflict would not arise if they were employed, not to make educational judgements, but to provide a picture of the state of standards and performance by representative sampling across the system. However, some form of educational inspection seems therefore to be necessary in order to ensure accountability in state-funded public education systems.

VI INSPECTION

In considering different ways of ensuring accountability, we seem to have rejected most, if not all, of the alternatives to state-backed inspection. What then, is educational inspection and how does it work? The first thing to be said about this is that bodies that are called inspectorates, commissions, councils or whatever else are not necessarily engaged in the pure business of inspection, which can be defined as *the gathering of evidence in order to make judgements about the quality of a service relative to accepted norms*. An inspectorate has some analogies with a police force. There are norms against which a service is to be judged (like the criminal law in the case of the police), evidence is gathered and, if necessary, a prosecution is initiated. Inspectorates, too, gather evidence, but, unlike the police, they also make definitive judgements about what is good or bad with very limited right of appeal. It can therefore be seen that the role with which they are vested can, potentially, be a very significant one indeed.

In Britain, Her Majesty's Inspectorate of Schools (HMI) until recently, formed such a body. It had a statutory duty to report on schools inspected but it was also used to carry out research (such as the 1978 primary survey and the 1991 report into the French educational system) and it had a significant advisory role within the schools. Although not a pure inspectorate, HMI was a quite flexible instrument of government which, nevertheless, enjoyed a fair degree of independence. One of its primary functions was to visit schools and colleges, inspect their work and report to the Secretary of State for Education on what it had seen and judged to be the case. Since the early 1980s these reports have been made available to the public. HMI generally commanded respect, although by no means universal respect, throughout the education system, even though its methodologies were not published and indeed could seem opaque. This respect arose from the fact that HMI was generally believed to recruit the ablest members of the teaching profession to its ranks and from its advisory role which, again, commanded wide if not universal respect within the teaching profession.

There were thought to be problems with the HMI system, however, both from the point of view of the government which employed the inspectors and from the point of view of accountability more generally. These problems eventually led to the demise of HMI as it had existed since the abolition of the Revised Code in 1898,[7] and it is in these problems that we can see how difficult it is to run a system of inspection that can satisfy all interested parties. It is necessary first of all to point out that HMI ran into difficulties at a time when neo-liberal ideas in British politics were very influential. At the same time, the ideology of progressivism was thought to be gaining influence throughout the education system and within HMI itself to an increasing extent.[8] One of neo-liberalism's main tenets is a suspicion of the self-serving nature of government bureaucracies, and HMI's perceived ideological bias only served to heighten those suspicions. The government's suspicion of HMI was further heightened by the fact that the inspectorate's behaviour appeared to match another tenet of neo-liberal thinking about government bureaucracies, that they would strive to gain extra financial resources for the areas for which they were responsible. From the early 1980s onwards, under the leadership of Sheila Browne in particular, HMI, in the newly public reports, drew repeated attention to the way in which its staff thought that educational standards were being compromised by a lack of resources.[9]

But the other major problem for HMI lay in its élite nature and something that was consequent on that, namely its small size. It was never even remotely possible for the organisation to run a system of universal and regular inspections of educational institutions in England and Wales. This meant that HMI, constituted as it was as a full-time corps of professionals, was unable to carry out the function of accounting for the activities of all the schools in the country. If it were to grow as a full-time corps of officials to be large enough to undertake such a function then it would have become a very costly institution to maintain. But its growth would also have taken place within the context of a professional culture that the Conservative government of the day would have found inimical to the kinds of reforms that it was putting through the education system, which were, in part at least, designed to limit and roll back the influence of the progressivism in which HMI was thought to be to some extent implicated.

It is possible for *researchers* to make inferences about the characteristics of a population on the basis of a sample, but *inspectorial* judgements of this kind have to be categorical and based on the relevant population if they are to inspire confidence; for example, parents want to know whether or not the school which *their* child is attending is good. They are not interested in whether or not schools with similar characteristics are. HMI was unable to provide this information on a universal basis and neither did it have a clear role for inspecting an identifiable subset of the school population, for example those schools identified as being in danger of falling below certain minimum standards. These limitations to and ambiguities in its role made it difficult to justify its continuance in the form in which it had existed for a hundred years or so, in a climate where *all* the functions of government were coming under increasing critical scrutiny.

VII REFORMS TO THE INSPECTION SYSTEM IN THE UNITED KINGDOM

For these reasons HMI in its old form as an élite multi-functional inspectorate of some 450 staff was doomed. The British government committed itself to the implementation of a Parent's Charter and the regular inspection of all schools, together with public reports on their performance. A new body called the Office for Standards in Education (OFSTED) was brought into being. OFSTED consisted of what was left of HMI and an administrative structure created to serve a new system of inspection.

This new system relies, not on a permanent corps of inspectors, but on accredited individuals who form teams to bid for contracts to inspect particular schools, each of which is to be inspected once every four years. OFSTED awards and supervises the contracts.[10] Inspections are guided by a document, *The Framework for Inspection*, which was largely drawn up by HMI personnel, so it could be argued that the HMI influence lives on in the form of this framework document.[11] It renders transparent what was previously opaque, namely HMI rules for inspection and reporting on inspection. In addition, it provides procedures for assessing the way in which schools deploy their resources, which was rendered necessary by the devolution of budgets to schools in the late 1980s by the 1988 Education Reform Act. The framework promised to make inspection a publicly accountable and transparent activity and the intention was for each inspection to stick very closely to the guidelines laid down in the framework document.

OFSTED put in place a programme for the selection and the training of inspectors and registered inspectors (those personnel who were entitled to lead inspection teams) and recruited mainly from ex-LEA inspectors and teacher-trainers. In addition, the 1992 Act required each inspection team to include a lay inspector, someone who had not previously been involved professionally in the education system. This proviso represented a conscious attempt to break down the inward-looking educational establishment culture that was felt to jeopardise objective inspection.

Under the OFSTED system, there are now no full-time inspectors except for those members of HMI who are responsible for training inspectors, for assuring the quality of inspections and for carrying out some inspections themselves.

LEA inspectors will still exist but, increasingly, they are being made independent and self-financing by their Local Education Authorities and are, in fact, becoming semi-permanent teams of OFSTED inspectors. OFSTED inspection teams exist only for the specific purpose of inspecting particular schools or clusters of schools. They have no further recognised existence and actual inspection and reporting on inspection is all that they are paid to do by OFSTED. The data that they gather, however, become the property of the government and Her Majesty's Chief Inspector (HMCI) makes periodic reports on the state of the nation's schools on the basis of these data.

OFSTED represents a new model of inspection that is quite different from what is available in most, if not all, comparable countries. It is still too early to evaluate its efficacy but the advantages that it offers seem to be quite clear. It allows for universal inspection in a relatively cost-effective way that HMI could never have hoped to attain had it been expanded. It is cost-effective because inspectors are employed only for the period of inspection and reporting and they have to operate in a competitive market which drives down the price of individual bids. Because its procedures are transparent, it should be possible to achieve procedural justice in the process of inspection; everyone — inspectors, schools, parents, OFSTED — should either know or be capable of finding out what the procedures are for carrying out inspections and what the criteria are for making inspectorial judgements about the quality of education in each school.

What, then, are the potential disadvantages of the OFSTED system? The first must be a disadvantage from the point of view of the reformers themselves. The new system was set up with a view to removing the prejudices of a discredited educational establishment from the critical business of quality assurance and control. A little thought, however, would show that this was going to be more easily said than done. The main problem here is with the range of personnel available to staff the new system of inspection. The majority of any such individuals would have to be teachers with senior experience at head or deputy head level in the case of primary schools, and heads of departments, at least, in the case of the secondaries. This is the pool of teachers from which local authority inspectorates and HMI recruited in the past. In fact, unless one assumes that current senior teachers will wish to leave their posts in order to become inspectors, this means that former HMI and local authority inspectorate personnel comprise the majority of the new OFSTED teams. The other group from which OFSTED could recruit are teacher-trainers, who often have the relevant senior experience in schools and who work in institutions which have the infrastructure to support economic bids for inspection contracts.

There is an irony in this. HMI and local inspectorates were abolished by the British government partly because they were perceived to be a malign influence on the classroom practice of the teachers whose careers they could influence (this was particularly true of local inspectors). As there is no widespread pool of qualified personnel which could be recruited from, apart from the teacher-trainers, OFSTED, initially at least, is obliged to recruit from the very people whose influence the government sought to eliminate. The importance of this fact will become clearer in the discussion below.

It might be said that the way in which the law lays down that OFSTED inspections are to be conducted means that the alleged subjective progressivist prejudices of former inspectors will not be given free rein in their judgements of schools. It is true that inspections must be conducted according to the protocols of a very thorough and detailed *Framework for Inspection*[12] in the use of which all prospective OFSTED inspectors are trained. There are, however, several important differences between earlier and more recent HMI practices which are taken account of in the framework. The first of these is the National Curriculum and its associated assessment procedures. The second is the devolved financial management of schools that now exists. Performance in the National Curriculum subjects, together with the effective use of all of a school's resources, is now the subject of inspection, as are the behaviour and discipline and attendance of the pupils.

For all the subjects on the curriculum, including Religious Education and Social, Moral, Spiritual and Cultural Education, a report on pupil's progress must be made. In 1993, there were four distinct ways of assessing the quality of education in each of these areas. First, pupils' achievement in relation to national norms must be assessed on a scale which expresses whether or not that achievement is average, below average or above average.[13] Second, pupils' achievement must be assessed in relation to their own capabilities. Third, the quality of learning must be assessed and, fourth, so must the quality of teaching. These last three aspects of a school's work are assessed in terms of whether or not they are good, satisfactory or unsatisfactory (this is to oversimplify: all assessments are made on a five-point scale).

How are these four critical features of a school's performance to be assessed by an inspection? Is there a measuring rod against which the school's performance can be laid and assessed? If there is not, then to what extent can the judgements that are made be considered to be valid and reliable? Training for inspection, it should be noted, does *not* include training in the correct application of these scales, although it does include a practice session which is then moderated by other members of the training group.

How then can we rely on the data generated by an OFSTED inspection? Let us look at the first question: pupils' achievement in relation to national norms. In order to answer this question it is necessary to have a picture of national norms and to have to hand the individual pupil data with which to compare it. No inspector could hope to carry with him or her an accurate mental picture of national norms for children of a particular age group, let alone for pupils of a particular age group in that kind of school with that kind of catchment area. Presumably, then, inspectors have access to that kind of data while they are on inspection so that they can make a judgement that inspires confidence. However, we know that the national norm data are not available both because the National Curriculum assessment system is not yet completely in place and because it will not cover every year of schooling even when it is. So inspectors do not, and indeed could not, have access to the critical data that would inform such an important judgement. Whatever they say about this must be subjective in nature, using a scale that does not relate to any data against which it could be set.

For the second judgement, of achievement against the capabilities of pupils, it is necessary to set the performance noted during the inspection against data which show the level of performance at which the pupils are capable of achieving. If anything, this is an even more difficult judgement to make than the first. It is difficult enough for an experienced teacher who has taught a class for a considerable period to assess what a pupil's real capabilities are, because of the variety of factors that are involved in learning and displaying that learning. One could perhaps infer from the fact that pupils were manifestly not achieving anything at all, were achieving very little or were making little discernible progress, that their performance was below their capability, but any finer-grained judgement could not be made with any degree of confidence. Once again, the judgements that are made are subjective in nature and limited in precision.

For the third, the question of the quality of learning, a great deal of reliance is placed on discussions with pupils to find out their attitudes to learning and their strategies for effective learning. Observation is also important in order to assess whether or not pupils are concentrating on what they are doing, whether or not they are using appropriate strategies to overcome difficulties, and so on.

Part of the problem here is a *logical* one: there are two distinct but related senses in which we speak of learning.[14] The first is the task sense. For example, when someone is said to be learning to drive a car or throw a pot, it is implied that they do *not yet know how to do these things* and that they are in the process of trying to do so. The same can be said for *knowing that*. A pupil can be said to be learning about the Napoleonic Wars without it being implied that he or she yet knows even the most important facts about those historical events. On the other hand, we speak of learning as an *achievement*. If I have learned to drive a car, then I am able to drive a car. If I have learned about the Napoleonic Wars, I can give a reasonably comprehensive and accurate account of those events. In most cases, the use of the past tense in the case of the achievement sense of learning, together with the context of discussion, will make it perfectly clear which sense of learning is being used. However, the OFSTED handbook does not seem to be clear about this. Although for the most part it is written as if it is the *task* aspects of learning that are uppermost, it is also the case that *achievement* aspects are to be noted.[15]

The main focus of the judgement must be on the task of learning and how effectively pupils carry out the various tasks on which they are engaged. One easy way of dealing with this would be to say that one can form judgements about the quality of learning (in the sense of task) on the basis of the quality of learning (in the sense of achievement). There would then be no need for inspectors to make judgements about the quality of learning in the task sense since there is no way of assessing it *independently* of doing so in the achievement sense. Although tempting, this approach is probably too easy and simplistic, for the logical connections between learning in the two senses are not entirely straightforward. One cannot simply say that if someone succeeds in learning something the quality of the learning was good and otherwise that it was not good, because there are various factors that may intervene which, nevertheless, do not necessarily detract from the quality of the work undertaken.

For example, what is learned may be forgotten due to the intervention of some unforeseen event, or the pupil may genuinely strive to learn but find that the material is too difficult to master. There are cases where the quality of the way in which the task is undertaken is high and where the learning in the achievement sense is not so good. At the same time, the way in which pupils learn is subject to ethical judgements. Whatever views we hold as to the most effective ways of learning, we are all prepared to say that not every method of getting pupils to learn is ethically acceptable.

The most that we can say here is that there is a *loose* conceptual connection between task and achievement senses of the term such that effective learning usually leads to the acquisition of knowledge, understanding and skill and that our concept of learning would be somewhat different from what it is were this not the case.

But a real problem was identified in Chapter 8. Learning practices are subject to moral evaluation in the light of criteria that relate to the value that is put on pupil autonomy and co-operation, for example. So it may well be that inspectors who value the fullest possible expression of personal autonomy in learning on the part of the pupil will judge the quality of learning against that particular criterion, while another one who values docility and obedience as effective ways of learning will make a quite different judgement. As they are looking at the matter not just from a pragmatic but also from a moral perspective, agreement between the two may be difficult, if not impossible, to achieve since each is applying different evaluative criteria.

In practice this need not turn out to be a problem since there is likely to be a large measure of agreement among inspectors as to what constitutes good quality of learning, but this in itself will not solve one of the problems concerning judgements of educational practice that were identified earlier: namely, how is subjectivity in judgement best avoided? Collective subjectivity is not necessarily an answer, for the judgements of all can be flawed. There is no analogy with the practice, described in Chapter 6, of setting standards and levels of performance against intersubjective agreement, because these in turn need to be moderated against synchronic and diachronic comparisons if they are to command conviction. Unless this is done in the case of inspection, the suspicion will remain that judgements are partly at the dictate of fashion.

Finally, inspectors are asked to make a judgement on the quality of teaching. Much the same issues arise concerning quality of teaching as they do concerning the quality of learning. *Teaching* can be taken in both the *task* and the *achievement* sense and it is the quality of teaching in the task sense that inspectors are asked to comment on. At first sight, it should not be possible for subjectivity to reign in the matter of making judgements as to the quality of teaching. The *Framework for Inspection* states that lessons should have clear aims and purposes; that they should cater for all abilities and interests and ensure the full participation of all; that the conduct of lessons should signal high expectations and challenging but attainable tasks; and that there should be regular feedback to pupils from their teachers. Finally, the teaching methods should suit the topic and subject as well as the pupils.[16] In addition, National Curriculum Programmes of Study and Attainment Targets should be fully taken into account.

Close inspection of these criteria suggests that, despite the apparent precision, much is left to the discretion of the inspector in forming a judgement. The authors of the criteria have been careful not to impose a specific pedagogy on teachers; in fact the criteria are all parameters for good teaching, rather than prescriptions for pedagogic practice. The giveaway here is that the teaching method should suit the topic and subject as well as the pupils. There is just a hint that a purely child-centred approach is not suitable. In a way all of this is admirable, since much discretion is left available as to teaching style.

Some at least of the criteria are part of what we mean by teaching. Teaching requires aims; likewise, a teacher who did not involve all the pupils could not be said to be teaching the whole of the class. Teachers who do not set attainable objectives or who set objectives that have already been reached are failing to provide learning opportunities. On a plausible account of teaching, therefore, it can be argued that all OFSTED is providing are the criteria for judging whether or not someone is teaching.[17] If OFSTED's role was to ensure *minimum* standards in all schools, then this would be an acceptable set of criteria, but they cannot be used to judge the quality of teaching.

Such criteria would be concerned with *whether* and *how well* a teacher met his objectives, the *degree* of involvement of all pupils, *how* high expectations were and the *quality* of the feedback given to pupils. This is implicitly admitted by OFSTED, for the *Handbook* states a couple of pages later:

> Teachers' work in the classroom will take many different forms, and it is important that judgements about the effectiveness of teaching are based on its contribution to outcomes and not on inspectors' preferences for particular methods.[18]

In this way, the whole of the debate about 'good practice' is circumvented and, in effect, good teaching practice is said to be the kind of practice that will contribute to desirable outcomes. But inspectors will not always be able to see outcomes, since these may not emerge in the lesson under observation. In addition, they may be asked to lay aside their own values as to good pedagogic practice without guidance as to what they should replace them with. There are further difficulties connected with making judgements about the aims of lessons: it can be the case that an inspector misinterprets what the objectives of a given lesson are or that he or she fails to identify the Statements of Attainment or Level Description that a child or group of children has reached. It is well known that teachers' judgements about these vary and need to be moderated if they are to be reliable. Subjective interpretation as to what constitutes good-quality teaching is likely to remain in inspectorial judgements.

It very often happens that judgements about the quality of learning suggest that it is of a higher standard than do judgements about the quality of teaching. Inspectors have a tendency to interpret such a finding as implying that the children are learning *despite* the efforts of their teachers. But the evidence for this would need to be detailed and highly specific if it were to counterweigh the major alternative possibility that inspectorial judgement is flawed on one or other of the quality of teaching or of learning. In practice, it is unlikely that inspectors are going to question their own judgements and so it is much more likely that teachers will be blamed for what are seen to be poor teaching styles even when their pupils are judged to be engaging in effective learning practices. It will be argued in the defence of inspectors that they must, according to the protocols of the *Framework*, be prepared to back up all their judgements with written evidence and that, therefore, they cannot just make arbitrary judgements of this kind. While it is true that the need to provide evidence does inhibit the making of completely arbitrary judgements, it is also true that evidence does not include reasons why that judgement is made.

All judgements are made on an ordinal scale similar to the kinds of attitudinal scales that are employed in psychological and social science research. This gives them an air of scientific authority which, perhaps, they do not deserve. Scales of this kind, such as Likert Scales and Semantic Differentials, have been frequently criticised on the grounds that they are of doubtful validity in measuring what they set out to measure.[19] But at least they can be standardised to produce *reliable* judgements. However the instruments used by the inspectorate have not, as far as is known, been independently standardised to produce judgements that are reliable. Inspectorial moderation at the team meeting (see next section) cannot do this precisely because it lacks the independence which is necessary to produce reliable results. As instruments, then, the scales for judgement are deeply flawed.

VIII INSPECTORIAL JUDGEMENT AND THE CONSTRAINTS OF INSPECTION

A key point about inspection is that inspectors should be able to report their findings rapidly to those they have inspected. The very credibility of inspectors rests on their ability to do this. Recall that a key characteristic of inspectors, as opposed to researchers, is that they have the authority to make judgements on behalf of those to whom a school is accountable. Their being *in authority* to do this depends, in large part, on their being *an authority* in the matter of judging the quality of teaching, learning and achievement within a school. This authoritative expertise derives from training and experience. OFSTED training does not include a study of whatever research evidence there might be, nor does the inspection procedure require it; it is essentially a form of trained intuition which should give an inspector the ability to form rapid judgements about the matter in hand. Without this power he or she might as well be a researcher. There is a more practical side to the need to be able to make rapid judgements, namely the fact that if it is reasonable to expect teachers to submit to this kind of scrutiny, then it is only fair that those inspected should learn, as quickly as possible, what the judgements are. Otherwise, their capacity to make judgements may be doubted.

There is, therefore, a need for the inspectorial team to report its findings and judgements to the school staff at the end of the inspection. This in turn means that the inspectors have to arrive at a consensual judgement at one team meeting. Individual inspectors need to form judgements, to present the evidence for them and to gain the acceptance of their judgements from their fellow team members in a very short space of time. These pressures, necessary to ensuring the credibility of the whole exercise, tend to work against the formation of objective judgements. At first sight, this might seem like a surprising statement, since the collective judgement of the team should flush out any arbitrary or unjustifiable judgements.

However, it is necessary to consider the pressures that the inspectorial teams and, in particular, the team leaders, the *registered inspectors*, are under. They are responsible for the success of the whole inspection and are also responsible for putting together a team that will carry out a successful inspection. There are, therefore, strong pressures on registered inspectors to compose a team whose members are likely to work in a consensual manner and to agree in the judgements that they make. This means that a collective subjectivity is likely to emerge, whereby the particular preferences for styles of teaching and learning, together with views about other matters such as achievement in relation to capabilities and behaviour and discipline, are likely to be shared to a large degree by all the members of the team. The alternative is too dangerous for the registered inspector to contemplate; the task of reconciling opposed views on matters on which the values of the inspection team differ means that the rapid arrival of a consensus about the school is likely to be difficult, if not impossible, within an extremely short time span.

The OFSTED system, then, appears to have built into it the kinds of problems that were thought to bedevil HMI and LEA inspectorates, namely the kind of collective subjectivity that ensured that educational judgements of a certain kind were imposed upon the schools. But such external pressures can only be partially successful because they do not address the main issue, which is the value system that informs the inspectorate and hence the work that it does. So long as an inspectorate is informed by a largely autonomous system of values, there is always the likelihood of a dissonance of views between an inspectorate and government. There seem to be two possibilities for remedying this. The first is to subject the inspectorate to very strong external political control, and the second is to develop a consensus about pedagogic issues so that the inspectorate's own culture is imbued with a broader perspective than would be the case if it were allowed to generate its culture internally.

Are inspectorates worth having? I have, in this chapter, looked at the alternatives and found difficulties with them. On the other hand, inspection, particularly on the HMI/OFSTED model, has its own difficulties. There are, however, several areas in which an inspectorate can make a useful contribution. The first is in looking at schools which are in difficulties, and the second is by acting as a research arm directed at looking at particular aspects of education, although this can also be done by a body such as the APU or by commissioned research. The first function is necessary for the maintenance of public confidence in the system: the public need to know that problems can be identified and that there is a corps of qualified people who can make recommendations as to how such difficulties can be put right. For the second function it is not so necessary that an inspectorate carry it out. A third function, which arises from the first two, is to tender advice to the government on specific policy issues, but this can be commissioned as well. It should also be borne in mind that an inspection, particularly OFSTED-style, does have the virtue of being comprehensive and of seeing the school as a whole. Fourthly, it should be possible for schools to employ consultants to advise them on particular aspects of school development and improvement. Inspectors would be one important group which could do this but, again, consultants could be privately employed.[20]

There is, then, a very limited role for inspectors as one club in the armoury of instruments for ensuring accountability. To summarise, these will include public testing and examination so that overall standards and effectiveness can be assessed, a research arm like the Assessment of Performance Unit to maintain a broad picture of standards without necessarily having an advisory role, commissioned research on specific issues from outside researchers and an inspectorate to identify and help schools in difficulties. The setting up of bodies like OFSTED, at least on a permanent basis, is probably an expensive mistake that will formally make schools accountable but will have a minor impact on standards of achievement unless there is also a procedure whereby the results of evaluation can be built into a programme of self-evaluation and self-improvement through working with the teachers in the schools or colleges (which incidentally would make the inspectors themselves accountable).[21] There is no provision for that in the OFSTED system.

NOTES

1. For a recent survey of different forms of school evaluation, including inspection, in seven OECD countries, see *Schools under Scrutiny: Strategies for the Evaluation of School Performance*, 1995.
2. See, for example, Alexander, *op. cit.*, 1994, p. 11; Goodson, *op. cit.*; H. Silver, *Good Schools, Effective Schools*, 1994, Chapter 4.
3. Such a system is to be distinguished, for example, from the system of HEFCE subject inspections in higher education institutions in England which operates through the recruitment of peers *as inspectors* for limited periods of time.
4. At the time of writing there is some dispute about the extent to which the integrity of researchers is compromised by the carrying out of research commissioned by the British Schools Curriculum and Assessment Authority (SCAA). See *The Independent*, 7 July 1994.
5. This is not to say that the same individual cannot be at one time academic researcher and at another an inspector. It is to say, however, that there may be tensions within an individual who tries to carry out both roles at the same time.
6. It is tempting to say that judgements made on behalf of the state have to command a certain amount of awe and respect if they are to be believed. For example, the legal system has to have that kind of authority if the vital functions that it has to carry out are to command the acceptance of the population.
7. Cf Alexander, 1994, *op. cit.*
8. The evidence for this is mixed as HMI responded to a variety of pressures, external governmental ones as well as internal cultural ones, but one publication that supports this interpretation is *The Teaching and Learning of Language and Literacy*, 1990.
9. See, for example, HMI, *Education in England: The Annual Report of HM Senior Chief Inspector of Schools*, 1992.
10. The original proposal was to allow schools to award the contracts, but this was amended by the House of Lords and the government accepted the amendment.
11. *A Framework for Inspection*, 1993, and subsequent updated editions.
12. Available in the *Handbook for the Inspection of Schools*, 1994.
13. This requirement has been modified in the more recent versions of the schedule.
14. For a discussion of this, see Gilbert Ryle, *The Concept of Mind*, 1949.
15. OFSTED, 1993, *op. cit.*, Part 4, pp. 9–10.
16. Ibid., Part 4, p. 48.
17. P. H. Hirst, What is teaching? In R. S. Peters (ed.), *The Philosophy of Education*, 1973; J. Kleinig, *Philosophical Issues in Education*, 1982, Chapter 3.
18. OFSTED, *op. cit.*, Part 4, p. 50.
19. For a discussion of Likert scaling, see H. W. Smith, *Strategies of Social Research*, 1981, Chapter 11, pp. 306–307.
20. For a description of inspectors acting in this mode, see OFSTED, *Improving Schools*, 1994.
21. OFSTED, *op. cit.*

Chapter 12
Conclusion: Education, Quality and Democracy

Politics is concerned with two issues: how a people should live together and the management of different points of view. It follows from the first that we cannot just consider individual self-interest, for that is but one answer to the question posed, namely how a people should live. If we accept that people do not just live lives devoted to individual self-interest then we are not just talking about different self-interests or agglomerations of self-interest in social or corporate groups, but about different *points of view* which will contain perceptions of self-interest to a greater or lesser degree, depending on the values of the society as a whole and the nature of the interest group and those who comprise it. Experience and observation suggest that people, acting either individually or in groups, are motivated for a wide variety of different reasons, which include the pursuit of values, the practice of particular virtues, the desire for social acceptance, for love, for a sense of service or of duty, for family life, *as well as* for financial or material reward.

But if these different points of view are not brought into contact with each other through a political process, a lack of balance will develop which means that differing points of view will not be able to take account of one another and adapt accordingly. The very openness and accountability that the gradual spread of democratic values implies will mean that certain practices and institutions that were thought to be valuable by some will be eroded over time. Accountability and the decline of deference leads to a situation in the public services where cherished practices and values are prised open for scrutiny and often changed in ways that those within the services find distressing. Democracy has its costs.

Democracies will not, in the long term, tolerate responsibility without power, and there are good moral reasons why they should not, when responsibility is tied to the provision of resources. There are societies which are democratic in certain respects but which nevertheless remain dominated by an almost deferential respect for certain institutions. But this does not stand up well to the spread of democratic values and tends to be eroded as those values spread. This is a pervasive feature of democratic societies and will remain so until the demand for the *power* that goes with responsibility and resource provision is abated.

In the nineteenth century states started to provide services such as education but did so against a social and moral background that had not yet accepted the democratic mentality. One influential view assumed that once money had been provided to professionals to carry out a service, then it was assumed that they could both be trusted to carry it out and to regulate and monitor their own activity.[1] Such, for example, was the attitude of John Stuart Mill, who thought that, although the state should provide some resources for education, it would be an unwarranted interference with individual liberty to dictate how those resources should be deployed.[2] However, different forms of ensuring quality and accountability grew during the nineteenth century, including both inspection and public examinations.

By the mid-twentieth century, however, the balance of power within education reflected the growing strength and confidence of teachers as a profession. In addition, because Britain operated a decentralised system there were relatively few countervailing tendencies at the national level and even local authorities did not make full use of their statutory powers to regulate the curriculum after the passing of the 1944 Education Act. By the 1970s, concern about economic decline, and about new pedagogical methods and the maintenance of a common culture, led to a measure of public concern about education and a growing willingness on the part of politicians to raise educational issues.

By a historical accident these demands gathered at a time when neo-liberal theories of economics, of public service behaviour and of government were in the ascendant. This ideological dominance became a political one in many Western democracies, particularly the English-speaking ones, shortly afterwards and it became a practical political project to put neo-liberal ideas of accountability into practice.[3] As a consequence of this it is tempting to see the demands for quality in public services as a phenomenon driven solely by neo-liberal ideas.[4] This temptation is mistaken, for the forces at work go deeper than that: they relate to the underlying practical logic of democratic forms of government. Engagement with the neo-liberal agenda alone will not, therefore, deal with the underlying issues of democracy and accountability that drive public concern with the worthwhileness of the services that they pay for.

Education is a particularly complex service and ensuring that it is working well is fraught with difficulties which require some philosophical attention in order to understand them. First, the public education service is seen to embody the values and cultural heritage of a society; secondly it is seen as a means of long-term individual transformation; thirdly it is seen as a way of ensuring long-term economic success. It thus has not only a deeply personal aspect, but also a commercially oriented one, not to mention a political role that grows as the issues of cultural pluralism and concern about national identity occupy more and more attention in democratic societies.

The poverty of psychological resources of the neo-liberal model of motivation together with a growing realisation of the limitations of markets acting alone as efficient allocators of resources, especially in the sphere of public goods, has meant that an opportunity has arisen to develop the language of accountability in a more overtly political way that pays attention to the underlying processes in a democratic political society, namely the negotiation of values and their implementation in the context of multiple points of view. The need is particularly acute in societies which have relatively low levels of consensus about social and political issues and indeed, in societies that develop politically through what Feinberg has called a 'culture of friction' — an example being the United States.[5]

Those who work within education and who wish to preserve some of the independence of schools, universities and colleges need to find a way of 'riding the tiger' of democratic accountability and quality issues in such a way that they can both accommodate the legitimate concerns of interest groups outside the service and also use their expertise and commitment to preserve the integrity of the educational service itself. The neo-liberal agenda has to be argued against and replaced with a democratic agenda of accountability that satisfies the above conditions.

The main features of such a democratic culture of accountability for public services, and for education in particular, would take into account the arguments advanced here and might be as follows:

(1) Acceptance of the need for pluralism — taking into account the different points of view of different parties, being amenable to change, and respectful of evidence.
(2) Negotiation about the implementation of values and their incorporation in aims needs to have some public presence which ideally should be within the normal political process but also within other institutions of civil society such as businesses, voluntary associations, trade unions and the media.
(3) The acceptance of negotiation as a way of doing business implies the acceptance of compromises as normal. In practice this implies a pluralism of aims and curricula.
(4) The need for formal mechanisms for accountability, and for an adequate provision of information to interested parties and the devolution of responsibility to those closest to the provision of the service wherever this is possible.
(5) The need for a balance of central and local ways of ensuring accountability. This balance would have to be argued for case by case. Aims, curricula and standards seem to be more appropriately the responsibility of the state, at least in their broad outline. On the other hand, the gathering of information can be shared between the state and more local bodies. Responsibility for teaching and classroom organisation should probably rest as near as possible to the classroom. Inspection probably needs to remain as a national service devoted to making sure that minimum service standards are maintained at all times.[6] Assessment has an institutional, local and national dimension, depending on what it is used for. But if, as I have argued, the concern for standards is central, not just to ensuring that education is worthwhile but to its being *seen* as worth while, then there has to be a national and even an international dimension to it in order to ensure that standards are not only maintained but also raised wherever possible.

The role of philosophy of education in these developments is both limited and varied. Insofar as political ideas contain within them philosophical assumptions, then philosophy has a role, both as advocate and critic. It will, therefore, not speak with one voice. It also has a role in showing what the logical, epistemic, ethical and political limits to debate about the nature and purpose of education actually are. Again, this will be done from different points of view and, if the argument of this book is correct, this is inevitable.

What philosophy cannot do is to provide conclusive reasons for making political decisions about education. These must depend on views about how people should live and on how their different interests and points of view should be accommodated. These are essentially matters of substantive politics and morality and not ones where philosophy has the final word.

NOTES

1. Such attitudes are more persistent in some sectors than in others. Indeed, a spread of the democratic attitude to all aspects of health care might, arguably, undermine the proper functioning of the service. If doctors are held to be accountable to line managers rather than to individual patients, this could have far-reaching consequences for health care.
2. J. S. Mill, *On Liberty*, Mary Warnock (ed.), London, Fontana, 1972, pp. 238–241.
3. There is, perhaps, some irony in the fact that the other dominant intellectual fashion of the time, namely Marxism, reinforced the perception that behaviour, especially in groups, is essentially driven by self-interest, rather than by any other factors.
4. Even a very recent collection takes this view: see I. Kirkpatrick and M. M. Lucio (eds), *The Politics of Quality in the Public Sector*, 1995, Introduction. It is also worth noting that radicals have begun to appropriate the quality agenda, making use of those anti-hierarchical features of it that were discussed in Chapter 2. See, for example, F. W. English and J. C. Hill, *Total Quality Education: Transforming Schools into Learning Places*, 1994.
5. Feinberg, *op. cit.*
6. Exactly how this is done must be a matter of national tradition as much as anything else. The relatively centralising traditions of France, for example, will produce one model, the regional consensus associated with Germany will produce another, while the Federal and more overtly conflictual system of the United States will produce yet another. Britain is still working towards a satisfactory balance between national and local control and there is also (still) a strong regional dimension to educational decision-making in Britain.

References

Alexander, R., *Primary Teaching*, London, Holt, 1984.

Alexander, R., *Policy and Practice in the Primary School*, London, Routledge, 1992.

Alexander, R., *Innocence and Experience*, Trentham, 1994.

Alexander, R., Wise men and clever tricks: a response, *Cambridge Journal of Education*, 24.1, 1994.

Abbs, P., Training spells the death of education, *Guardian*, 7 January, 1987.

Aspin, D. and Chapman, J. D. with Wilkinson, V. R., *Quality Schooling*, London, Cassell, 1994.

Bantock, G. H., *Culture, Industrialisation and Education*, London, Routledge, 1968.

Barnett, R., *Improving Higher Education: Total Quality Care*, Buckingham, Open University Press, 1993.

Barrow, R., *The Philosophy of Schooling*, Brighton, Harvester, 1981.

Barrow, R., *Common Sense and the Curriculum*, London, Unwin, 1976.

Barrow, R., *Intelligence and Education*, David Elgar, 1993.

Barrow, R. and Woods, R., *An Introduction to the Philosophy of Education*, London, Methuen, 1974.

Barry, N., *Introduction to Modern Political Theory*, London, Macmillan, 1981.

Beard, R., *Developing Reading 3–13*, London, Hodder & Stoughton, 1987.

Bentham, J., *Economics*, 5th edition, London, Pitman, 1960.

Bennett, S. N., *Teaching Styles and Pupil Progress*, London, Open Books, 1976.

Bernstein, B., *Class, Codes and Control*, volumes 1 and 2, London, Routledge, 1973, 1977.

Boot, R. L. and Hodgson, V. E., Beyond distance teaching — towards open learning, in V. E. Hodgson, S. J. Mann and R. Snell (eds), *Open Learning: meaning and experience*, Milton Keynes, Open University Press, 1987.

Brown, A., *Modern Political Philosophy*, London, Penguin, 1985.

Brown, G. and Desforges, C., *Piaget's Theory: a psychological critique*, London, Routledge, 1979.

Cameron, D. and Bourne, J., No common ground: Kingman, grammar and the nation, *Language and Education*, 2.3, 1988, pp. 147–160.

Carr, D., *Educating the Virtues*, London, Routledge, 1991.

Carr, D., Wise men and clever tricks, *Cambridge Journal of Education*, 24.1, 1994.

Caulkin, S., Hezza's quality drive, *Observer*, 6th February 1994.

Central Advisory Council for Education, *Children and Their Primary Schools* (The Plowden Report), London, HMSO, 1967.

Coleman, J. L., *Markets, Morals and the Law*, Cambridge, Cambridge University Press, 1988.

Cooper, D., *Illusions of Equality*, London, Routledge, 1980.

Coote, A. and Pfeffer, N., *Is Quality Good For You?*, London, IPPR, 1991.

Crosby, P. B., *Quality is Free*, Maidenhead, McGraw-Hill, 1979.

Dahrendorf, R., *On Britain*, London, BBC Books, 1982.

Darling, J., *Child-Centred Education and its Critics*, London, Chapman, 1994.

Davis, A., Criterion-referenced assessment and the development of knowledge and understanding, *Journal of Philosophy of Education*, 29.1, 1995.

Dearden, R. F., *The Philosophy of Primary Education*, London, Routledge, 1968.

Dearden, R. F., *Means and Ends in Education*, London, Routledge, 1984.

Dent, N., *Rousseau*, Oxford, Blackwell, 1988.

Dewey, J., *Democracy and Education*, New York, Macmillan, 1916.

Donaldson, M., *Children's Minds*, London, Fontana, 1978.

Donaldson, M., *Sense and Sensibility*, Reading and Language Information Centre, University of Reading, 1989.

Education Reform Act 1988, London, HMSO, 1988.

English, F. W. and Hill, J. C., *Total Quality Education: transforming schools into learning places*, Thousand Oaks, CA, Corwin, 1994.

Entwistle, H., *Education, Work and Leisure*, London, Routledge, 1970.

Entwistle, H., *Child Centred Education*, London, Routledge, 1970.

Feigenbaum, A., *Total Quality Control*, Maidenhead, McGraw-Hill, 1991.

Feinberg, W., *Japan and the Pursuit of a New American Identity*, New York, Routledge, 1993.

Fitzgibbon, C. T., Analysing examination results, in C. T. Fitzgibbon (ed.), *Performance Indicators*, Clevedon, Multilingual Matters, 1990.

Flew, A., *Sociology, Equality and Education*, London, Macmillan, 1976.

Flew, A., Democracy and education, in R. S. Peters (ed.), *John Dewey Reconsidered*, London, Routledge, 1977.

Gaita, R., *Good and Evil: an absolute conception*, London, Macmillan, 1991.

Gallie, W. B., Essentially contested concepts, *Proceedings of the Aristotelian Society*, 1955–1956.

Galton, M., Simon, B. and Croll, P., *Inside the Primary Classroom*, London, Routledge, 1980.

Goldstein, H., *Multilevel Models in Educational and Social Research*, Oxford, Oxford University Press, 1987.

Goodson, I. F., *Studying Curriculum*, Buckingham, Open University Press, 1994.

Gordon, J. C. B., *Verbal Deficit*, London, Croom Helm, 1981.

Gould, S. J., *The Mismeasure of Man*, Harmondsworth, Penguin, 1981.

Gramsci, A., *Selections from the Prison Notebooks*, (eds Q. Hoare and G. Nowell Smith), London, Lawrence & Wishart, 1971.

Gray, J. and Wilcox, B., *Good School, Bad School*, Buckingham, Open University Press, 1995.

Hall, N., *The Emergence of Literacy*, Sevenoaks, Hodder, 1988.

Hamm, C., *Philosophical Issues in Education*, London, Falmer, 1989.

Her Majesty's Inspectorate of Schools, *Aspects of Vocational Education in the Federal Republic of Germany*, London, HMSO, 1990.

Her Majesty's Inspectorate of Schools, *The Teaching and Learning of Language and Literacy*, London, HMSO, 1990.

Her Majesty's Inspectorate of Schools, *Education in England: The Annual Report of H. M. Senior Chief Inspector of Schools*, London, DES, 1992.

Herrnstein, R. and Murray, A., *The Bell Curve: intelligence and class structure in American life*, London, Free Press, 1994.

Hirsch, D., Lesson one: Hobson's choice, *Independent*, 12 May 1994.

Hirsch, D., *School: a matter of choice*, London, HMSO, 1994.

Hirsch, E. D., Jr., The primal scene of education, *New York Review of Books*, Vol. XXXVI, No. 3.

Hollis, M., *The Philosophy of Social Science*, Cambridge, Cambridge University Press, 1994.

Jensen, A., *Educability and Group Differences*, Edinburgh, Constable, 1973.

Johns, E. A., *The Social Structure of Modern Britain*, 3rd edition, London, Pergamon, 1979.

Jonathan, R., State education service or prisoner's dilemma: the 'hidden hand' as a source of educational policy, *British Journal of Educational Studies*, XXXVIII.2, 1990.

Juran, J., *Quality Planning and Analysis*, Maidenhead, McGraw-Hill, 1993.

Kant, I., *Groundwork of the Metaphysic of Morals*, in H. J. Paton, *The Moral Law*, London, Hutchinson, 1948.

Kirkpatrick, I. and Lucio, M. M. (eds), *The Politics of Quality in the Public Sector*, London, Routledge, 1995.

Kleinig, J., *Philosophical Issues in Education*, London, Croom Helm, 1982.

Lane, H., *Talks to Parents and Teachers*, London, Allen & Unwin, 1954.

Lawton, D., *Class, Culture and the Curriculum*, London, Routledge, 1975.

Letwin, O., *Education: the importance of grounding*, London, Centre for Policy Studies, 1988.

Lewis, D., *Convention*, Cambridge, MA, Harvard University Press, 1969.

List, F., *The National System of Political Economy*, New York, Augustus Kelley, 1991.

Locke, J., *The Second Treatise of Government*, in *Two Treatises of Government*, London, Dent 1924. First published 1690.

Maistre, Joseph de, *On Sovereignty*, in J. Lively (ed.), *The Works of Joseph de Maistre*, London, Allen & Unwin, 1965.

Malcolm, N., *Memory and Mind*, Ithaca, Cornell University Press, 1977.

Mayston, D. and Jesson, D., Developing models of educational accountability, *Oxford Review of Education*, 14.3, 1988.

McPeck, J., *Critical Thinking and Education*, Oxford, Martin Robertson, 1984.

Merriman, L., *The Transition from Degree to Diploma in the Professions Allied to Medicine*, unpublished Ph.D. thesis, Nene College, Northampton, forthcoming.

Mill, J. S., *On Liberty*, London, Dent, 1974. First published 1859.

Morgan, C., *A Practical Guide to Quality and Quality Systems*, Northampton, Nene College, 1994.

Mortimore, P., Sammons, P., Stoll, L., Lewis, D. and Ecob, R., *School Matters: the junior years*, Wells, Open Books, 1988.

Muir, J., The Isocratic idea of education and the irrelevance of the state versus market debate, *Proceedings of the Philosophy of Education Society of Great Britain*, 1994.

National Commission on Education, *Learning to Succeed*, London, Heinemann, 1993.

Naish, M., Education and essential contestability, *Journal of Philosophy of Education*, 18.2, 1984.

Neill, A. S., *Summerhill: a radical approach to education*, 1965.

Niskanen, W., *Bureaucracy and Representative Government*, Chicago, Aldine-Atherton, 1971.

The Norwood Report 1943, *Curriculum and Examinations in Secondary Schools*, London, HMSO, 1943.

Nozick, R., *Anarchy, State and Utopia*, Oxford, Blackwell, 1974.

Office for Standards in Education, *A Framework for Inspection*, London, HMSO, 1993.

Office for Standards in Education, *Improving Schools*, London, HMSO, 1994.

Peters, R. S., *Ethics and Education*, London, Allen & Unwin, 1966.

Peters, R. S. (ed.), *The Philosophy of Education*, Oxford, Oxford University Press, 1973.

Peters, T. and Waterman, R., *In Search of Excellence*, New York, Harper & Row, 1982.

Prais, S. J., Mathematical attainments: comparisons of Japanese and English schooling, in B. Mood (ed.), *Judging Standards and Effectiveness in Education*, London, Hodder & Stoughton, 1990.

Pring, R., Standards and quality in education, *British Journal of Educational Studies*, XL.3, 1992.

Quinton, A., Inquiry, Thought and Action: John Dewey's theory of knowledge, in R. S. Peters (ed.), *op. cit.*

Ranade, W., *Future for the National Health Service? Health Care in the Nineteen Nineties*, London, Longman, 1994.

Rawls, R., *A Theory of Justice*, Oxford, Oxford University Press, 1971.

Rawls, R., *Political Liberalism*, New York, Columbia University Press, 1993.

Reid, J., Reading and spoken language: the nature of the links, in R. Beard (ed.), *Teaching Literacy, Balancing Perspectives*, London, Hodder & Stoughton, 1993.

Reynolds, D., School effectiveness and school improvement: a review of the British literature, in B. Moon, J. Powney and J. Isaac (eds), *Judging Standards and Effectiveness in Education*, London, Hodder & Stoughton, 1990.

Rutter, M., Maughan, B., Mortimore, P. and Ouston, J., *Fifteen Thousand Hours: secondary schools and their effects on children*, London, Open Books, 1979.

Ryle, G., *The Concept of Mind*, London, Hutchinson, 1949.

Ryle, G., Intelligence and the logic of the nature-nurture issue: reply to J. P. White, *Proceedings of the Philosophy of Education Society of Great Britain*, 8.1, 1974.

Sanderson, M., *The Missing Stratum: Technical Education in England 1900–1990*, Athlone Press, 1994.

Schon, D., *Educating the Reflective Practitioner*, New York, Basic Books, 1987.

Sharpe, K. and Winch, C., Equal opportunities and the use of language: a critique of the new orthodoxy, *Studies in Higher Education*, 19.2, 1994.

Selleck, R. J. W., *English Primary Education and the Progressives, 1914–1939*, London, Routledge, 1972.

Silver, H., *Good Schools, Effective Schools*, London, Cassell, 1994.

Smith, A., *The Wealth of Nations*, Harmondsworth, Penguin, 1970. First published 1776.

Smith, F., *Reading*, Cambridge, Cambridge University Press, 1985.

Stowell, M., Equal opportunities, access and admissions: tensions and issues for educational policy, *Journal of Access Studies*, 7, 1992.

Stretton, H. and Orchard, L., *Public Goods, Public Enterprise and Public Choice*, London, Macmillan, 1994.

Taylor, F., *The Principles of Scientific Management*, New York, Norton, 1911.

Tizard, B., Blatchford, P., Burke, J. Farquhar, C. and Plewis, I., *Young Children at School in the Inner City*, Hove, Lawrence Erlbaum Associates, 1988.

Tooley, J., The prisoner's dilemma and educational provision, *British Journal of Educational Studies*, XL, 1992.

Toulmin, S., *The Uses of Argument*, Cambridge, Cambridge University Press, 1957.

Tullock, G., The welfare costs of tariffs, monopoly and theft, *Western Economic Journal*, 3, 1967.

Waterland, L., *Read With Me*, Stroud, Thimble Press, 1985.

Whitfield, R. C. (ed.), *Disciplines of the Curriculum*, McGraw Hill, 1971.

White, J., *The Assessment of Writing*, APU, 1986.

White, J. P., *The Aims of Education Restated*, London, Routledge, 1982.

White, J. P., *Education and the Good Life*, London, Kogan Page, 1990.

White, J. P., Education and the limits of the market, in D. Bridges and T. McLaughlin (eds), *Education and the Market Place*, London, Falmer, 1994.

White, J. P., The dishwasher's child: education and the end of egalitarianism, *Journal of Philosophy of Education*, 28.2, 1994.

Wilson, J., Equality revisited, *Journal of Philosophy of Education*, 27.1, 1993.

Winch, C., The curriculum and the study of reason, *Westminster Studies in Education*, 10, 1987.

Winch, C., Reading and the process of reading, *Journal of Philosophy of Education*, 23.2, 1989.

Winch, C., *Language, Ability and Educational Achievement*, New York, Routledge, 1990.

Winch, C., Should children's books be censored?, *Westminster Studies in Education*, 16, 1993.

Winch, C. and Gingell, J., Dialect interference and children's difficulties with writing: an investigation in St. Lucian primary schools, *Language and Education*, 8.3, 1994.

Winch, C., Vocational education: a liberal interpretation, *Studies in Philosophy of Education*, 1995.

Woodhouse, G., The need for pupil-level data, in C. T. Fitzgibbon (ed.), *op. cit.*

Woodhouse, G. and Goldstein, H., Educational performance indicators and LEA league tables, *Oxford Review of Education*, 14.3, 1988.

Quality and Education
Index